Praise for *The Big Questions*

"Steven E. Landsburg's latest book of economic brain teasers re-
sembles one of those Hanayama metal puzzles that you're supposed
to pull apart: They drive me crazy, yet I can't put them down. Landsburg is the University of Rochester professor who brought us *The
Armchair Economist* and *More Sex Is Safer Sex.* . . . In *The Big Questions,* he attempts something more ambitious and slightly less flip: to
sum up his ideas about 'the nature of reality, the basis of knowledge,
and the foundations of ethics.' Be prepared for a diverting journey
into the maze of one man's mind, a supply-and-demand version of
the movie *Being John Malkovich.*"

—*Bloomburg News*

"In *The Big Questions,* Steven Landsburg ventures far beyond his
usual domain to take on questions in metaphysics, epistemology,
and ethics. . . . [T]his must make Steven Landsburg history's most
courageous mathematician because for Landsburg mathematical
abstractions are not like Mount Everest, rather Mount Everest is a
mathematical abstraction. Indeed, for Landsburg, it's math all the
way down—math is what exists and what exists is math, A=A. Read
the book for more on this view, which is as good as any metaphysics
that has ever been and a far sight better than most."

—MarginalRevolution.com

"*The Big Questions* is a funky book, like an intellectual roller-coaster
ride through some of the most fascinating ideas in science, math,
and economics. These are the ideas, says the author—a University of
Rochester professor of economics—that unlock the most perplexing
mysteries in philosophy and life, in general. His book is a thought-
provoking blast."

—David E. Henderson

"*The Big Questions* is one of the strangest and most compelling books I've ever read. Whatever you think and believe about any one of dozens of the biggest questions in life, be prepared to have your deepest presuppositions challenged and your most cherished beliefs shaken, if not overturned. Landsburg fearlessly wades into icons and ideologies with fresh insights I've encountered nowhere else. Landsburg's mind is like a bizarre amalgam of Gödel, Escher, and Borat, with a little Wittgenstein thrown in for good measure. I'll buy a beer for anyone who can read this book and not be stunned by its originality."

—Michael Shermer, publisher of *Skeptic* magazine, monthly columnist for *Scientific American,* and author of *The Mind of the Market*

fP

THE
BIG
QUESTIONS

Tackling the Problems of Philosophy

with Ideas from Mathematics,

Economics, and Physics

STEVEN E. LANDSBURG

FREE PRESS | NEW YORK LONDON TORONTO SYDNEY

Free Press
A Division of Simon & Schuster, Inc.
1230 Avenue of the Americas
New York, NY 10020

Copyright © 2009 by Steven Landsburg

First Free Press trade paperback edition October 2010

FREE PRESS and colophon are trademarks of Simon & Schuster, Inc.

For information about special discounts for bulk purchases,
please contact Simon & Schuster Special Sales at
1-866-506-1949 or business@simonandschuster.com.

The Simon & Schuster Speakers Bureau can bring authors to your live event.
For more information or to book an event contact the Simon & Schuster Speakers
Bureau at 1-866-248-3049 or visit our website at www.simonspeakers.com.

Designed by Level C

Manufactured in the United States of America

10 9 8 7 6 5 4 3 2 1

Library of Congress Cataloging-in-Publication Data
Landsburg, Steven E.
    The big questions : tackling the problems of philosophy with ideas from mathematics,
economics, and physics / Steven E. Landsburg. —1st Free Press hardcover ed.
       p. cm.
1. Philosophy.   I. Title.
BD21.L29 2009
100—dc22   2009022560

ISBN 978-1-4391-4821-1
ISBN 978-1-4391-4822-8 (pbk)
ISBN 978-1-4391-5359-8 (ebook)

Philosophy begins in wonder. And at the end, when philosophic thought has done its best, the wonder remains. There have been added, however, some grasp of the immensity of things, some purification of emotion by understanding.

—*Alfred North Whitehead*

Sometimes the light's all shinin' on me.
Other times I can barely see.

—*The Grateful Dead*

Contents

Introduction
The Beginning of
the Journey

I like very much people telling me about their
childhood, but they'll have to be quick or else I'll be
telling them about mine.

—*Dylan Thomas*

On the first day of kindergarten, Mrs. Rosenberg explained
the routine: nap time, playtime, snack time—and every day, at
2 P.M., a collective "walk through the hall."

She didn't say where we'd be going and she didn't say why, but
I don't think it occurred to me to wonder. Failure to wonder, in
fact, plagued me through my entire elementary school career: In
sixth grade I mastered everything there was to know about the
textile industry without ever asking what a textile was, and for
that matter without its ever having occurred to me that a textile
had to *be* anything at all. If I'd been forced to guess, I probably
would have said that a textile was something like linoleum, but
I never got so far as guessing, or even realizing that there was
anything to guess about.

Anyway, when 2 P.M. rolled around we all lined up outside

the classroom and followed Mrs. Rosenberg through the hall. I was cheerfully keeping pace until we turned a corner and faced the most ominous thing I'd seen in my five years on earth: a sign on the wall—a sign that was *all lit up* so that you could not doubt its importance—with the words FIRE EXIT and a big red arrow pointing in the *exact direction we were walking*.

Now, I had no idea what an "exit" might be, but I certainly knew what a fire was, and there was no way I was going to follow Mrs. Rosenberg or anybody else directly into one. So I turned around, returned to the classroom, and waited quietly for news of the mass incineration to come.

I don't think it ever occurred to me to warn the others. Maybe I thought it was their own fault for coming to kindergarten without first learning to read. Maybe I thought it was best not to call attention to myself, lest the powers that controlled Mrs. Rosenberg come find me and cast me into the flames. I don't remember being particularly agitated. I just sat calmly in the classroom, and when the others returned, even though it was contrary to all my expectations, I don't think I was particularly surprised or curious about how they had managed to avoid disaster.

Every day from then on, 2 P.M. would roll around, the rest of the class would line up for its walk through the hall, and I would sit quietly at my desk. Mrs. Rosenberg never said a word. She and the class took their walk through the hall and a little while later they returned. I never doubted that sooner or later, they'd all be burned to ashes. I did start to wonder where they went every day.

That was one of the two great mysteries of kindergarten. The other great mystery was this: Every day at about 2:30 P.M., Mrs. Rosenberg would assign one of the other students to take me to the bathroom. I could never figure out why I was singled out to be taken to the bathroom; surely the other students were as needy in that department as I was. Or maybe they weren't. Maybe they were all robots made of metal. That would explain why they could walk through fire and survive.

One day, Mrs. Rosenberg pulled up a chair across from my desk and asked me, "Why don't you ever come with us on our walk through the hall?" I was mortally embarrassed to tell her that I was afraid of the fire, so I said, "I just don't like to." With just the right blend of gentleness and firmness that must be the stock in trade of any great kindergarten teacher, she said, "Well, you *have* to." And I said, "Okay."

I had no trouble sleeping that night; I felt no panic, I made no plans to escape. I accepted with Zen-like serenity the fact that I would follow the class down the hall and none of us would be heard from again; the dozen round-trips that the others had already successfully negotiated never entered my consciousness as relevant data. Tomorrow we would walk through the hall and we would never return. So be it.

But when 2 P.M. rolled around the next day, my serenity began to dissipate. I had to steel up my courage to take my place in line. But Mrs. Rosenberg had said I had to. So I did.

We walked through the hall. Past the unambiguous sign, pointing the way to our doom. But—and here the reader might have anticipated me—at the end of the journey, there was no fire. Instead, there was: a bathroom!

And in that bathroom, I had the most astonishing intellectual revelation of my life. Here were two entirely separate mysteries: Where does the class go every day? and: Why do I, and only I, get escorted every day to the bathroom? And it turned out that the two mysteries had *exactly the same answer*. That was the moment when I learned that the world was an intricately woven place, beautiful in its complexity, that everything touched on everything else, and that real understanding somehow depends on seeing how everything fits together.

When I told Mrs. Rosenberg that I "just don't like" to walk through the hall, I'm sure she sensed my embarrassment, and I'm sure she thought it was the bathroom itself that embarrassed me. Unlike me, poor Mrs. Rosenberg never learned the real truth.

After that day, I never worried about the fire-exit sign again. Life was far too rich to waste time on trivia like why someone had posted such a misleading sign or what a textile might be. At age five, I had my priorities straight.

———————

Determined as I was to stay focused on the big picture, I felt sure by the age of ten that I would devote my life to studying philosophy. All other paths seemed fraught with peril. You could build bridges or write poems or cure cancer, but without a lifetime steeped in philosophy, how could you ever know that a bridge, a poem, or a medical breakthrough is a worthy achievement?

A few years later, I had the twin "Aha!" insights that diverted me from my chosen career: First, *all* paths are fraught with peril. What if you devote your life to philosophy only to determine, at age ninety-two, that yes, you *should* have gone to medical school? And second, why should it take fifty years of intense study to figure out whether a cancer cure is a good thing?

Having dashed my own ambition with these insights, I drifted along for a few years until, sometime in my teens, I stumbled onto a little book called *Space and Time in Special Relativity* by a Cornell professor named N. David Mermin, and discovered that it is possible to think. I mean really think. With exceptional clarity—and in sparkling prose—Professor Mermin showed me how to start with a couple of simple and unambiguous assumptions, and then tease out their logical consequences to build a majestic and entirely unexpected vision of the nature of time and space. The material was the stuff of any freshman physics course, but to this pre-freshman, it was jaw dropping.

Many years later, I was thinking about the problem of population, and more specifically the question "What does it mean for the world to have the 'right number' of people?" Which, for example, is better: a world with a billion deliriously happy people or a world with ten billion who are somewhat less happy? Should we aim to maximize total happiness (whatever that means), or average happiness, or some other measure?

I started with a few simple and unambiguous assumptions that I thought everyone could agree to, and teased out their logical consequences. Although I achieved only a very partial solution to the problem, I was delighted to discover that my chain of reasoning led to exactly the same set of equations Professor Mermin had been led to in another of his papers on relativity. There was, then, an unexpected structural similarity between my problem and his. I sent Professor Mermin a copy of my paper, with a cover letter thanking him for his lifelong inspiration, and I still treasure his very gracious reply.

Smitten as I was with Professor Mermin's book, it never occurred to me that I should study physics; I doubted—and continue to doubt—that I am the sort of person who should be let loose anywhere near a sensitive piece of laboratory equipment. So I went off to college and stumbled around from one major to another (English, history, political science) until the day my friend Bob Hyman, an exceptionally talented math major, told me that infinite sets come in a great variety of infinite sizes, some much bigger than others. This sounded so intriguingly bizarre that I had to know more about it, and on Bob's recommendation I took a course in set theory and fell in love with math.

I loved math for the same reasons I'd loved that book on relativity—for its beauty, its logical clarity, and its profound and indisputable truth. From then on, I loaded up on math courses, to the point of neglecting the college's distribution requirements, and failed to earn my degree.

Fortunately, by the time it became clear I wouldn't be graduating, I'd already been accepted to graduate school at the University of Chicago; doubly fortunately, nobody at Chicago ever asked me whether I'd actually finished college.

While I was studying math at Chicago, I happened to fall in with a gang of scrappy economics students who invited me to join their daily lunchtime intellectual free-for-alls. Think of the Algonquin Round Table, but with substance—wit that not only sparkles, but illuminates. Economists, too, I learned, had techniques for advancing by logical steps from simple assumptions to unexpected conclusions. I wanted to master these techniques, and my friends proved to be good and patient teachers.

I've spent the rest of my life seeking—and, to my delight and astonishment, finding—lunchtime companions with the same mix of energy, brilliance, humor, and passion for truth that I first found in graduate school. For thirty years, I've counted my lunch companions among the greatest blessings of an exceedingly blessed life.

I went on to a career of research and teaching in both mathematics and economics, with a little dabbling in physics along the way, but I never lost sight of my fascination with the big questions of philosophy: Where did the Universe come from? Why is there something instead of nothing? How is knowledge possible? What justifies a belief? How can we tell right from wrong, and good from evil? How should we live our lives?

Philosophers have useful ways of thinking about these questions, but so do people who are not philosophers. Physicists know something about the origins of the Universe; mathematicians know something about the patterns of reality; economists know something about how our choices affect the lives of others, which is not distinct from the problem of distinguishing right from wrong. I've come to believe these disciplines provide some of the best available tools for chipping away at the problems of philosophy.

When a man with a hammer tells you that everything looks like a nail, you should doubt his objectivity. When a man who knows some math and economics tells you that the problems of philosophy can be solved with math and economics, you're entitled to exactly the same reaction. But in this case I believe the causality runs the other way: I was drawn to math and economics *because* they illuminate the big questions. I saw the nails and went out to find a hammer.

In this book, I'll tell you what I believe about the nature of reality, the basis of knowledge, and the foundations of ethics. I'm not sure any of my beliefs are right, but I'll explain why I think they're plausible—and more likely to be right than any other beliefs. (Though of course I might eventually be convinced otherwise by new arguments.)

Along the way, I'll digress into illuminating bits of science, math, and economics—sometimes to illustrate a point and sometimes just for fun. So we'll learn something about the lore of very large numbers, the mechanism of color vision, the real meaning of the Heisenberg uncertainty principle, the Talmudic prescription for dividing a bankrupt estate, and much more.

Like the memories of childhood, a ramble through philosophy has no order and no end. Sometimes, following a digression, I'll return to the main topic; other times, I'll move on to something new.

An original idea is a great rarity and I'm sure this book contains very few. Others will have had—and perhaps rejected—these thoughts long before I did. But I hope I've packaged them in a way that will intrigue and challenge you, and that we can enjoy ourselves along the way.

Part

I

Reality and Unreality

The economist John Kenneth Galbraith once explained the division of labor in his marriage: His wife settled the small issues and he settled the big ones. So while Mrs. Galbraith decided where to live and how many children to have, Mr. Galbraith decided how to formulate foreign policy and restructure the tax code.

This book is about even bigger questions, and Part I is about the biggest questions of all: What exists, and why? What are we made of, what are our minds made of, and what is the Universe made of? How should we think about God, and the ultimate causes of things?

Along the way, we'll wander down some side paths to talk about the foundations of mathematics, the prospects for artificial intelligence, the nature and purpose of economic models, and the origins of life.

1 On What There Is

God wrote the Universe in the language of
mathematics.

—*Galileo Galilei*

Why is there something instead of nothing? Why is there a
Universe, and why isn't it empty? Whence all these galaxies and
mountain ranges, centipedes and rainbows? Where did all this
stuff come from?

For many years these questions struck me as fascinating but
impossible to think about. I couldn't even imagine what an answer might look like. This bothered me, but there didn't seem to
be much I could do about it.

It's possible there *are* no answers. Perhaps the questions are
simply misguided, like "Why does my computer hate me?" Your
computer doesn't hate you; it just seems that way when you run
Microsoft products. But when your cursor freezes, some part of
your brain makes the mistake of looking for malicious intent.
Perhaps it's some equally misguided part of my brain that looks
for fundamental causes. Perhaps the Universe just *is*, and that's
all there is to it.

But I think it's generally good policy to assume that things have causes. They often do, and even when they don't, you generally learn more by looking for nonexistent causes than by refusing to look for existent ones. Besides, I can't seem to stop myself.

So I assume—at the risk of grave error—that the Universe is no mere accident. There must be some reason for it. And if it's a compelling reason, it should explain not only why the Universe *does* exist, but why it *must*.

A good starting point, then, is to ask whether we know of *anything*—let alone the entire Universe—that not only does exist, but must exist. I think I know one clear answer: Numbers must exist. The laws of arithmetic must exist. Two plus two equals four in any possible universe, and two plus two would equal four even if there were no universe at all.

I'm not just saying that the laws of arithmetic are eternal and immutable; I'm saying more than that. *Eternal* means for all time, but mathematics exists outside of time. Even if there were no time, there would still be mathematics.

Why do I say that? Maybe it's just another brain malfunction. You could argue that numbers are a human invention, and the laws of arithmetic are empirical regularities, not necessary truths. You put two stones on the table, you put another two stones on the table, you notice there are now four stones, the same thing happens over and over, you summarize your results by saying "two plus two equals four," and that's all there is to it. I feel quite sure that's wrong. I take my stand with those who believe that "two plus two equals four" is not a truth about stones or about physical objects generally, but a truth about *numbers,* which existed long before there was anyone around to count with them.

The philosopher Paul Benacerraf once proposed a thought experiment that neatly distinguishes the two points of view. Suppose you put two stones on your kitchen table, then two more, then count and discover that there are five stones altogether. Whenever you've done this in the past there have been four stones, but this time, oddly enough, there are five.

Your first thought will probably be that you miscounted, or failed to notice that there was already a stone on the table before you began. But over the course of the day, the same thing keeps happening. Two friends join you for lunch, then another two, and somehow you've now got five companions. You climb two flights of stairs from the basement, then another two, and somehow you're on the fifth floor.

Eventually you're forced to conclude that something has drastically changed. But what? You might say that *mathematics* has changed—two plus two used to make four, but now it makes five. Or you might say that *physics* has changed—two plus two make four, just as always, but the physical world no longer seems to care.

In many ways, it doesn't matter which description you pick. Either way, all you're saying is that the old laws of mathematics are no longer useful for describing physical reality. But your choice of description says a lot about your instincts. If you view mathematics as a human construction, designed to explain the world, then you'll be comfortable saying, "Okay, it's time to throw out the old math and create a new math," and to believe that once we stop maintaining it, the old math sort of falls into disrepair and rusts away to nothing.

But if, like me, you view the laws of mathematics as necessary truths, you'll describe things very differently. Instead of throwing out the old *math*, you'll want to throw out the old *physics*. The old physics said that when you put two bunches of objects together, you could predict the total by using *addition*. The new physics says you've got to use something more complicated than addition. But addition itself has not changed.

I believe, then, that arithmetic is both immutable and necessary. Numbers exist, and they exist because they must. Admittedly, I'm being a little vague about what I mean by *existence*.
Clearly numbers don't exist in exactly the same sense that, say,
my dining-room table exists; for one thing, my dining-room
table is made of atoms, and numbers are surely not. But not
everything that exists is made of atoms. I am quite sure that my
hopes and dreams exist, but they're not made of atoms. The color
blue, the theory of relativity, and the idea of a unicorn exist, but
none of them is made of atoms.

I am confident that mathematics exists for the same reason I
am confident my hopes and dreams exist: I experience it directly.
I believe my dining-room table exists because I can feel it with
my hands. I believe numbers, the laws of arithmetic, and (for
that matter) the ideal triangles of Euclidean geometry exist because I can "feel" them with my thoughts.

Better yet, I believe in numbers because I know some facts
about them. For example, every positive integer is the sum of
at most four squares. That's been true forever, though it wasn't
proved (by the French mathematician Joseph Lagrange) until the
year 1770. Because the facts of arithmetic were true long before
humans existed, arithmetic cannot be a mere human invention.[1]

That, then, is my first assertion: Mathematical objects—such
as the natural numbers and the laws of arithmetic—are real.[2]
I cannot give you an absolute proof of this assertion, just as I
cannot give you an absolute proof that I am a thinking being

---

1 The distinction between what's *true* and what we can *prove* lies at the heart
   of Gödel's famous incompleteness theorem, which I'll have a lot to say about
   in later chapters. For more on this distinction, feel free to skip ahead to Chapters 9 and 10; Chapter 10 offers an explicit example of a statement that's true
   but not provable.

2 This assertion represents a mainstream viewpoint—arguably the *only* mainstream viewpoint—among working mathematicians. See the appendix for
   more on this point.

and not a zombie. For that matter, I'm not sure I can even give a completely coherent account of what it means (though I promise to come back to this in Chapters 9 and 10). Nevertheless, I know it to be true.

And so do you. When you add a column of numbers in two different directions and get two different answers, you never seriously entertain the notion that mathematics is inconsistent; instead you are 100 percent certain that you made a mistake. Why is that? If arithmetic were just a system of arbitrary rules, it could very well be self-contradictory. The reason you're sure it's *not* self-contradictory is that deep down, you're sure the rules of arithmetic are *about* something. That "something" is the natural numbers (i.e., the counting numbers 0, 1, 2, and so forth). You and I know that the natural numbers are real. Not only are they real, they are necessary. By their very nature, they could not fail to exist.

And likewise for other mathematical structures, of varying degrees of complexity. A point is a mathematical structure, though there's not much to say about it. Euclidean geometry—the geometry you learned about in high school, with its lines, angles, and circles—is a richer structure.[3] The natural numbers together with the laws of arithmetic form a mathematical structure of profound complexity. The human genome, with its combinatorial structure of A's, C's, G's, and T's, can be described entirely in the language of arithmetic, so at the very least, arithmetic is

---

3 Euclidean geometry provides another good example of how mathematics can exist independently of any physical manifestation. The universe we live in is not accurately described by Euclidean geometry. The angles of a Euclidean triangle add up to exactly 180 degrees. But if you build a triangle from three steel girders, its angles will never add up to exactly 180 degrees. That's partly because space itself is (slightly) curved, so the theorems of Euclidean geometry are (slightly) inaccurate descriptions of the physical world; it's also partly because, unlike the sides of a Euclidean triangle, no steel girder has ever been either perfectly straight or infinitely thin. The Euclidean triangle exists, but its existence transcends the merely physical.

as complex as human life, and therefore as complex as your brain and the pattern of your consciousness.

I believe that everything—you, your consciousness, and the Universe that you and I inhabit—exists because everything *is* a mathematical structure. First I'll explain what it means for your consciousness to be a mathematical structure; then I'll move on to the rest of the Universe.

Patterns are mathematical structures, and the idea that consciousness is a pattern—the pattern of neural activity in your brain—is a mainstay of the approach to artificial intelligence that is sometimes called "strong AI" and sometimes called "functionalism." Your brain contains about a hundred billion neurons, which spend their time sending signals to each other. Depending on the mix of signals it's recently received, a neuron might or might not send a signal to another neuron down the line. According to the functionalists, it's the pattern of activity (as opposed to, say, the makeup of the neurons themselves) that generates your consciousness. If you were to build an artificial brain, with artificial neurons made of silicon, scrap metal, or cascading marbles, and if those artificial neurons interacted in the same pattern as the neurons in a human brain, your creation would be as conscious as you are.

In his magnificent book *Consciousness Explained,* Daniel Dennett imagines a wine-tasting machine. You pour a sample wine in through a funnel, and the system responds: "A flamboyant and velvety Pinot, though lacking in stamina." Dennett summarizes the functionalist philosophy thus:

> If you reproduced the entire "functional structure" of the
> human wine taster's cognitive system (including memory,
> goals, innate aversions, etc.), you would thereby reproduce

all the mental properties as well, including the enjoyment, the delight, the savoring that makes wine-drinking something many of us appreciate.

It might seem implausible that something as subtle and ethereal as a sense of delight could arise from a mere pattern of firings. But one thing I've learned from Dennett is that a world of prejudice is built into that word *mere*. It is quite thoroughly impossible for you or me to begin to imagine the complexity of a network of a hundred billion neurons. So when we try to imagine it, we conjure up images of, say, several dozen neurons, interacting in complicated ways, and that image leads us badly astray. It completely fails to account not just for the *amount* of complexity, but for the *kind* of complexity that can arise in a system with trillions of potential connections, containing systems and subsystems reflecting and modifying each other's activity.

According to the strong AI crowd, it's that pattern—the software that runs on your brain as opposed to the hardware (i.e., neurons) on which it's implemented—that accounts for consciousness. Your neurons communicate through chemical and electrical signals, but those are irrelevant details. If you replaced the neurons with tubes full of marbles that communicated by propelling those marbles through the air, the experience of consciousness would be the same. Dennett and others, including Douglas Hofstadter, have elaborated on all this in great and fascinating detail. You should read all their books.

If you do that, you'll come across Hofstadter's essay "A Conversation with Einstein's Brain," where he envisions a book with about a hundred billion pages—one for each of the neurons that resided in Albert Einstein's brain on the last day of his life. On each page is a series of numbers, detailing which other neurons this neuron is capable of signaling, which incoming signals cause which outgoing signals, and so on. The book also includes a set of rules for altering these numbers in response to signals that have been sent and received (this is meant to model the way the brain stores memories—as changes in the rules for which neurons will fire under which circumstances). And there's also a preface, detailing the exact pattern of neuron firings that went on in Einstein's brain in response to any given visual or auditory stimulus.

Now you can converse with Einstein. You say: "Hello, Professor Einstein; how do you feel today?" Your voice registers as a series of tones. And then:

We'd take the first tone . . . and [using the Preface] see which cells it would make fire, and how. That is, we'd see precisely how each number on each page would change. Then we'd go through the book painstakingly page by page, and actually *effect* those changes. You might call that "round one". . . . We've gone through the book once, neuron by neuron. But there is the fact that some of the neurons are firing, you know, so we have to take that into account. Which means we have to proceed to the pages [that receive those signals] and modify *those* pages in the way that is directed by the "structure-changing numbers." That is round two. And those neurons, in turn, will lead us to still others, and lo and behold, we're off on a merry loop around the brain. . . .

Perhaps on each page the time taken for the neuron in question to fire is specified—the time it took to fire in real life, in Einstein's brain—a quantity best measured, probably, in thousandths of a second. As the rounds progress, we sum up all the firing times, and when the times add up to the length of the first tone, we start in on the second tone. . . .

[Eventually], certain of the "speech neurons" will begin to fire. . . .

Then we consult tables showing how the firing of speech neurons affects the shape of the mouth and the tension in the vocal cords, and we calculate what Einstein is "saying."

The process in practice would take many hundreds of millennia, but in principle, there's no reason to doubt that we'd get exactly the same responses that we'd have gotten had we spoken to Einstein himself. After all, his responses are entirely determined by the movements of his mouth and vocal cords, which are entirely determined by the firing of speech neurons, which is entirely determined by the firing of other neurons, all the way back to the initial firings caused by the tones coming from the questioner.

Better yet—instead of following Hofstadter's recommendation to do all the painstaking lookups by hand—imagine employing a family of demons who zip through the book at near light speed doing your lookups for you. Now you can talk with Professor Einstein in real time.

The system responds to every stimulus, every question, every sound, and every sight, exactly as Einstein would. Why, then, asks Hofstadter, should we doubt that the system experiences consciousness exactly as Einstein did?[4]

Your mind, in other words, is software, while your brain is

---

4 I've told the story as Hofstadter tells it, though I am sure an accurate story would be far more complex. The real Professor Einstein's answers would have depended not just on our questions, but the temperature in the room, the pretty girl passing through his peripheral vision, and the states of everything from his sinuses to his bladder. In principle, though, we could simulate all those inputs, too.

mere hardware. The same software running on completely different hardware would still be you.

Or maybe not. The philosopher John Searle believes that conscious thought is fundamentally a *biological* process, a product of flesh and blood. He warns against confusing *simulations* of that process with the process itself. You could write a computer program that simulates every cell in your stomach and all of their interactions, but it still couldn't digest food. Why, then, should a computer program—even one that simulates every neuron in your brain and all their interactions—be able to think?

If Searle is right, then consciousness is more than just a pattern of neuron firings. But it can still be a pattern at a deeper level—say the pattern of interactions among the atoms in your brain, as opposed to the neurons. If consciousness is not a pattern at *some* level, I'm not sure what else it could be.

Consciousness, then, is apparently software. But the Universe is hardware. Where does all the hardware come from? I suspect that the hardware, too, is made of pure mathematics. I was led to this insight by a series of side comments in the physicist Frank Tipler's wonderfully provocative and original book on *The Physics of Immortality:* If consciousness can emerge from sufficiently complex software, and if it makes no difference what hardware the software runs on, then the hardware ought to be dispensable altogether. Once you've granted that the hardware is insignificant, why do you need it in the first place? Complex software is a purely mathematical object, so if mathematics exists, then the software that constitutes your mind exists—quite independent of the hardware that it runs on. And sufficiently complex software should, just by existing, be enough to generate consciousness.

Part of my job as a professor of economics is to write down

mathematical descriptions (we call them "models") of simple (in other words, imaginary) economies and figure out how the inhabitants of those economies would react to, say a change in tax policy.[5] Some of my colleagues like to program their models into their computers so they can actually *watch* the model-people's reactions to different policy experiments.

Now, suppose my models were unfathomably more detailed, and unfathomably more complex: Instead of assigning a separate mathematical symbol to each inhabitant of the model-world, I assign a separate symbol to each neuron in the brain of each inhabitant, and I keep careful track of all the interactions among all the neurons. Then, according to the strong AI view, if my colleagues implement this model on their computers, the inhabitants of the model will experience real consciousness.[6] Not only that, but they will experience the model-world as a physical reality. That's because this more detailed model contains more than just descriptions of the actors' neurons; it contains also equally detailed descriptions of the physical environment and the actors' interactions with it.

In fact, I believe that even if my colleagues *don't* implement the model on their computers, the inhabitants will *still* experience real consciousness and experience the model-world as a physical reality. This is a leap, but it strikes me as not a very big one; if a model can generate consciousness on *any computer,* then the computer itself can't be an important part of the process. So why shouldn't the model generate consciousness with no com-

---

5 In case that sounds a little vague, I'll give you an example of a such a model in the next chapter.

6 I am sure there are AI researchers who will object to this summary as a caricature, but I am also sure that it captures the spirit of what many of them believe.

puter at all? (On the other hand, everyone I know thinks this is a much bigger leap than I do.)

But any model I can write down exists—as a mathematical structure—long before I ever conceive of it. So my model-people are already alive someplace, living in a world that, to them, is the only reality. And conceivably, we are they.[7]

The Universe itself, in other words, is a mathematical pattern, containing your consciousness and mine as subpatterns. The Universe exists because it can; a logically possible Universe is a mathematical object, and mathematical objects exist by necessity. Most of those objects are pretty tame. A point is a mathematical object, but it's as boring an object as you can imagine. It's a rare pattern indeed that contains subpatterns capable of consciousness. Frank Tipler makes the marvelous suggestion that we take the presence of such subpatterns as the *definition* of physical (as opposed to purely mathematical) existence. In other words:

A Universe physically exists if its inhabitants know it's there.

So I believe your dining-room table, your pornography collection, and your mother-in-law are all mathematical objects—subobjects of a larger mathematical object called the Universe. Is there something odd about observing a mathematical object

---

7 There remains a critical difference between the inhabitants of an economic model on the one hand, and you and me on the other hand: An economic model can be implemented on a computer and can unfold over time. By contrast, the Universe *can't* unfold over time, because time is a *part* of the Universe. The Universe can no more unfold over time than it can be located in Alaska.

A computer program is two things: It is a set of instructions for a computer to follow and it's also an abstract pattern in its own right. The Universe—if I am right—is analogous not to the set of instructions, but to the abstract pattern. Time and space, along with our perceptions of time and space, are pieces of that pattern. The pattern does not unfold; it just *is*.

and perceiving it as physical? No odder, I claim, than observing a physical object and perceiving it as green. Color is not a physical property; it's a property imposed by your nervous system.[8] If your brain can conjure colors into existence, why can't it conjure physicality?

None of this is meant to deny that the Universe we live in is governed by the laws of quantum mechanics, natural selection, and the rest of orthodox science. All of those things—along with our methods for discovering them—are part of the mathematical structure that is our Universe.

There is nothing radical here. Every modern cosmological theory begins with the assumption that the Universe is a mathematical object—usually a geometric object, where fundamental forces like gravity and electricity are aspects of the geometry. Gravity, for example, is curvature: Apples fall from trees because they're trying to travel along the straightest possible paths in a curved space. Nobody has the slightest idea how to describe the Universe as anything *but* a mathematical object. All I'm suggesting is that we listen to what the physicists' theories are trying to tell us.

Many cosmological models posit that our Universe is part of a grander structure called the *multiverse,* which contains many universes similar to our own, but with histories that differ in detail. In some of those universes, Al Gore was elected president of the United States in the year 2000. In others, he was elected in the year 2008. In others, he is currently the president of Kazakhstan. When I say that "every possible universe exists," I am not talking about the multiverse. The multiverse itself is a mathematical structure, containing our Universe as a substructure, but it is just one of many mathematical structures. I assert that every

---

8 More about this in chapter 5!

mathematical structure exists. Some have no physical manifesta-
tions. Some are too bizarre for us to contemplate. Some are universes. One of them is our Universe. Some are multiverses. If we
live in a multiverse, then one of them is our multiverse.

I love this idea, not just because it explains where our own
Universe came from, but because it obliterates the distinction between possible existence and actual existence. If some universes
are merely possible while others are real, what distinguishes the
real ones? The theory I've outlined makes it unnecessary to ask
such uncomfortable questions. Any universe that *can* exist *does*
exist; there's no longer any need to explain why ours was granted
special privileges. They're all real.

I'd be happiest if someone could prove that there is only one
possible universe—or one possible multiverse—that is, only
one mathematical structure containing conscious substructures
something like us. Then we'd know not only why there's a Universe, but why we live in *this particular* Universe. But I hold out
little hope for such a satisfying discovery.

I've made no attempt to catalog the many writings by cosmologists, physicists, mathematicians, and philosophers that express
visions similar or related to mine. But I do want to mention an
exceptionally well-argued paper by Max Tegmark (a cosmolo-
gist at MIT) called "The Mathematical Universe," which was
recently published in the journal *Foundations of Physics*.

Professor Tegmark argues in essence as follows: Let's think
about the content of science, starting with, say, biology. Biology has two parts: the part that is chemistry and the part that
organizes information into categories that are easier for humans
to understand. Chemistry describes what's going on in your
heart and lungs at the molecular level. The dividing line between
"heart" and "lungs," by contrast, is a human invention; at the
molecular level, your body is a teeming mass of trillions of par-

ticles, with no natural division between "heart particles" and "lung particles." Our brains *create* a clear distinction between lungs and hearts, and the science of biology enshrines that distinction, even though it's not a fundamental aspect of reality. (What I've said about the distinction between hearts and lungs could equally well be said about the distinction between mammals and reptiles, or between living and nonliving beings, or for that matter between "parts of me" and "parts of you.") Professor Tegmark (nonpejoratively) calls such distinctions the "baggage" of biology. So biology has two parts: the part that is chemistry and the part that is baggage.

Chemistry in turn has two parts: the part that is physics and the part that is another level of baggage. Physics gives us fundamental particles like protons and electrons; chemists draw lines around certain collections of particles and call them "molecules." Then they draw lines around certain collections of *kinds* of particles and call them "metals" or "noble gases." The particular lines that get drawn are dictated not by anything fundamental but by the patterns that appeal to human brains. Erase that baggage and all that's left is physics.

Now take this a step further. Physics in turn has two parts: the part that is mathematics and the part that is baggage—the part that is expressed in equations, and the part that is expressed in verbal concepts (like "mass" and "speed") that appeal to human brains. Erase the baggage and only the mathematics remains.

Now there are only two possibilities: Either *everything* is baggage, in which case there is no external reality *whatsoever* beyond the subjective creations of human brains. Or *something* is real completely independent of us humans. If we reject the first possibility—if we insist, in other words, that there must be *some* external reality—then what could that reality consist of? It can't include baggage, because baggage is *by definition* a creation of the human mind. But without the baggage, all that's left is the math. So math must be the fabric of the Universe.

One more reason I like the Universe-as-mathematical-object theory is that it suggests an answer to one of the most vexing problems in philosophy: the unreasonable effectiveness of mathematics in the natural sciences.

The Nobel laureate Eugene Wigner wrote a famous essay on this topic, asking (and failing to answer) why the language of mathematics should be able to describe the physical world with such accuracy. A second-order differential equation is a purely mathematical construction with no obvious intuitive content to anyone who got less than a B in calculus; mathematicians study such equations as a pure intellectual game. Nevertheless, second-order differential equations are the language of motion; they provide an astonishingly compact and accurate description of everything that moves, be it a flying arrow, a falling apple, or an orbiting planet. Other examples abound. Mathematicians invent a concept because they think it's beautiful or elegant, and a generation later, physicists discover that the same concept is exactly what's needed to describe some fundamental regularity in the way the Universe works. Functional analysis is the language of quantum mechanics; differential geometry is the language of relativity; my own sometime specialty of algebraic K-theory, developed as a tool for exploring purely geometric questions in a highly abstract setting, turns out to have applications in the physics of string theory.

As Wigner stressed, it is an extraordinary mystery—and an extraordinary bit of good luck—that mathematics can describe the Universe. Perhaps there is a clue to the mystery in the recognition that the Universe is *made* of mathematics.

It's often argued that complexity can arise only by evolving from simplicity. This cannot be right, because mathematics is complex and it didn't evolve from anything; I'll talk much more about this observation in Chapter 3. Mathematics had its complexity built in from the get-go, and it contains within itself the most complex patterns ever observed, from the evolution of galaxies to the structure of the human brain to the salary-cap regulations of the National Football League. Why look elsewhere for their origins?

2 Unfinished Business

Going Bananas

> Economists are generally wrong with complicated
> models but right about concepts. . . . By analogy, a
> mechanic knows that changing your oil is good for
> your engine, but he can't tell you what problems you
> will have with your car next year. You shouldn't ignore
> the mechanic's advice on changing oil just because he
> doesn't know when your battery will die.
>
> —*Scott Adams*

I am eager to say more about the three R's of 'rithmetic, religion, and reality, but first I'll take care of some unfinished business from the preceding chapter: I promised you an example of an economic model.

A model is a story about an imaginary world that's both simple enough to understand completely and complicated enough to teach us something about the world we live in—like a fable, only more compelling. If I tell you that "slow but steady (at least sometimes) wins the race," and if you stubbornly refuse to believe me, I can say, "Well, let's imagine a hare and a tortoise. . . ." That's a fable, not a model, because it's not fully imagined. To turn it into a model, I might say, "Let's imagine a hare who runs twenty miles an hour but takes a one-hour nap after each five minutes of running, and a tortoise who runs five miles an hour but never stops to rest. Now let's *compute* how long it takes each of them to run a thirty-mile race." That's a model.

To keep our models tractable, we have to keep them simple, and to keep them simple we have to keep them unrealistic. If you've never studied economics, that blatant unreality is liable to drive you bonkers. To illustrate, here is a model adapted from the work of Nobel laureate Robert E. Lucas Jr.:

Every year, exactly twenty people are born, each of whom lives for exactly two years and then dies. So in any year, there are twenty old people (the ones who were born a year ago) and twenty young people (those who have just been born). These people are randomly distributed across two cities. There's also a government, which occasionally hands out money to old people. Young people earn their livings by growing bananas, which they can either eat or sell to old people—in exchange for money, which they'll use to buy bananas when they themselves are old.

I've just described this model in words, but all of the words can be translated into pure mathematics. After making some standard assumptions about people's preferences (e.g., bananas are good, work is bad), you can *calculate* the way rational individuals would behave in such a world. You can determine how they bargain with each other and how prices get set.

Professor Lucas earned his Nobel Prize largely for that model, which set the agenda for a generation of research in macroeconomics. Why? Why are economists so enamored of a model that is so thoroughly and obviously divorced from reality?

First, the Lucas model does capture some important aspects of reality: People start out young and end up old; they work when they're young, and they save money to spend when they're old.

They make decisions about how much to work and how much to save. And most important, they face uncertainty. In this particular model, the uncertainty is centered on two questions: "How many people live in my city?" and "How much money do those people have?"

Uncertainty makes planning difficult. If you're a young person and you notice an uptick in the price of bananas, you could respond in either of two perfectly reasonable but very different ways:

- Maybe I got lucky and landed in a city with very few young people—so bananas are in short supply. This is my chance to cash in. I think I'll work like crazy.

- Maybe the government just handed out a whole lot of money to old people. Those old people are feeling rich, and they're buying bananas like crazy. But the money they're spending has been devalued by inflation, and it's likely to *stay* devalued. Why work hard to earn a bunch of inflation-ravaged dollars? I'll just keep doing what I'm doing.

Young people waver between the two explanations—and therefore compromise in their behavior. They don't work like crazy, but they do work a bit harder.

Now suppose the government *has* just handed out a whole lot of money. Then everyone is very happy for a while. Old people are happy because they just got handed a bunch of money. Young people are happy because they think they might be getting rich.

But next year, when those young people have become old and try to *spend* their riches, they're in for a rude shock. The money they earned isn't worth very much, and all that hard work was— well, not for naught, but certainly for less than expected. And if only they'd known, they'd have chosen to take life a little easier. In short, they've been snookered.

Bottom line: When the government prints money, everyone is temporarily happier. But a lot of them are being tricked, and eventually they're going to regret their former "good fortune."

Is that exactly what happens in the real world? Of course not. The real world is more complicated in at least a trillion different ways.

And yet there is perhaps an important moral here for the real world: When the government prints money, prices go up. When prices go up, workers notice they're getting paid more and are at least partly oblivious to the fact that they're earning debased currency. They respond by working more, but in the end, they regret their choices. On balance, the quality of their lives suffers.

That's an insight. Now you might ask: If this was Lucas's insight, why didn't he express it this way? Why didn't he just write down the last few sentences of the preceding paragraph, instead of positing a bunch of imaginary people who live exactly two years and eat only bananas?

Answer: Because there is simply no way to know by looking whether those sentences are logically consistent. There's no *obvious* contradiction there, but contradictions have a way of lurking in the bushes.

There's also no way to know by looking whether these few sentences have other implications that are clearly false, in which case they must be false as well.

The only way to be sure you're telling a logical, coherent story is to translate your story into mathematics and to simplify it down to the point where you can calculate all its implications. That's exactly what a model is.

Sometimes your model suggests additional implications that you'd never have thought of on your own. Lucas introduces one more character into his model: An econometrician who studies the economy, using statistical techniques that were standard before Lucas burst on the scene. The econometrician notices (correctly) that whenever the government hands out more than the usual amount of money, people scurry around growing a lot more bananas. He concludes (spectacularly incorrectly) that if the government makes a *habit* of handing out large amounts of money, banana production can be kept at a permanently high level.

The econometrician's problem is that he doesn't understand *why* the money supply affects the banana crop. He doesn't realize that people are being fooled into overestimating the demand for bananas, or that people can be fooled only when the money supply changes *unpredictably*. When the government takes the econometrician's advice and adopts a policy of injecting lots of money on a predictable schedule, nobody's fooled anymore and the policy is 100 percent ineffective.

By studying the mistakes of this hapless econometrician, Lucas and others were led to profound insights about what real-world econometricians were doing wrong, and a revolution ensued.

I sometimes hear economists defend the unrealism of their models thusly: "Economics is an infant science. Today our models are unrealistic; a decade from now, they'll be a little less so, and a decade from then a little less. Eventually we'll have realistic models that make accurate predictions."

That, I think, is pure poppycock. Our predictions are not,

and never will be, based on models; they're based on informal reasoning. We study models because they hone our reasoning skills. We can figure out what happens in those models and thereby develop a good intuitive feeling for what sorts of reasoning are likely to be productive.

In this we are no different from, say, physicists. Ask a physicist what will happen if you hit your brakes while accelerating around a sharp curve. He will tell you, with sufficient precision to convince you not to do it. He will feel no need to draw a diagram, construct an equation, or perform a computation. He knows the answer because he has a sure intuition, honed by years of analyzing highly stylized artificial examples. Physicists study weights falling in perfect vacuums, billiard balls gliding on frictionless tables, and the behavior of charged particles isolated from the rest of the Universe. The point of these exercises is not that they are real, but that it is possible to understand them completely. That complete understanding hones the physicist's intuition so that he can guess with reasonable accuracy how real cars behave on real roads.

Economists aspire to the same sort of insight. For example: Over the past twenty years, there's been an outpouring of models that predict a consumption tax is far more conducive to long-term prosperity than an income tax. It would be insane to take any one of those models as a guide to public policy. But the fact that so many different models, coming from so many different starting points, all seem to arrive at the same conclusion is suggestive. It's forced economists to start thinking about *why* such disparate models all reach the same conclusion. In the process, we've learned new ways of thinking that *are* likely to apply to the real world.

What economists *can't* do is tell you what interest rates will be eighteen months from now. Neither can the physicists. You could, I suppose, point to that as a failure of modern physics. After all, interest rates are determined by physical processes in the brains of bond traders; isn't that the stuff of physics? The answer, of course, is that physical (or economic) models are not designed to make precise predictions of complicated phenomena outside the laboratory. They are designed to hone the intuition.

Economics is an art, but it's a disciplined art. You're not allowed to just say anything that sounds good. Our models keep us honest.

3 How Richard Dawkins Got It Wrong

The Case Against God

Dear Intelligent Design People:
　　Complexity is the hallmark of *unintelligent* design.
　　Please rethink your arguments.
　　　　　　　　Sincerely,
　　　　　　　　Steven E. Landsburg

I believe the Universe is made of mathematics, but there is no lack of alternative theories. For some odd reason, the most durable of these—those with names like Judaism, Christianity, and Islam—seem to be the ones devised by illiterate shepherds.

In this chapter, I'll ask whether there's any reason to believe that religious theories of creation might be *true*. I am not, of course, the first author to address this question; antireligious screeds have been a staple of the recent bestseller lists. The best seller of the bunch is a lively entry by Richard Dawkins called *The God Delusion*.

Now, Richard Dawkins is an international treasure. He first came to public attention with a masterpiece called *The Selfish Gene* that made modern evolutionary biology accessible and fascinating to an audience of millions, including me. How can a willingness to die for one's countrymen have survived natural selection? Answer: Because natural selection operates not at the level of the organism, but at the level of the gene. Genes prosper when they have effective survival and reproduction strategies— such as predisposing you to sacrifice yourself to save others who are likely to be carrying the exact same gene.

Because you are the sort of person who's reading this book, you've probably heard that story before, along with some of its more sophisticated variations. Thirty years ago, pre-Dawkins, you probably wouldn't have. It was Dawkins who translated this great body of thought from the obscurity of academic journals to the forefront of public consciousness.

But in his public crusade against religious belief—and in particular in *The God Delusion*—I believe that Dawkins has stumbled badly. Not only has he got his arguments wrong; he's got them exactly backward.

Let's start with the argument from Intelligent Design. First I'll explain why the Intelligent Design argument is wrong; then I'll explain Dawkins's objections and why they are equally wrong—and wrong for exactly the same reasons!

Here is a one-paragraph summary of the argument from In- telligent Design:

The Universe (or Life, depending on whether the speaker is more hostile toward physics or biology) *is extraordinarily and irreducibly complex. Such complexity requires a designer. Orthodox science fails to account for that designer. Ergo ortho- dox science is at best incomplete.*

Here "irreducible" complexity refers to the interaction of many parts, any one of which is useless without the others. If a lens is no good without a retina, and a retina is no good without a lens, how could either have evolved first? [1]

Intellectuals generally have been far too quick to ridicule this argument. Except perhaps for the fact that complexity is the hallmark of *un*intelligent design, the argument is not fundamentally silly. Its problem, I think, is that it proves too much.

After all, if Intelligent Design theory is correct, then *everything* that's irreducibly complex must have been designed. That would include, for example, arithmetic. Arithmetic is so complex that no system of axioms—not even an infinite set of axioms—can fully describe it. [2] It is most assuredly an *irreducible* complexity (eliminate the number three and all of arithmetic falls apart!). By contrast, the human genome is so simple that you can easily fit a complete description on a single DVD. And the emergent patterns in arithmetic—the patterns that emerge just from the existence of the natural numbers (zero, one, two, three, four . . .)—are infinitely (and I use that word advisedly) more dazzling than the patterns that produce bacterial flagella or the human eye.

Indeed arithmetic *must* be more complex than life, because all the complexity of life derives from the complexity of arithmetic—in particular, the combinatorial patterns that manifest themselves in DNA and protein synthesis.

Of course, some people think life is more than DNA and protein synthesis; some even claim that life requires an immortal soul. But immortal souls are beyond the purview of science,

---

1 The retina/lens example is for illustration only; Intelligent Design proponents prefer to point, for example, to bacterial flagella consisting of about forty critical proteins.

2 See Chapters 9 and 10 for more on this point!

whereas the whole point of Intelligent Design theory is that the irreducible complexity of *scientifically observable* processes is already so great as to require a designer. Every one of those observable processes can be described as an arithmetical pattern. So if your argument is that anything as complex as life requires a designer, then you must be prepared to conclude that arithmetic required a designer.[3]

That's devastating, because almost nobody is prepared to believe that arithmetic was designed. If God designed arithmetic, he must have made some choices along the way; if you're not making choices, you're not designing. But a choice is not a choice unless you could have chosen differently, which suggests that, for example, God could have arranged matters so that two plus two makes five. And at least in my experience, even people who claim to be very religious have trouble swallowing *that* much omnipotence.

Indeed, the mainstream view among theologians of all stripes is that God can do anything *logically possible* but cannot violate the laws of logic. If you accept that the laws of arithmetic are dictated by logic, then even God can't change them.

If arithmetic couldn't have been different, it can't have been designed. If arithmetic wasn't designed, then at least one irreducibly complex structure exists without a designer. If an irreducibly complex structure can exist without a designer, then the Intelligent Design argument is wrong.

That, I think, is sufficient refutation. The only way out is to allow that arithmetic *was* designed. But I don't think the Intelligent Design people want to go there.

---

3 As in Chapter 1, I'm invoking both the complexity of arithmetic and the fact that arithmetic was not designed. But nothing in this chapter depends on anything else I claimed or speculated about in Chapter 1.

Here's why: The leaders of the Intelligent Design movement have consistently and adamantly denied that the Intelligent Designer must be God. Presumably this is so they can divorce their argument from religion and sneak it into public school classrooms. But that denial is untenable. Once you argue that irreducible complexity implies a designer, you're forced to conclude that arithmetic itself, no less than the physical Universe, required a designer. And who but God could design the very laws of arithmetic?

I'm willing to concede that *life* could have an Intelligent Designer who isn't God—maybe we were designed by mortals from another planet, for example. And maybe they were designed by mortals from still another planet and so on ad infinitum. That theory contradicts a lot of known physics (e.g., cosmologists are pretty sure that time doesn't stretch infinitely backward), but at least it doesn't contradict *itself*. So as long as you're willing to throw a lot of science out the window, you can consistently believe in that kind of Intelligent Design without God.

But that won't work for arithmetic. Only God—or an entity so Godlike we might as well call it God—could create numbers and tinker with the laws of addition. If the Intelligent Design argument is right, God must exist. Whatever the movement's founders might like, Intelligent Design cannot be divorced from religion.

That's a huge political problem if you're trying to sell Intelligent Design as a secular theory. But it leaves the Intelligent Design movement on the horns of a dilemma: The Intelligent Designer either did or did not design arithmetic. If he didn't, then irreducible complexity does not require a designer, and the whole argument goes out the window. But if he did, then he's clearly God, and the whole claim that Intelligent Design is a secular theory goes out the window. Either way, the Intelligent Design movement is hosed.

Richard Dawkins offers a very different argument against Intelligent Design: According to Dawkins, an Intelligent Designer would have to be even more complex than the Universe he/she/it designed. Instead, he argues, the First Cause—if First Cause there be—must have been simple, and complexity must have arisen over time (presumably through natural selection).

Here, I think, Dawkins starts off right and veers off very wrong. Partly, he is saying: "*If* your argument is that complexity requires a designer, then God, being complex, also requires a designer." That part is right. But he seems also to be saying that all complexity must arise, through one process or another, from simple antecedents. I do not believe that, because mathematics is the most complex thing we know of, and it surely did not arise from simple antecedents.

Dawkins and the Intelligent Design proponents are entirely in agreement—and, I think, entirely in error—on this crucial point: They both believe that complexity cannot arise *ab initio*. For the Intelligent Design people, complexity can arise only by design; for Dawkins, complexity can arise only from simplicity. But if either of these conclusions were correct, it would apply equally well to arithmetic. Not even religious people believe that arithmetic was designed by God, and not even Dawkins believes that arithmetic evolved through natural selection. Therefore Dawkins and his opponents are equally wrong.

So much, then, for Intelligent Design. What about other arguments for the existence of God? One of the most durable is the "ontological argument," devised by Saint Anselm in the eleventh century.

Anselm defines God as "the greatest thing imaginable." Now, existence is really really great, so if God didn't exist, he couldn't be the greatest thing imaginable, now could he? Therefore, *by definition* God exists! Case closed!

Inspired by Anselm, I am going to prove there is a number that's bigger than any other number. I call this number *G,* and I *define* it to be the biggest number ever! Now, if *G* didn't exist, it could hardly be the biggest number ever, could it? So *by definition G* exists! Case closed!

Just think of it! The biggest of all numbers! Once you've counted to *G* you can count no further. If you've got *G* nickels and somebody gives you another nickel, how many nickels have you got? It can't be *G*+1 because that would be an even bigger number, and that's impossible!

In other words, the conclusion is wrong. In fact there is no biggest number. ("Infinity" does not count; there is no such number as infinity.) No matter how big *G* is, *G*+1 must be even bigger. But what about my airtight argument? Answer: The argument was ridiculous on the face of it. You can't call a thing into existence simply by defining it. If you could, I'd define a new kind of remote control that automatically removes Adam Sandler from any movie.

Regardless of what Anselm chooses to "define," there can instead be something very great, and then something even greater, and then something greater than that, ad infinitum—just as there are numbers, and then larger numbers, and then numbers that are larger still, ad infinitum. Anselm starts by assuming that there *is* a greatest thing imaginable. Start with an unjustified assumption and you're sure to reach an unjustified conclusion.

Richard Dawkins, once again, rejects the religionists' argument for reasons I find as unconvincing as the argument itself. "Isn't it too good to be true," asks Dawkins, "that a great truth about the cosmos should follow from a mere word game?"

Dawkins confesses to an "automatic, deep suspicion of any line of reasoning that reache[s] such a significant conclusion without feeding in a single piece of data from the real world."

But great truths about the cosmos *are* discoverable by mere "word games." Take, for example, the great truth that there are infinitely many prime numbers. Nobody has ever observed all of those infinitely many primes; nobody has ever observed even more than a negligible fraction of them; yet we know they exist, and we know they exist without referring to a single piece of data. Euclid knew it, too, and he recorded the proof over two thousand years ago.

Suppose you've run up against an Implacably Hostile Person who believes that 2 and 3 are the only primes. How might you refute him?

> You: I think you overlooked some primes. What about 7, for example?
>
> IHP: I don't think 7 is prime.
>
> You: Hrm. Well, surely you remember the elementary school fact that every number is divisible by some prime. So if your theory is right, 7 must be divisible by either 2 or 3. Which is it?
>
> IHP: Oh. Hrm. Well, maybe 7 is also prime. I'm pretty sure the only primes are 2, 3, and 7.
>
> You: And if I could show you a number not divisible by 2, 3, or 7, you'd have to admit you were wrong again, wouldn't you?
>
> IHP: Yes. But how would you ever hope to find such a number?
>
> You: Well, there are a whole lot of ways. But here's one that comes to mind: If I multiply 2 times 3 times 7, I get 42. That's divisible by 2, 3, *and* 7. So the number next door,

namely 43, can't be divisible by any of them.[4] So much for your theory that 2, 3, and 7 are the only primes.

IHP (after much thought): Okay. Here's my new theory. The only primes are 2, 3, 5, 7, 11, 13, 17, 19, 23, 29, 31, 37, 41, and 43.

You: *Sigh.* If I multiply those numbers together, I get 13082761331670030. The number next door, namely 13082761331670031, can't be divisible by anything on your "complete" list of primes.

IHP: Oops.

Coming up with an even longer finite list won't do your friend any good; no matter *what* list he comes up with, you're going to use the same trick to prove him wrong. The trick always works, so no finite list of primes can be complete. The complete list of primes must be infinite.

There. A great truth about the cosmos, derived from a "mere word game." Dawkins aside, Anselm's argument suffers not from being a word game, but from being *wrong*.

There are other arguments for God's existence, but they all strike me as too silly to mention, and in any event, they've all been eloquently refuted by Dawkins and many others. So I won't mention them here.

Still, I can't resist saying a few words about "Pascal's Wager," which is not an argument for the *truth* of God's existence but for the wisdom of *assuming* it.

The argument is that God *might* exist (which I suppose is true, in the same sense that the dark side of the moon *might* be populated by purple dinosaurs), so everyone—believers and dis-

---

4 In fact, numbers divisible by 2 (2, 4, 6, 8, . . .) always live at least two doors apart; numbers divisible by 3 (3, 6, 9, 12, . . .) always live at least three doors apart, and so on.

believers alike—runs the risk of being wrong. Whether we like it or not, we're all gamblers. And the wise gamble is to believe in God because—*even if God is unlikely to exist*—the potential pay-off (eternity in paradise!) is so great. When the rewards are good enough, you go with the long shot.

Pascal's Wager, then, presents God as a sort of Nigerian e-mail scammer. Even when his promises seem too good to be true, they're also too good to walk away from.[5] For those who buy this kind of argument, the economist Alex Tabarrok has proposed another wager. There's an (admittedly small) chance that God exists and really really wants you to give Alex Tabarrok all your money. In fact, there's *some* chance that your admission to heaven depends on this. Since there's so much at stake, the wise gamble is to send him all your money. I'll take 10 percent as a finder's fee.

---

5   I like to tell people that those Nigerian e-mail solicitations are so unlikely to be for real that I never bother to respond unless they're offering at *least* $50 million.

Part

Beliefs

Most of your beliefs are ill-considered. That's because you're no fool. Your time and energy are limited, and you prosper by focusing on a few well-chosen areas.

Fortunately, most of your beliefs don't matter. You can believe the most outlandish things about the origin of the Universe, or extrasensory perception, or the implications of the trade deficit, and still perform brilliantly as an accountant, a cabdriver, or a professor of English literature. And you can still be a good friend and a great parent, too.

The next several chapters are about the beliefs that most people would discard in a moment if they had any occasion to think hard about them. Whether the subject is religion, biology, economics, morality, or our everyday pictures of how the world works, I claim that most people would jettison many of their most cherished "beliefs" in a heartbeat if anything really hung in the balance. I'll concentrate on the few areas I've thought hard about myself so that I can try to explain not just why many widely held beliefs are wrong, but which alternative beliefs seem to be right.

Those areas include science and economics (Chapters 4 and 5), religion (Chapter 6), metaphysics—things like free will, ESP, and life after death (Chapter 7), and virtually every other area where beliefs differ, from baseball to crime solving (Chapter 8).

Along the way, we'll learn something about color vision, water waves, the case for free trade, cognitive science, and how to identify a spy.

4 Daydream Believers

It is hard enough to remember my opinions without also remembering my reasons for them.

—*Friedrich Nietzsche*

When your beliefs don't matter, it's costless to cling to them. So that's what people do. "Jesus was divine." "Free will is an illusion." "Protectionism can make us prosperous." We're tenacious about such beliefs precisely because nothing hangs in the balance. Misunderstanding protectionism can make you an unwise voter, but so what? Your vote never swings an election anyhow. It makes perfectly good sense for you to get these things wrong.

At worst, your false beliefs will earn you the scorn of the few people who have actually thought about the issues—and perhaps of the many who take their cues from those few. In some circles, a professed belief in creationism will make you a laughingstock, and you'll probably deserve it. There might be some good arguments for creationism, but most creationists are just plain ignorant of the many knock-down arguments for natural selection that have won over virtually everyone who thinks hard about biology. A professed belief in protectionism (or, in its modern guise "antiglobalization") merits exactly the same response.

There might be some good arguments for protectionism, but most protectionists are just plain ignorant of the many knock-down arguments for free trade that have won over virtually everyone who thinks hard about economics. I'll share some of those arguments in the next chapter.[1]

I spend a lot of time on university campuses, where it's de rigueur for ardent protectionists to ridicule the ignorance of ardent creationists, all the while oblivious to the fact that, to anyone who knows what he's talking about, both belief systems sound exactly equally flaky. Even among intellectuals, there's not usually much incentive to care about ideas.

When you were in elementary school, you probably learned about the color wheel—all the colors arrayed around in a circle, from red to green to blue to violet and back around to red again. When you were in junior high school, you probably learned about the spectrum of colors ranging from red (with the longest wavelength) down through orange, yellow, green, blue, indigo, and violet (with the shortest)—all lined up in a row, as anyone who's looked at a rainbow can plainly see. I was in graduate school when my friend Bob Bruner pointed out the contradiction. Which is it? Do colors naturally form a circle or a line? I remember being mildly disturbed that I didn't know the answer and majorly disturbed that I'd never thought to ask the question. (Today I know the answer, which I'll share in the next chapter.)

Disturb the surface of a pond (say by dropping in a pebble) and you create water waves. One crest washes up to shore, then another, then another. Disturb the air (say by shouting, "You're

---

1 You could argue that creationism and protectionism are in different categories, because creationism is a scientific theory—theory of what *is*—whereas
protectionism is a set of policy prescriptions—a theory of what *ought* to be.
But protectionism, as I'm using the term here, also makes a lot of assertions
about the causes of poverty and prosperity that are on quite the same scientific footing as creationism's assertions about the causes of intelligent life.

It!") and you create sound waves (this time it's the air that's waving). One crest washes up against my ear and I hear your message. Where's the next crest? Why don't I hear your message again? And again and again and again? Why doesn't the entire world sound like a Wagnerian opera? And most important—having known at least since junior high school that sound is a wave—how could I have reached adulthood without ever asking this question?

I have tried and failed to devise a plain English explanation for why the pebble in the pond creates ripples while your voice in the air doesn't. If you're really interested—and if you've got a taste for advanced mathematics—you might try Googling for "Huygens's Principle." The bottom line is this: The surface of a pond is two-dimensional. The air is three-dimensional. A disturbance creates ripples when the number of dimensions is even; it creates a single wave—without ripples—when the number of dimensions is odd.

If we lived in a six-dimensional world, where ponds had five-dimensional surfaces, then sound waves would ripple and ponds would not. A pebble dropped into the odd-dimensional surface of the pond would create a single crest; an exclamation in the even-dimensional air would resound, and resound, and resound, and resound . . .

Why do waves care whether the world is even or odd dimensional? That's the part I can't explain without more mathematics than you want to see.[2] But the explanation has nothing to do with my point, which is the ease with which we all adopt self-contradictory beliefs. We all learned in school that "sound is a wave"; we've all dropped pebbles in ponds and know what

---

2 If you *do* want to see some of the mathematics—and some additional subtleties about the physics of ripples—see the appendix, or visit www.the-big-questions.com/ripples.html.

waves are like; yet somehow most of us never notice the blatant discrepancy.

Our ability to hold contradictory beliefs about the nature of the physical world is another instance of our tendency to embrace ideas without questioning them—or stopping to think about whether we really believe them. As I've already said, there's nothing unreasonable about this behavior; if you're going to survive in the world, you've got to pick and choose what you're going to think hard about.

The next few chapters concern a few of the small number of subjects that *I've* chosen to think hard about, followed (in Chapter 8) by a general argument that seems to indicate that pretty much *all* of our beliefs are ill-considered. But first, some unfinished business.

5 Unfinished Business

> The color yellow is a mystical experience shared by everyone. Discuss.
>
> —*Tom Stoppard*

I promised to tell you a little more about color vision and the economics of protectionism. First, color.

HOW COLOR VISION WORKS

In elementary school, I was issued a color wheel—all the colors of the rainbow, arrayed in a circle, with, for example, green located halfway between blue and yellow to remind me that "blue and yellow make green." In junior high school, we studied the rainbow itself, and learned that each color corresponds to a different wavelength of light, ranging from red (the longest) down through orange, yellow, green, blue, indigo, and violet.

As I've mentioned, it wasn't till I was in graduate school that my friend Bob Bruner asked me this question: If colors correspond to wavelengths, longest to shortest, what business do we have arranging them in a circle? Shouldn't it be a color *line*? As a graduate student, I was well accustomed to being asked questions

I couldn't answer. But I was flabbergasted that I could have lived my entire life without noticing such a glaring inconsistency.

Bob knew the answer, and was kind enough to share it. Now I'll share it with you.

First, light does indeed come in a variety of wavelengths; infinitely many of them, in fact. We say that red is followed by orange, but actually, as you move across the rainbow, red fades gradually into orange, passing through infinitely many shades along the way. Keeping track of infinities requires fancier mathematics than you probably want to deal with right now, so I'll stick with the harmless fiction that there are just seven wavelengths: our old friends red, orange, yellow, green, blue, indigo, and violet. If you're British, you were taught the mnemonic "Richard of York gave battle in vain"; Americans get by with the succinct "Roy G. Biv."

Objects acquire color by reflecting light of many wavelengths. That flower you're looking at reflects, let's say, 8 units of red light, 4 of orange, 3 of yellow, 2 of green, 7 of blue, 6 of indigo, and 5 of violet; call it (8,4,3,2,7,6,5) for short. We need seven numbers to describe the light coming off a flower.

Now, seven numbers are more than your brain wants to keep track of, so your eye boils the information down from seven numbers to three. First it averages the 8, 4, and 3 (getting 5); then it averages the 4, 3, 2, and 7 (getting 4); then it averages the 7, 6, and 5 (getting 6). (Notice that some of the seven numbers are used more than once.) These averages—(5,4,6)—are what get sent to your brain.[1]

Your brain converts the (5,4,6) to a color—in this case, let's

---

1 Of course I am oversimplifying. Your eye actually receives a string of infinitely many numbers, not just 7; moreover it takes *weighted* averages, so that it might count 6 twice when it averages 6, 4 and 3. Nothing important depends on these simplifications. The bottom line is that your eye computes three averages and sends those three numbers to your brain.

suppose, a somewhat gaudy shade of magenta. Only those three numbers matter. Therefore different flowers, reflecting very different light distributions, can appear identical in color. Imagine a flower with reflected light distribution (9,5,1,6,4,7,7). Your eye averages 9, 5, and 1; then it averages 5, 1, 6, and 4; then it averages 4, 7, and 7. It sends along the resulting (5,4,6) to your brain, and you say, "Oh, look! These two flowers are exactly the same shade of magenta!"

Like so:

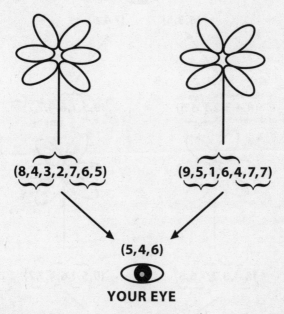

The first flower reflects 8 units of red, 4 of orange, 3 of yellow, and so forth; the second reflects 9 units of red, 5 of orange, 1 of yellow, and so forth. In each case, your eye averages the first three numbers to get 5, the second through fifth numbers to get 4, and the last three numbers to get 6. Either way, the same (5,4,6) is reported to your brain, so your brain sees the two flowers as identical in color.

The moral so far is that it takes an eye and a brain to create a color—and a different eye and a different brain might use very different rules. Imagine some other creature—say a vole—whose eye receives the same seven numbers yours does, but bunches them differently for averaging. Let's say that on receiving (8,4,3,2,7,6,5), the vole's eye averages the 8 and 4 (getting 6), then the 4, 3, and 2 (getting 3), then the 2, 7, 6, and 5 (getting 5).

Like so:

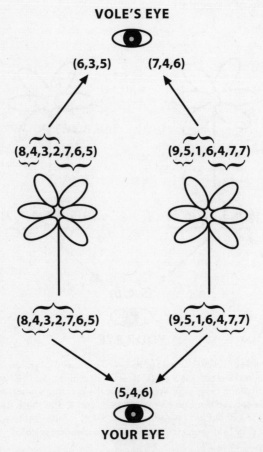

VOLE'S EYE

(6,3,5)　　(7,4,6)

(8,4,3,2,7,6,5)　　(9,5,1,6,4,7,7)

(8,4,3,2,7,6,5)　　(9,5,1,6,4,7,7)

(5,4,6)

YOUR EYE

Your eye computes one set of averages; the vole's eye computes another. These two flowers look exactly the same to you, but not to the vole.

As you can see in the diagram, the vole's method of averaging gives the set of numbers (6,3,5) for the flower on the left, and the very different numbers (7,4,6) for the flower on the right. To a vole's eye, the colors of these flowers appear quite different, though to a human's they appear identical.

(Meanwhile, there are other pairs of flowers whose colors appear different to humans, but identical to voles.)

Color, then, is a biological phenomenon—it's created in the brains of living things. Light, by contrast, is a physical phenomenon—it's there whether or not anyone's around to see it. The rainbow is physics. The color wheel, as we shall see, is biology.

More specifically, the color wheel is *human* biology; it illustrates the colors that arise in the human brain. Each color, as we've seen, is encoded by three numbers. Three numbers specify the *x, y,* and *z* coordinates of a point in space. So you can imagine each point of space colored with the corresponding color. For example, the point with coordinates (5,4,6) gets that gaudy magenta color.

Here's a picture of three-dimensional space; you can imagine that each point has been assigned a color:

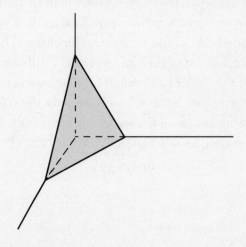

The origin, where all three axes meet, is black. As you move out along any straight line through the origin, the colors of the points become more intense, but they don't change hue.

Now look at the shaded triangular surface I've wedged in against the three axes. Every line coming outward from the origin crosses this surface exactly once—so every hue appears exactly once on the surface.

Lay the surface down flat and it's filled out with every hue your brain can manufacture. Smooth out the corners, and voilà, you've got a color wheel.

The bottom line: The colors of the rainbow correspond to light of specific wavelengths, which can be arrayed in order from longest to shortest. But the color of almost anything else in the world arises from a *mixture* of wavelengths. Your eye looks at this mixture and does some arithmetic to compute three numbers that get passed to your brain. Those three numbers determine a color, so the colors perceived by your brain fill out a three-dimensional space. The color wheel is a surface wedged into that space.

Incidentally, some animals (like eagles) have eyes that compute four or five separate averages, rather than three. This means the eagle can see a much richer array of colors than you can. An eagle's "color wheel" would be a three-dimensional ball. To the eagle's eye, each point of the ball represents a different hue.

Of course this "color ball" would be quite useless to a creature without X-ray vision, because you'd see only the colors on the surface, missing out on all the wondrous hues inside. Perhaps it's just as well that eagles don't go to elementary school.

CRAZY TALK

It takes a profound ignorance of science to believe that God created the world six thousand years ago. It takes an equally profound ignorance of economics to believe that protectionism—the use of quotas and tariffs to discourage the importation of foreign goods—can make us more prosperous.

It's true that a small number of working scientists manage to embrace some form of creationism, and a small number of working economists manage to embrace some form of protectionism—but in each case we're talking about tiny (though sometimes vocal) minorities. The vast majority of the time, scientific knowledge precludes creationism and economic knowledge precludes protectionism.

There's a difference, though: The case against creationism relies largely on *facts* about the fossil record and geologic strata, while the case against protectionism relies primarily on *logic*. The facts that refute creationism are discovered and reported by scientists; the rest of us have to take it on faith that those scientists are being truthful. By contrast, the logic that refutes protectionism is available for anyone to evaluate from scratch.

Therefore it seems to me that the protectionist's position is even less respectable than the creationist's. If you're convinced that most scientists are liars—that everything they say about fossils, for example, is false—then you can be a logically consistent creationist. But you can't be a logically consistent protectionist.

Like stem-cell research, another potentially transformative force for good, free trade is held in check largely by the stupid, the ignorant, and the superstitious. At least when it comes to stem cells, there's a limit to the damage the U.S. government can cause; research projects that are banned or discouraged here can migrate to Europe and Asia, and Americans can still partake of the benefits. When it comes to free trade, there is no such safety valve.

You can find the complete self-contained argument against protectionism in any intermediate-level microeconomics textbook, with all the accompanying graphs and equations. Those graphs and equations are critically important for making sure the argument is airtight. But the main ideas are easy to express in words.

Take an example. Suppose American manufacturers sell digital cameras for $100 each. One day a new Chinese supplier starts offering identical cameras for $75. Now each American seller faces an unpleasant choice: Match the Chinese price or lose your customers.

Suppose for the moment that everyone decides to match the Chinese price, and let's tote up the gains and losses to Americans. If you're buying a camera, the Chinese just saved you $25. If I'm selling you that camera, the Chinese just cost me $25. Your gain equals my loss. In toto, we're neither more nor less prosperous than before.

If that were the end of the story, the gains and losses from foreign trade would wash out. But the story goes on. I'm not so happy selling cameras at $75, so I'll start considering alternatives. Maybe I'll switch to making cell phones. Maybe I'll retire early and devote the rest of my life to playing World of Warcraft. Whatever I decide, *my decision cannot make me additionally worse off, because it's voluntary.* If getting out of the camera business made me worse off, I'd stay in the camera business.[2]

To be clear here: All sellers have clearly been hurt by the

---

2 You might object that I can't stay in the camera business because the Chinese have stolen my customers, but that objection is silly. As long as I match the Chinese price—or beat it by a penny—I can stay in business.

Chinese—but those who leave the camera industry must be hurt less (or at least not more) than those who stay.

Now let's retotal those gains and losses. Consumers are still ahead by $25 per camera. Those manufacturers who stay in the camera business are behind by $25 per camera. But those manufacturers who leave the industry are behind by something *less* than $25 per camera. Every American consumer gains $25; every American producer loses $25 *or less*. American consumers have gained more than American producers have lost.

That alone is enough to prove that trade makes Americans more prosperous on average. But it gets even better. There are plenty of Americans who won't pay $100 for a camera, but will happily pay $75. Without trade, those people don't buy cameras. With trade, they do. Their enjoyment is an additional gain to Americans, and it comes at *nobody's* expense.

If the populations of camera sellers and camera buyers were fixed, the introduction of cheap Chinese cameras would be exactly as good for buyers as it is bad for sellers. But the detriment to sellers is lessened when the seller population shrinks, and the benefit to buyers is magnified when the buyer population grows. Therefore the benefits must exceed the costs.

Virtually all economists consider this argument a slam-dunk proof that trade makes us richer (and therefore tariffs and quotas, which limit trade, make us poorer). According to a recent survey, 89 percent of professional economists (of all political stripes) oppose restrictions on international trade. Presumably some substantial fraction of the remaining 11 percent agree that trade enhances prosperity but believe that prosperity should sometimes take a backseat to other values. As for the remainder, there are probably a few who are paid to say things they don't believe and a few who are "professional economists" in name only. I'm sure there are "professional biologists" who deny evolution.

But I don't intend to make an argument from authority. If you think I've put something over on you, you're welcome to dissect my reasoning. All the logic is out in the open. You don't have to trust my honesty or anyone else's.[3] You can't dismiss logic by reciting calumnies like "economists are nothing but shills for special interests." (If you think I'm being overly defensive here, you should see some of my e-mail.) In the words of President Abraham Lincoln (himself no free trader):

If you have ever studied geometry, you remember that by a course of reasoning, Euclid proves that all the angles in a triangle are equal to two right angles. Euclid has shown you how to work it out. Now, if you undertake to disprove that proposition, and to show that it is erroneous, would you prove it to be false by calling Euclid a liar?

---

3 The argument I've given here is close to airtight but not perfectly. In principle, you can evade the conclusion by arguing that trade restrictions make Americans more prosperous by conferring monopoly power on American exporters. Economists love this kind of mental exercise, but few think it has much to do with the real world.

6 What Do Believers Believe?

> You do not believe; you only believe that you believe.
> —*Samuel Taylor Coleridge*

Every morning, my friend Misha, like other Orthodox Jews around the world, concludes his morning prayers with this declaration: "I believe with perfect faith in the coming of the Messiah, and though he may tarry, nevertheless I believe." Myself, I believe with perfect faith that the square root of two is an irrational number, but I have never felt an ongoing need to announce that conviction to the Universe. That's why I suspect Misha is a liar.

Almost always, the "beliefs" I go around repeating are the ones I don't really believe. If you pass me on the street at an unguarded moment, you might hear me muttering something like "I believe this plaid goes just *fine* with the paisley" or "I believe I can lose another five pounds by Thanksgiving" or "I believe she likes me!", but you'll never catch me muttering, "I believe two plus three makes five." I *know* two plus three makes five. That's why I don't have to remind myself of it.

The "beliefs" I echo are those I might *want* to believe, or those I'm trying to talk myself into, or those that I'm trying on for size. But when I pass the threshold to actual belief, I stop reviewing the matter.

So when congregations gather to pronounce the Thirteen Principles of Faith, or the Nicene Creed, or the Testimony of Islam, all I see is evidence that none of these people believes in God.

Of course there are degrees of belief. Some of my beliefs are more disposable than others. I believe that Abraham Lincoln was first elected to Congress in 1846, and went on to become president of the United States. It wouldn't take much evidence to convince me I'm wrong about the date. It would take considerably more to convince me Lincoln was never a congressman, and vastly more to convince me he was never president.

My shakiest beliefs are the ones I've never much thought about, which is often because I don't find their subjects very interesting. I believe, based on a hazy recollection from elementary school, that Pierre is the capital of South Dakota. But because I've never had much reason to *care* whether Pierre is the capital of South Dakota, I've never given the matter much thought, and I wouldn't be terribly surprised to learn that I'm mistaken.

And precisely *because* I don't give much thought to South Dakota (apart from occasional reminiscing about a wonderful vacation in the Badlands and the Black Hills), I'm generally unaware of how shaky my belief about its capital is. Ask me the capital of South Dakota and I'll say, "Pierre." Ask me, "Are you sure?" and I might suddenly realize—for the first time—that I'm not.

That's what I think religion is like for most people. They *believe* that they believe, but their "beliefs" are of the easily disposable kind. Suppose you could take a devoutly religious person, ask him, "Are the tenets of your religion true?" and somehow convince him that the life of his child depends on getting the answer right. I'm guessing that nine times out of ten, you'd find yourself confronting a born-again infidel. The only reason that rarely happens is that there's rarely an occasion when getting the right answer actually *matters*.

What's my evidence? I'll offer it in a minute, though I'm not even sure it's necessary. To me, all religions are such patent hokum that it's clear nobody could possibly believe this stuff. Case closed. I am confident that almost no adult could buy into Christianity (or Judaism or Islam or Wicca) for the same reason I am confident that almost no adult could buy into the story of Santa Claus.

Necessary or not, I believe there *is* a lot of evidence that true belief is rare, though little of that evidence has been collected systematically. First: Most religions assert that God sees all our actions, punishes us when we're bad, and rewards us when we're good. The punishments tend to be quite draconian. So you'd expect religious people to behave better than nonreligious people, especially in circumstances where nobody human is watching. How can the proceeds of a liquor store robbery be worth an eternity in hell?

You might respond that the sort of people who rob liquor stores are notoriously shortsighted, so they can believe in hell but still put it out of their minds, focusing on present rewards and ignoring future punishments. The problem with that response is that it flies in the face of what we know about deterrence. The fact is, deterrence works. For this there is much evidence and room for little doubt; you can find decades of evidence by hundreds of researchers summarized in the three-volume compendium *The Economics of Crime,* edited by Isaac Ehrlich and Zhiqiang Liu. The bottom line: When jail sentences get longer, crime falls. When conviction rates rise, crime falls. But conviction rates are what really matter: A 10 percent increase in the conviction rate is a considerably stronger deterrent than a 10 percent increase in the average jail sentence.

Now, to a true religious believer, the conviction rate is 100 percent. God sees all, knows all, and punishes all. Based on everything we know about deterrence, true believers should almost never commit crimes. But I have not been able to uncover a shred of evidence that those who profess belief are any more law-abiding than their atheist neighbors. To be fair, I've found no evidence to the contrary either. But here we have a testable implication of the hypothesis that religious beliefs are sincere, and I look forward to seeing that test conducted.

Richard Dawkins (one of my very favorite writers) has written an entire book called *The God Delusion* to refute the claims of religion. His arguments strike me as quite unnecessary, because nobody believes those claims anyway. (Do we need a book called *The Santa Claus Delusion*?) [1] Indeed, Dawkins undercuts his own position when he points to statistics showing that, at least on a state-by-state basis, there is no correlation between religiosity and crime. His point is that religion does not make people better, but he misses the larger point that if religion doesn't make people better, then most people must not be terribly religious.

As Dawkins is quick to acknowledge, his statistics (quoted from Sam Harris's *Letter to a Christian Nation*) are far too crude to actually prove anything, but insofar as they're even suggestive, they suggest that his book is directed against a nonexistent enemy.

---

1 I argued in an earlier chapter that Dawkins's attempted refutation of Intelligent Design is as flawed—and, ironically, flawed in exactly the same way—as the Intelligent Design argument itself. My complaints about Dawkins in this chapter are quite separate from those earlier complaints.

Many religions promise not just punishment for the wicked, but a glorious afterlife for the righteous, and if believers are sincere, this, too, should affect their behavior. Surely people who expect to survive their own deaths should be less reluctant to die, and should therefore invest fewer resources in self-preservation. Do those who call themselves religious spend less on health care than the rest of us? Do they buy fewer smoke alarms? Are they more likely to jaywalk? Less likely to flinch when a foul ball is hit in the direction of their foreheads? I'm guessing not, and if my guess is right, it becomes almost impossible to imagine that their "belief" in an afterlife could be sincere.

Here's where someone always asks: "What about suicide bombers? Surely voluntary martyrdom is a symptom of sincere belief in an afterlife." And here's where I always reply: "Yes, my point exactly. If religious belief were as widespread as people claim it is, there should be millions upon millions of voluntary martyrs. Where are they all?"

There are a billion Muslims in the world, of whom at least several million profess to believe that martyrdom is the most direct path to heaven. Why, then, have Islamic terrorists managed to carry out no more than about five hundred suicide bombings in the past fifteen years? Why so few volunteers? Is it possible that only a negligible fraction of those several million actually mean what they say?

Even among those five hundred bombers, a large fraction were children, and I do not deny that many children believe in God, just as I do not deny that many children believe in Santa Claus. Adult suicide bombers are a great rarity indeed. Among the nineteen hijackers of September 11, 2001, a majority were not told the nature of the mission and were led to believe they'd return alive. Why was this necessary? Apparently, the leaders of

Al Qaeda, with all their resources and all their fanatical support-
ers, were unable to dig up nineteen men who actually bought
into the whole seventy-two-virgins bit.

Moreover, you don't need religion to create a suicide bomber.
The most prolific suicide bombers in modern history have been
the Tamil Tigers of Sri Lanka, who were motivated by politics,
not religion—as is likely to have been the case for at least some
of those whom we categorize as "Islamic extremists." Take out
the children and the politically motivated, and we're down to
a couple of hundred suicide bombers over fifteen years. That's a
big deal in a lot of ways, but as "evidence" that tens of millions
of people believe in God and heaven, it's negligible.

Consider next the curious phenomenon of "interfaith dialogue": Catholics and Protestants, or Jews and Christians, or
Christians and Muslims, gathered to learn more about each other's beliefs in an atmosphere of mutual respect. Respect for what,
exactly? For each other's beliefs, or for their right to hold those
beliefs? If the latter, there's no need for dialogue; I can respect
your right to be wrong from a respectful distance. No, interfaith
dialogue is about respect for the *beliefs themselves,* which entails
some acknowledgment that those beliefs might be right. (What
else could it possibly mean to respect a belief?) But as soon as
the Christian admits the Muslim might be right, he admits that
Christianity might be wrong. So much for perfect faith.

Orthodox Jews have traditionally shunned interfaith dialogue,
on the ground that there's no point in discussing issues that are
already definitively settled. We all know Jesus wasn't divine,
so why waste time talking about it? I take this as evidence that
Orthodox Jews typically mean what they say about their religion
(though I continue to think that this evidence is outweighed by
all the evidence to the contrary). But in most other religions—
including other flavors of Judaism—mainstream leaders have

frequently encouraged and participated in these debates and dialogues.

To a true believer, what purpose could such dialogues possibly serve? At the end of the evening, does anyone ever switch religions? Or do they simply present opposing viewpoints ("Jesus died on the cross for our sins," "Jesus ascended bodily into heaven," "Jesus was an ordinary mortal"), after which everyone nods sagely and then goes home? That's not how people act when they actually believe they're right. In my experience, if you fill a room with people who have conflicting beliefs about important matters of fact, they don't leave until they've either figured out who's right or collapsed from exhaustion.

What's curious about interfaith dialogue, then, is that it tends not to involve dialogue. In fact, actual dialogue about religion is conspicuous by its absence throughout polite society. If people really believed this stuff, they'd want to defend it. Yet only a small fraction of so-called believers are vigorous proselytizers.

Why don't believers work harder to spread the truth to their unenlightened neighbors? Is it simply a matter of politeness? I could accept that if we were talking about politics, but not religion. Religious disagreements are quite unlike political disagreements, because religious disagreements always hinge on matters of *fact*. Not so in politics, which sometimes hinge on matters of *self-interest;* farmers prefer policies that enrich farmers while bankers prefer policies that enrich bankers. Seat them next to each other at dinner, and the farmer and the banker might (or might not!) decide to steer clear of politics for the sake of amity. But if they disagree about the capital of South Dakota, neither etiquette nor common practice requires them to hold their tongues. They offer evidence; they try to figure out who's mistaken, and if anything important hangs in the balance, they keep at it till they've resolved the matter. If they disagreed about the divinity of Jesus, I'd expect them to do the same—unless, of course, the disagreement is all for show in the first place, in which case they might as well move on to some equally unimportant topic.

Now let's turn from *interfaith* dialogue to *internal* dialogue. Generally speaking, the subjects we care most about are those we've studied and meditated on. Cosmologists get worked up over the size of the Universe, accountants about just-in-time inventory management, and seventeenth-century historians about Oliver Cromwell. That's true for two reasons: First, passion inspires study, and second, study inspires confidence and renewed passion.

Religious believers, then, should, by and large, be students of—well, of what, exactly? Religion is first and foremost a *physical* theory—a theory of how the Universe was formed, what keeps it going, how it will end, and what sort of stuff (souls? angels?) inhabits it. I predict, then, that true religious believers should have a passionate interest in fundamental physics—even if only to figure out what's wrong with the mainstream theories. But I also predict that the bookshelves of the average churchgoer are no more likely than anyone else's to contain a good survey of, say, quantum chromodynamics. I conclude that the average churchgoer is not a believer.

Likewise, creationists, if they are really interested in the origins of life, will have read Darwin—or better yet (because he's more concise and writes for contemporary readers) Dawkins. I can (barely) imagine someone who has read *The Selfish Gene* and soundly rejected its contents, but I cannot imagine someone who cares passionately about the origins of life and has no interest in learning what Dawkins has to say.

Of course, the problem here is that once you're acquainted with the spectacular success of modern physics or modern biology, it's hard to keep on being religious. As the psychologist Paul Bloom has pointed out, "religions consistently make claims—about the age of the Earth, the nature of mental illness, the origins of species, the nature of consciousness, and so on—that turn out to be wrong." You'd expect the people most aware of these errors to be those most interested in the nature of mental illness, the origins of species, the nature of consciousness, and so on. There you see the paradox: People who are deeply curious about the origins of species, the nature of consciousness, the nature of mental illness, and so on will tend to be aware of those errors and hence tend to reject religion. People who are *not* deeply curious about those things might embrace religion, but they cannot embrace it deeply, because they're not really interested in the things that religion is *about*. Who's left to be religious?

Against all of this, where is the evidence for widespread belief? The best evidence is the testimony of the supposed believers themselves; survey data indicate that a good 90 percent of Americans believe in God. But social scientists have long known that raw survey data tell you almost nothing, because most survey respondents have almost no incentive to examine their own beliefs very carefully. In one recent survey, 39 percent of New Yorkers said they would leave the city "if they could"! Every one of them was in New York on the day of the interview, so we know that at a minimum, 39 percent of New Yorkers lie to pollsters.

Likewise, when survey analysts ask businessmen whether they set prices to maximize profit, the answer is almost always an overwhelming no. Then when they ask, "If you changed your prices, would your profits increase?", the answer is an equally overwhelming no.

If people don't believe in God, why do they say they do? Let me point out that people say things they don't believe *all the time.* On the morning of election day, I turned on the news and watched a national politician declare that "it doesn't matter who wins; it only matters that everyone gets out and votes." This was a politician who had fervently devoted the previous six months of his life to making sure his side won. If he didn't think it mattered, why did he bother?

Sometimes we lie; sometimes we mouth platitudes. Many an atheist has thanked God for a Red Sox victory or promised to keep a sick friend in his (nonexistent) prayers. And sometimes we express our instincts instead of our thoughts. We scold and threaten our computers, even though we don't believe for a moment that they actually hear us.

Now, the cognitive scientists will tell you it's not that simple—depending on what you mean by belief, it's perfectly possible for different parts of your brain to believe contradictory things. One part says, "I think I'll have another cashew," while another says, "No! Don't you dare!" Perhaps some part of your brain *does* believe your computer is listening, even while the more thoughtful parts know better. But here's the sense in which I mean you don't believe for an instant in your computer's sentience: If you had to bet all your wealth (or your child's life) on the matter, there's no question which side of the bet you'd take.

In a fascinating *Atlantic Monthly* article, Paul Bloom laid out a seductive theory of these instinctive beliefs. In brief, the human brain contains the equivalent of two quite separate computers, running two quite separate programs for understanding causality. One is well suited for understanding causality in the physical world ("The bullet fired because he pulled the trigger") and the other is well suited for understanding causality in the social world ("He pulled the trigger because he was angry"). In Bloom's words: "The understandings develop [in children] at different rates: the social one emerges somewhat later than the physical one. They evolved at different points in our prehistory; our physical understanding is shared by many species, whereas our social understanding is a relatively recent adaptation, and in some regards might be uniquely human." The social system is particularly attuned to searching for *intent*. According to Bloom, supernatural beliefs arise when the social system tries to understand physical phenomena. What caused that tornado? The social system insists on rewording the question: Who *wanted* that tornado—and why? Ask the question and you're poised to discover an angry God.

Bloom offers this as a theory of why 96 percent of Americans are religious. I prefer to see it as a theory of why 96 percent of Americans *say* they're religious. The instinct to believe in God comes, perhaps, from the same brain system as the instinct to believe in malevolent software. But an instinct to believe is not the same as a belief.

One important difference between God and our computers is that we actually have to live with our computers. If you cling to the instinctive belief that you can bully your computer into submission, you're in for endless frustration. But whether you cling to the instinctive belief that God sees all, knows all, and guides all is of little consequence—as long as you don't much let it affect your behavior. You can tell the pollster you believe or disbelieve, and he walks off just as surely and quickly either way.

Another of my very favorite writers, the philosopher Daniel Dennett, has written a thoughtful book called *Breaking the Spell*, where he searches for the evolutionary origins of religious belief. Dennett observes that religious beliefs reproduce, they sometimes reproduce in slightly mutated form, and they are subject to natural selection—precisely the three conditions necessary for evolution to occur. It's important to recognize that Dennett is talking about the evolution of religion itself, not the evolution of religious people, though the two histories are surely intertwined. Therefore a search for religion's evolutionary origins is not at all the same thing as a search for religion's evolutionary "value" to people. As Dennett also observes, the common cold certainly evolved, but that doesn't make it valuable to humans.

I think there is much to be learned from this sort of inquiry, though I'd give it a slightly different emphasis. Where Dennett asks, "Why do (most) people believe in God?", I'd prefer to ask, "Why do (most) people have a powerful instinct to believe in God?" To the believers themselves, that instinct might feel exactly the same as an actual belief. But it seems to me, for the reasons I've outlined, that most people also have plenty of cognitive machinery that rejects that belief.

It's very easy for people to *claim* they're religious—to pollsters, to neighbors, and even to themselves—when nothing of importance hangs in the balance. But beliefs affect behavior. Believers in hell should commit fewer crimes; believers in heaven should take more risks; believers in one religion should interact in predictable ways with believers in another; believers in God should have a powerful interest in the alternatives. Those implications are testable. I am moderately confident that carefully gathered statistics could refute the hypothesis that religious beliefs are widely or deeply held. Are there exceptions? Genuine true deep-down believers? Probably. Are there many? I doubt it.

7 On What There Obviously Is

I believe in looking reality straight in the eye and
denying it.

—*Garrison Keillor*

You'd think the things we experience directly would be the hardest to deny. Descartes observed that even if you're so skeptical as to doubt the existence of the external world, it's quite impossible to doubt the existence of your own sensations. Maybe you're imagining that ice-cream sundae, but if you can taste it, at least the taste is real.

It takes a lot of intellectual contortion to deny the obvious, but never underestimate the contortions of an intellectual. Somehow a large class of people—most of them highly educated—have contrived to deny the existence of phenomena that they, along with the rest of us, experience every day.

Nobody, with the possible exception of a schizophrenic or two, has a shred of doubt that free will and ESP are real phenomena, though large classes of people vociferously *express* doubt, not just to others, but to themselves. In certain societal strata, it is de rigueur to deny the theory of evolution; in others, it is de rigueur to deny the existence of ESP. The difference is that, given sufficient ignorance, one *can* doubt evolution, whereas nobody who has experienced human existence can possibly doubt the existence of ESP.

Start with free will. No college sophomore has ever turned in a paper denying the existence of free will without first choosing to do so. Acts of choice are as fundamental to human experience as any visual or aural sensation. You simply cannot be a conscious human being without making choices *all the time*. And deliberating over them, too.

That's free will, and you've got it, and you know you've got it. So why does anyone deny it? Here I rely on introspection and memory, because I remember denying it myself, or at least being troubled by it, at the age of sixteen. The argument seems to be something like this: Physics, at least at the level of neurons, is essentially deterministic: If you know the state of a system on Monday, and have sufficient computational power, you can predict with certainty the state of the system on the following Friday.[1] Human beings are physical objects. Ergo, if you know the state of a human being and his surroundings on Monday, and have sufficient computational power, you can predict with certainty the actions of that human being next Friday. Where, then, is there room for free will?

The final question is posed as if it were unanswerable, whereas in fact the answer is easy: There is room for free will on Tuesday, Wednesday, Thursday, and Friday, as the human being in question engages in deliberations that ultimately cause his actions.

---

1 Quantum mechanics might introduce a bit of randomness into this equation, but that randomness is probably irrelevant here, both because there's arguably not enough of it to make a noticeable difference and because, in any case, nobody wants to equate random behavior with free will.

Those deliberations are physical acts (they consist largely of chemical and electrical signals being passed around the brain, and perhaps partly of pencil marks appearing in two columns marked "Pros" and "Cons" on a legal pad), and are subject to the laws of physics. Where's the problem?

To paraphrase the philosopher Robert Nozick: Determinism is true but thermostats can still control the temperature. And nobody *denies* that thermostats control the temperature. They do it via laws of physics, which, when analyzed at the subatomic level, are indescribably complex, but which (fortunately) can also be analyzed at a much grosser and less precise level where we're able to make sense of them. Likewise, determinism is true but you can still control your life. You do it via laws of physics which are indescribably complex, but which can be analyzed at a much grosser and less precise level in terms of concepts like "intention" and "choice."

What caused Hurricane Katrina? Water vapor rising from the ocean's surface condensed to form clouds, releasing heat and causing an area of low pressure, sucking in air and creating winds that caused still further evaporation and fed the cycle. An insane person might object that that can't be it at all, because evaporation is just a shorthand term for an indescribably complex process involving trillions of air and water molecules. Sure. But that doesn't mean evaporation isn't real.

What caused your decision to get drunk and watch *Mystery Science Theater* the night before your philosophy final? Free will. An insane person might object that free will can't be it at all, because free will is just a shorthand term for an indescribably complex process involving trillions of neurons, which in turn can be described in terms of quadrillions of atoms and quintillions of subatomic particles. So what? You still have free will, and you know it.

My memory's a little hazy on the subject of how I outgrew my own teenage angst about free will, though reading Daniel Dennett's books probably had something to do with it. But my main point here is not that we have free will. It's that we *know* we have it; at the deepest core level, we never doubt it for a second, and yet we're silly enough to *claim* we doubt it, and even—at least if we are sufficiently geeky to care about these things in the first place—to convince *ourselves* that we believe something we never *could* believe.

I'm sure free will is part of your everyday experience; I suspect extrasensory perception is also. I know it's part of mine.

I have an extrasensory perception that the ratio of a circle's circumference to its diameter is somewhere between 3.1415 and 3.1416. Better yet, I have an extrasensory perception that the same ratio is exactly four times the limit of the infinite sequence

$$1 - \frac{1}{3} + \frac{1}{5} - \frac{1}{7} + \frac{1}{9} - \frac{1}{11} + \cdots$$

My perception of this fact is as immediate, as powerful, and as incontrovertible as my perception of the remarkably attention-grabbing shade of green they've used for the new OBEY THE CROSS-WALK signs on the roads near my office. And my perception is quite extrasensory; it's based on mental processes that have taken place entirely inside my brain, with no input from any of my sensory apparatus.

You probably have extrasensory perceptions, too. Surely you perceive that $2 + 3 = 5$, though I'm not sure whether that counts as extrasensory; maybe you discovered it by combining two stones with three stones and using your eyes to see what happened. (Though even then, it's a big step from the sensory data to the generalization.) But your perception (if you have one) that there are infinitely many primes is fundamentally extrasensory.

Sure, you might have arrived at this perception by studying marks on paper—perhaps even by studying marks on paper in an earlier chapter of this book. But you *could* have arrived at it by pure thought, and it's entirely likely that Euclid or one of his precursors did just that.

Whether or not you give much thought to the subtleties of arithmetic, you probably have a pretty strong perception that arithmetic is internally consistent. Even without calculating, you can be quite sure that 234324324 plus 9418438 is not equal to both 243742762 *and* 342859152. Whether or not you believe there are infinitely many primes, you probably believe that the number of primes is not both finite and infinite simultaneously.

Unless you are an expert in mathematical logic, you probably have no idea how to *prove* the consistency of arithmetic, and if you *are* an expert in mathematical logic, then you are well aware that any such proof relies on principles that are no easier to accept than the conclusion itself—so that if you're willing to buy the proof, you might as well just skip ahead and buy the conclusion.[2] In other words, your perception of consistency does not rely on proof. If it does not rely on proof, it surely cannot rely on having *seen* or *heard* a proof. In other words, it is purely extrasensory.

Everyone knows this. More precisely, everyone who is a thinker sophisticated enough to deny the existence of ESP is also a thinker sophisticated enough to perceive mathematical truths in an extrasensory way. If you've got the cognitive apparatus to deny ESP, you've got the cognitive apparatus to experience it.

At this point, you might be tempted to accuse me of playing

2 The best argument for the consistency of arithmetic, as I suggested in Chapter 1 and will suggest more forcefully in Chapters 9 and 10, is that arithmetic describes the natural numbers and the natural numbers are, in some important sense, *real*. But of course our awareness of the natural numbers is itself extrasensory.

a silly word game. After all, you might say, when people speak about ESP, they don't mean extrasensory perception in general; they mean a certain *kind* of extrasensory perception that is quite unlike my mathematical examples. As my friend Roger Schlafly put it: "Saying you believe in ESP because you can perceive mathematical truths without using your senses is like saying you believe in UFOs because you believe there are flying objects that have not been identified."

I appreciate the wit but I think the analogy is quite thoroughly misguided. In everyday parlance, *UFO* means something like "flying object designed and controlled by intelligent extraterrestrial creatures." Such things are logically possible; we can disagree about their existence, and it's useful to have a word for them.

By contrast, the everyday usage of the term *ESP* refers generally to a broad range of phenomena, having in common only two characteristics: They are perceptions, and they are extrasensory. Some of those phenomena have one additional characteristic: They are physically impossible. But if you're going to *define* ESP by its impossibility, then of course there's no point in debating it. People do have serious conversations about the reality of ESP. Therefore the generally accepted definition of ESP cannot require impossibility. And if impossibility is not a criterion, then mathematical insight is as good an example of ESP—*in the everyday sense of the term*—as any instance of clairvoyance or telepathy.

Likewise with free will. Some people *define* free will by its physical impossibility—and then go on to debate whether it exists or not. Talk about playing silly word games! Let me introduce a note of common sense here: If you require free will or ESP or anything else to be impossible by definition, then it doesn't exist. But according to the ordinary definitions that ordinary people use in ordinary life, these things not only exist, they exist *undeniably*. That people continue to deny them is a curious phenomenon indeed.

Similar considerations apply to "life after death." At one level, the question is trivial: You can no more believe in a literal life after death than you can believe in a round square or a married bachelor; death is *defined* to be the cessation of life. If you're still alive, you're not dead.

So when people ask, "Do you believe in life after death?", they can't possibly mean the question literally. What, then, do they mean?

Apparently they mean something like: "Do you believe that if you die on Sunday, your consciousness will still exist on Monday?" Here the answer is either obviously yes or obviously no, depending on what you mean by consciousness.

Take an analogous question: I own a quilt with a unique and quite beautiful geometric pattern. If my quilt is destroyed in a fire on Sunday, will that pattern still exist on Monday?

It depends on what you mean by "that pattern." If you mean a certain abstract mathematical structure—triangles overlaid with circles according to certain complicated rules—then of course the fire can't destroy the pattern. Patterns do not exist at particular times any more than they exist in particular places. Asking whether an abstract pattern exists on Monday makes no more sense than asking whether it exists in Nebraska. It exists, period.

But if you mean a particular *instance* of the pattern—a bunch of dyed threads arranged according to the pattern's rules— then of course the fire destroys the pattern. Obviously.

Likewise, your "consciousness" can refer to an abstract pattern of connections and stimulus-response rules, or to the specific instance of that pattern that constitutes your brain. Does that pattern exist after you're dead? No, but only because it doesn't exist *before* you're dead, either; it exists outside of time. Your death is irrelevant. Does your brain still exist? Surely not, at least after a very short time passes and decay sets in.

People seem to think there's more to this life-after-death question than that, but I can't imagine what they could possibly be talking about. Neither, I suspect, can they.

8 Diogenes' Nightmare

I would never die for my beliefs, because my beliefs might be wrong.

—Bertrand Russell

I think, therefore I am perhaps mistaken.

—Sharon Fenick

Someone's been passing state secrets to a terrorist group. Through some quirk of fate, it's your responsibility to identify the most likely culprit. Your two best agents, each an honest truthseeker, have been investigating the case and have arrived to deliver their reports in your office:

> *Agent 86: I can't share my evidence with you, but I'm pretty sure the culprit is a man named Curly.*
> *Agent 99: I can't share my evidence with you either, but I'm pretty sure the culprit is a man named Shemp.*

Based on what you've heard, who's the more likely culprit?

Surely you've had this experience: You meet up with an intelligent and knowledgeable friend, and before long you've fallen into an amiable disagreement. Who's most likely to win the World Series or the next election? Is global warming a problem? Does your cousin Fred have the hots for my sister Wilma? Is a caribou the same thing as a reindeer? You argue for a while, nobody's mind is changed, and you cheerfully agree to disagree.

Over the course of the argument, you share all your relevant evidence. You're both smart enough to evaluate what the evidence does and does not imply. So how can you possibly disagree?

When two well-functioning computers run identical programs with identical input, they produce identical output. Likewise, you might expect that when two thoughtful people apply identical rules of logic to analyze identical evidence, they should reach identical conclusions. Sometimes the conclusion is indefinite ("The Yankees will *probably* win the World Series"); sometimes—if the evidence is misleading—the conclusion might be wrong, but at least the conclusion should be *shared*.

The moral of the story, at least so far, is that you and your friend are not logic machines. Your opinions must be shaped by something other than logic and evidence. At least one of you is relying on something like intuition, revelation, ESP, or good old-fashioned stubbornness.

I'm not particularly fond of this moral. I often like to think that, outside of pure mathematics, most of my own beliefs are grounded firmly in logic and evidence. Other times, I like to think I look good on a dance floor.

But disturbing as the moral may be, a far darker moral lies ahead: Not only do our disagreements prove we're not logic machines; those same disagreements prove we're fundamentally dishonest, in the sense of not caring whether our positions are correct.

It's going to take a few pages to get to that darker moral. The first step is to say something a little more surprising about how we'd behave if we *were* logic machines.

I've already pointed out that two logic machines analyzing identical evidence should reach identical conclusions. But the Nobel Prize–winning game theorist Robert Aumann has made the more startling observation that two logic machines analyzing entirely *different* evidence must *still* reach identical conclusions—as long as they're aware of each other's opinions.

Let me explain.

Suppose I have good reasons for betting on the Yankees; you have equally good, but entirely different, reasons for betting on the Red Sox. I don't know your reasons and you don't know mine. Nevertheless, the instant I hear you're betting on the Red Sox, I should question my faith in the Yankees. True, I don't know *why* you're betting on the Red Sox—but surely you have *some* reasons. So, to put this bluntly, why should I trust my own opinion any more than I trust yours?

Well, here's why: Maybe I have some very good reasons to stick with the Yankees. (Maybe I met a doctor who's treating the Red Sox's best starting pitcher for bursitis.) That's fine. So I stick with the Yankees. And as soon as I *announce* that I'm sticking with the Yankees, you can *infer* that I've got some very good reasons for my opinion. You have no idea what those reasons are, but you know I find them quite convincing—convincing enough to overcome the momentary shock of hearing that you favor the Red Sox. Now *your* faith is shaken. Are you sticking with your opinion? If so, that tells me that *you* must have very good reasons, which shakes my faith even further. Do I still stick with the Yankees? Only if my reasons are very *very* good, in which case you *know* that my reasons are very very good. So our conversation goes something like this:

> You: I'm betting on the Red Sox.
> Me: I hear you. But I'm betting on the Yankees.
> You: Well *I* hear *you,* but I'm still betting on the Red Sox.
> Me: I still say Yankees.
> You: I still say Red Sox.
> Me: Yankees.
> You: Red Sox.
> Me: Yankees.
> You: Red Sox.
> Me: Okay. Red Sox.

Appearances to the contrary, new information is conveyed at every stage of this conversation. When you start off with "I'm betting on the Red Sox," I know very little about the quality of your reasons—but it's still enough to shake my confidence in the Yankees, at least a little bit. After I shake *your* confidence by declaring for the Yankees, you stick with the Red Sox *even though your confidence is shaken.* Now I know your reasons must be pretty good. But so are mine, so I stick with the Yankees, shaking your confidence even further. By sticking with the Red Sox for another round, you reveal even more about how good your reasons must be.

"I still say Yankees even though I know that you say Red Sox" means one thing. "I still say Yankees even though I know that you know that I know that you say Red Sox" means something stronger. The more you reaffirm "Red Sox," the more I doubt "Yankees"; the more I reaffirm "Yankees" in the face of this doubt, the more you doubt "Red Sox." Eventually, the party with the weaker evidence backs down.[1]

(That last sentence—"Eventually, the party with the weaker evidence backs down"—requires proof, and the proof requires more sophisticated mathematics than is appropriate for this book. That's where Professor Aumann's work comes in; if you're interested in seeing the mathematics, Google for "Aumann" plus "agreeing to disagree.")

More precisely, Professor Aumann proved that the conversation cannot end with an agreement to disagree. That leaves two possibilities: Either the conversation ends in agreement, or we're trapped in an endless Monty Python sketch ("Yankees!" "Red Sox!" "Yankees!" "Red Sox!"). But shortly after Aumann's publication, the economists John Geanakoplos and Herakles Polemarchakis ruled out the latter possibility by proving that the conversation can*not* go on forever; it must eventually end in agreement.

Real-world conversations do not always end in agreement. Why not? One guess is that reaching agreement takes more time than it's worth. Nobody is going to sit through twenty million rounds of "Yankees!" "Red Sox!" "Yankees!" "Red Sox!" just to find out who's right; by the time that conversation ends, the World Series will be over. But the computer scientist Scott Aaronson largely disposed of this loophole by proving that when both parties are honest, they can reach agreement after a reasonable amount of time.

So why don't we always reach agreement? Perhaps because we're not being honest. I'll come back to that thought in a moment, but first let me point out that we've now got the tools to

---

1 More precisely, everybody backs down. Coming in, I thought the Red Sox had a 20 percent chance and you thought the Red Sox had a 90 percent chance. Walking away, we agree that the Red Sox have a 70 percent chance.

solve the brainteaser at the head of this chapter. If your agents had submitted their reports in sealed envelopes, they'd be (as far as you know) equally reliable. But that's not what happened. Agent 86 went first, announcing that he believes Curly is the culprit. That means he's got pretty good evidence; it must be at least, say, a seven on a scale of ten. Then 99 tells you that she believes Shemp is the culprit *even after hearing 86's opinion to the contrary*. To be that sure of herself, 99 must have evidence that's at least, say, an eight. There's no way to be sure whose evidence is stronger, but if you must play the odds, you should go with 99.

Now, if 86 comes back with "I still think it's Curly"—even after learning that 99's evidence is at least an 8—you can infer that 86's evidence is at least, say, an 8.5, and you should lean toward 86. If 99 comes back with "I still think it's Shemp," you should lean back toward 99. But there's no need to think too hard about it; just let the agents fight it out and eventually they're sure to agree.

That's the theory. In the real world, of course, both agents get increasingly defensive, despise you for doubting them, and denigrate each other's competence. The almost inescapable conclusion is that at least one of the agents—more likely both of them—is more a show-off than an honest truthseeker.

And likewise, it would appear, for all of us who live in the real world. Chances are you've disagreed with someone today, and walked away without settling your differences.[2] I'm forced to conclude that at least one of you is not an honest truthseeker. Chances are the same thing happened yesterday and the day

---

2 "I think the bathroom should be blue, not pink" does not count as a disagreement; we actually agree that blue looks better to me and pink looks better to you. For this discussion, the only relevant disagreements are over matters of fact, not matters of taste. Still, I'm confident you've disagreed with someone over a matter of fact in the past day or so.

before. Either you're the one and only honest truthseeker in your entire social circle, or you're just as corrupt as the rest of us.

If the arguments I've given here are right, then honest truthseeking must be almost vanishingly rare. That disturbing conclusion has inspired dozens of economists to work overtime searching for some logical loophole in Aumann's argument.

First potential loophole: Our search for truth is guided by more than just logic and evidence; we rely also (sometimes mistakenly, perhaps sometimes not) on intuition, revelation, and ESP. If my belief that God created the world in seven days is based on evidence, I can point to the evidence and say, "Look here!" But if my belief is based on revelation, there's nothing to point to. I've had my revelation; you've had your revelation to the contrary; we both honestly believe our revelations are accurate, and there's no middle ground.

Nice try, but no cigar. Even when we rely on revelation, we're forced to ask: Why should I trust my own revelation any more than I trust yours? Sure, my revelation came to me in a way that makes it seem certain, but no more so than your revelation seems certain to you. Why should I be persuaded by my own certainty and not be persuaded by yours?

All the arguments that apply to evidence apply equally well to revelation. Each time I reaffirm my revelation, I reveal a higher level of certainty; each time you reaffirm yours in the face of my higher level of certainty, you reveal an even higher level. The process should escalate until someone backs down—just as it does with evidence.[3] And the same thing works in mixed cases,

---

3 For Bayesian learning theorists, the formal translation of this observation comes down to: "Why should I trust my own prior any more than I trust yours?" (If you're not a Bayesian learning theorist, by all means skip this footnote.) For a more detailed discussion, see the references in the appendix, especially the work of Robin Hanson.

where, say, I'm relying on revelation and you're relying on evidence, or we're each relying on some mixture.

What other loopholes might there be? Do we perhaps argue inconclusively because, despite our honesty, we make logical errors, or because, try as we might, we don't fully understand the evidence that's right in front of us? The economist Robin Hanson has emphasized that this apparent loophole is no loophole at all, essentially because honest truthseekers would correct for the possibility that they've made logical errors or misconstrued the evidence.

Hanson's best guess is that disagreements persist because we tend to overestimate our own intelligence, and therefore tend to put too much weight on our own opinions. One sees this in academic circles all the time. Every year, the members of my department devote prodigious amounts of energy—perhaps half our working hours over a period of several months—to evaluating the qualifications of applicants for faculty positions. At the same time, the faculties of MIT and Stanford are evaluating pretty much the same pool of candidates. Yet we persist in making offers to the candidates *we* believe are strongest, as opposed to the candidates our Stanford colleagues believe are strongest—even though they're surely as well qualified to make judgments as we are. We could save ourselves a lot of time and effort by just announcing a policy that we're willing to hire anyone with an offer from Stanford.

Of course, an unjustified faith in your own opinions is just another form of dishonesty. If 99 believes 86 is an idiot, 86 should at least entertain the possibility that 99 is correct. Eventually, they should agree about who's smarter.

But perhaps there's something in our evolutionary makeup that won't let us admit—even to ourselves—that we might be stupid. Admitting you're stupid can be a poor strategy for attracting mates.

On the other hand, many arguments *do* end in consensus. Criminal juries, for example, usually manage to agree on a unanimous verdict. Academic seminars (at least in the departments I'm familiar with) are often scenes of sharp disagreement, but more often than not we hash things out until everyone's figured out who's right and who's wrong.

Even so, we reach consensus not by reasserting our positions until someone backs down, but by explaining our reasoning until we understand each other. We do this primarily because we're more interested in the reasoning than in the conclusions. Indeed, we are so eager to understand each other's reasoning that we often play devil's advocate. If a brilliant mathematician who has spent years thinking about the problem assures me that a certain equation has no solutions, I believe him. But if I want to understand his reasoning, I am likely to demand an explanation in language that expresses false doubt. I'll say, "This step in your argument makes no sense," even though I'm quite sure that it will make perfect sense once it's explained to me.

Sometimes I'll even say, "I don't believe you," when what I really mean is "I think you're probably right, but I don't understand why." So an apparent disagreement is really no disagreement at all.

Academics, then, are frequently "dishonest truthseekers"—we take adversarial positions from which we fully expect to retreat. Lawyers, by contrast, have a very different culture. Following an impassioned argument by the prosecutor, you'll never hear the defense attorney say, "Good Lord, you're right! I hadn't thought about it that way before!" The reason, of course, is that lawyers, as they themselves will be the first to admit, are not truthseekers at all. You've had a good day in the courtroom when you've changed someone's mind. You've had a good day in the seminar room when someone changes yours.

I much prefer the latter, which is why I chose a life in the academy. But I can imagine that in some circumstances and for some issues, the lawyers' approach—two dishonest advocates submitting arguments for the perusal of a (presumably) honest jury—could be an efficient way to uncover truth.

Lawyers are dishonest because they're paid to be, and they fail to agree at least partly because they're dishonest. But we're left with a nagging puzzle: Why is consensus so rare in *other* walks of life? Why do professional gamblers bet against each other, rather than treating each other's opinions as seriously as their own? With all that money on the table, you'd expect them to try to get things right.

The answer, I guess, is that gamblers aren't in it only for the money. They're in it also for the prestige of being right when the other guy was wrong. You can't earn that prestige without staking out a contrarian position now and then. Ditto for stock-market investors. Virtually all economists agree that if you're out to make money, it's crazy to try to "beat the market"; lionizing the man who *does* beat the market is like lionizing the man who manages to flip heads twenty times in a row. Nevertheless, men and women who beat the market are lionized. If you want to be admired for your investment prowess, you've got to act as if you disagree with the crowd—and then hope for good luck.

Or maybe gamblers and stock-market players are simply superstitious and irrational. But what about physicists?[4] Ask two

---

4 Physicists, of course, are never superstitious. Niels Bohr, one of the founding fathers of quantum mechanics and among the greatest of twentieth-century physicists, kept a horseshoe over his door for good luck. He explained that he didn't believe in it, but he'd heard that it works even if you *don't* believe.

theoretical physicists whether string theory is likely to yield productive insights and you'll get three different answers.[5] They've all seen the same evidence; why don't they all have the same opinion?

You might reply that there's not yet enough evidence to be definitive, but that misses the point. True, there's not yet enough evidence to justify a full-fledged acceptance or rejection of string theory—but there could well be enough evidence to support some level of optimism or pessimism. How can the same evidence support both the optimism of some scientists and the pessimism of others? Perhaps, like gamblers, stock-market investors, and even (gasp!) economists, physicists sometimes care more about the glory of vanquishing an opponent than the glory of discovering truth.

---

5 String theory is a branch of modern physics which—speaking very roughly—posits the existence of tiny strings whose vibrations create matter in something like the same way that a vibrating guitar string creates music.

Part

Knowledge

Some beliefs matter. Believe what you will about free will or free trade, but please don't believe that stomping on the accelerator will make your car slow down. It's important to get that right—so we do.

My basement contains a hot-water heater. My upstairs bathroom contains a stall shower. How does the hot water get to the shower? According to a recent informal survey (taken in the lounge where I eat lunch every day), six out of six Ph.D. economists believed that "there's a pump." No plumber shares that misconception. On the other hand, the world teems with plumbers who think protectionism can make us prosperous. Because our time and energy are limited, we get a few things right and most things wrong.[1]

When it's important to get things right, we try to replace our mere *beliefs* with actual *knowledge*. In the next few chapters, I'll talk about where knowledge comes from: mathematical insight (Chapters 9 through 11), logical reasoning (Chapter 12), and the

---

1 My colleague Mark Bils observes that the hot-water-pump survey raises a thorny economic question, namely: How can there possibly be a positive rate of unemployment in a world where you can obviously make a living by knocking on people's doors and offering to inspect their hot-water pumps? You go down to the basement, smoke a cigarette, come back upstairs, announce that the pump looks good for another two years, and charge thirty dollars.

analysis of evidence (Chapter 13). Chapters 14 and 15 are about the limits to knowledge (if any) imposed by quantum physics.

Along the way, I'll tell you a little about Gödel's incompleteness theorem, the lore of very large numbers, the most counterintuitive theorem in all of mathematics, why the world is overpolluted, the importance of attending preschool, the effects of Internet porn, the Heisenberg uncertainty principle, and why game theorists care about the oddness of the quantum world.

9 Knowing Your Math

God exists since mathematics is consistent, and the
Devil exists since we cannot prove it.

—*André Weil*

If a "religion" is defined to be a system of ideas that
contains unprovable statements, then Gödel taught
us that mathematics is not only a religion, it is the only
religion that can prove itself to be one.

—*John Barrow*

When I add a column of numbers twice and get two different
answers, I believe I've made a mistake. That's because I believe
arithmetic is consistent. It doesn't contradict itself.

Why should I believe that? Here's the most convincing argument that anyone knows: The laws of arithmetic are consistent
because they are *true*, and true statements can't contradict each
other.

To buy that argument, you must believe that the laws of
arithmetic are true.[1] To buy *that*, you must believe the laws

---

1 Later in the chapter, I'll list the "laws of arithmetic" for you.

of arithmetic are *about* something. The statement "All glorphs are gumbels" is neither true nor false, because there is no such thing as a glorph. The statement "A column of numbers has only one sum" can be true only if there is such a thing as a number.

There are other ways to prove arithmetic is consistent, but those other ways all rely on principles that are less self-evident (and therefore more suspect) than the simple observation that the natural numbers exist and the laws of arithmetic are true. If, like 99.8 percent of all working mathematicians, and 99.8 percent of everyone who's ever used a calculator, you trust the consistency of arithmetic, it's almost surely because deep down you believe the natural numbers are in some important sense *real*.

Admittedly, the word *real* is a little vague. If it makes you feel better, let's give it a precise definition: "The natural numbers are real" *means* that the laws of arithmetic are consistent.

Like you, I believe that the natural numbers are real. Like you, I have precious little evidence for this belief. True, I've been working with numbers my whole life and have never found an inconsistency. But that evidence is so paltry it's negligible: All the numbers I've ever worked with are highly atypical. I have added columns of four-, five-, and six-digit numbers, but I have never added columns of billion-digit numbers. Yet almost all numbers have more than a billion digits. I therefore have no direct evidence of how most numbers behave.

A die-hard skeptic might conclude that because we have no experience of large numbers, we cannot know that they behave consistently, or even that they exist at all. That die-hard skeptic is named Alexander Yessenin-Volpin, an eccentric mathematician and courageous former Soviet dissident who did a stint in a psychiatric hospital for writing "anti-Soviet poetry." According to Yessenin-Volpin, we should have faith only in those numbers that are "small enough to think about." This doctrine is called "ultrafinitism," and few mathematicians take it seriously.

By way of objecting to ultrafinitism, a mainstream mathematician might ask: "How on earth are we to decide which numbers are 'small enough to think about'? Surely one- and two-digit numbers are small enough to think about; surely thirty digit numbers aren't. Where's the cutoff?"

One such mainstream mathematician is Harvey Friedman, notable both for his contributions to mathematical logic and for having been appointed to a professorship at Stanford when he was not yet nineteen years old. Friedman once tried to debate Yessenin-Volpin; here's his account of what happened:

> I . . . proceeded to start with 2 and asked him whether this is "real" or something to that effect. He virtually immediately said yes. Then I asked about 4, and he again said yes, but with a perceptible delay. Then 8, and yes, but with more delay. This continued for a couple of more times, till it was obvious how he was handling this objection. Sure, he was prepared to always answer yes, but he was going to take 2^{100} times as long to answer yes to 2^{100} than he would to answering 2. [2^{100} is a thirty-digit number.] There is no way that I could get very far with this.

In the end, Friedman and Yessenin-Volpin agreed to disagree. Nearly every mathematician shares Friedman's faith in the reality of large numbers; few could even name a single ultrafinitist other than perhaps Yessenin-Volpin himself. We believe not only in arithmetic, but in algebra, geometry, and the rest of mathematics. But we have not a shred of logic and no more than a shred of evidence to support that belief.[2]

Our belief, then, must rest on some other basis; call it faith, intuition, gut instinct, revelation, or ESP (I'm not sure how many of those are just different names for the same thing). For that matter, it might be an illusion—or a truth—that is built into the way the human brain (or at least *my* brain) is wired. In one sense, then, my knowledge of arithmetic is on the same footing as the pope's (purported) knowledge of God. The one key difference, I feel confident, is that I'm right and the pope is wrong.[3]

One reason to doubt people who claim direct knowledge of God is that they have so much trouble agreeing about the details. Admittedly, the same caveat applies, though perhaps in a more limited sense, to people like me who claim direct knowledge of mathematics. The question of which mathematical truths are clearly accessible to the intuition has been answered differently by different people in different times and different places. In 1888, the great German mathematician David Hilbert proved his "Basis Theorem," which is the foundation for much of modern algebra. He did so by the unprecedented technique of treating infinite sets of infinite sets as if they were con- crete objects, leading Hilbert's contemporary Paul Gordan to sneer that "this is not mathematics; it is theology." But the tech- niques proved sufficiently fruitful that just a few years later, even Gordan allowed that "theology has its uses."

Hilbert's techniques were controversial in 1888 but main-

2 On reflection, it seems unsurprising that we can know things without the aid of logic or evidence. A spider, after all, knows how to spin a web without either reasoning it out from first principles or meticulously observing the work of other spiders. You could argue that the spider's instincts are uncon- scious and hence don't count as knowledge, but if spiders can be hardwired to spin webs, I see no reason in principle why people can't be hardwired to understand mathematics.

3 I'll have a little more to say about this in Chapter 13.

stream a decade later; nowadays almost no mathematician (surely excepting Yessenin-Volpin) would question them. There are great gaps between what Yessenin-Volpin would allow, what Gordan allowed, what Hilbert allowed, and what most of us allow today. My own faith in modern algebra—and in the techniques used to prove Hilbert's Basis Theorem—is extremely strong, though probably not as strong as my faith in the consistency of basic arithmetic.

But at its core, mathematical intuition has not substantially changed through the ages. The basic facts about counting and arithmetic that Pythagoras "just knew" are the same as those that you and I just know. Euclid's idea of a proof was more or less the same as ours. And though many of Euclid's proofs are now considered inadequate, they are inadequate in ways that Euclid himself would have acknowledged if they'd been pointed out to him. Euclid sometimes failed to meet modern standards, but that's not because his standards were different; it's because he made mistakes. So do we all.

In other words, there's been very little change over the millennia in the mathematical truths we hold to be self-evident. When we study arithmetic, we single out those truths and call them "axioms." The axioms of arithmetic are infinite in number; nevertheless, in case you're interested, I can describe them all for you. (If you're *not* interested, by all means skip ahead a page or two.)

Here are the first four axioms:

- 0 is a number.

- Every number has an immediate successor.

- No two numbers have the same immediate successor.

- 0 is not the immediate successor of any number.

That's four down and infinitely many to go. Here are some of the others:

- If there are any even numbers, then there is a smallest even number.

- If there are any prime numbers, then there is a smallest prime number.

- If there are any numbers that can be written as the sum of two cubes in more than one way, then there is a smallest number that can be written as the sum of two cubes in more than one way.

- If there are any numbers that are not equal to themselves, then there is a smallest number that is not equal to itself.

And so forth. For any property you can think of (like "even" or "prime," or "able to be written as a sum of two cubes in more than one way" or "not equal to itself"), there's a corresponding axiom. Incidentally, the smallest even number is 0, the smallest prime number is 2, the smallest number that can be written as a sum of two cubes in more than one way is 1729 (which is equal to 1 cubed plus 12 cubed, and also to 9 cubed plus 10 cubed), and there are no numbers that are not equal to themselves.

This infinite family completes the list of axioms for arithmetic. When I say *the* list of axioms, all I mean is that this list is in common use. You are, of course, welcome to write down your own competing list. This particular list was first written down about a century ago by the Italian logician Giuseppe Peano, and they're usually called the Peano axioms.

Starting from the Peano axioms, and using the rules of logic, we can prove certain theorems. We can prove, for example, that the sum of two even numbers is even, that every number can be factored into primes, and that there is no largest prime number. We know those theorems are true because they follow logically from the axioms, and the axioms are true. But that's not *why* the theorems are true; the sum of two even numbers would be an even number whether or not this fact happened to follow from the axioms we (or Professor Peano) chose to write down.

What's *true* is a matter of mathematical fact. What's *provable* depends on our (somewhat arbitrary) choice of axioms.

In fact, Kurt Gödel, as part of his celebrated incompleteness theorem, gave an explicit example of a sentence in arithmetic that is true but not provable. Gödel's example is a little too complicated to include here, but I'll give you an equally good example in the next chapter.

If Gödel's sentence isn't provable, how could he have known it was true? Answer: He knew it was true because he proved it. But he "cheated" by using an extra axiom that's not on Peano's list.

Here's the extra axiom; let's call it the SuperAxiom: *Peano's axioms are consistent.* That is, you can't use Peano's axioms to prove something self-contradictory, such as "not all even numbers are even."

It's easy to write down lists of axioms that are *in*consistent: You could, for example, take "zero does not equal one" as your first axiom and "zero equals one" as your second. Those axioms contradict each other, and the reason they're able to contradict each other is that one of them is *false*.

Peano's axioms, however, cannot contradict each other because all of them are *true*. Therefore the SuperAxiom is true, and anything that follows from it is true. What Gödel found is a sentence that, on the one hand, follows from the Peano axioms plus the SuperAxiom (so we know it's true) but on the other hand, does *not* follow from the Peano axioms alone (so by the usual standards, it's not provable).

Do you feel cheated? Gödel's celebrated "nonprovable" sentence is actually quite provable—as long as you allow yourself to use the quite uncontroversial SuperAxiom.

So let's add the SuperAxiom to our list of axioms. Now Gödel's sentence is both true and officially provable—just as the sentence "one plus one equals two" is both true and provable. There's nothing extraordinary about that. What's become of Gödel's great accomplishment?

"Go right ahead," replies Gödel. "Add the SuperAxiom to Peano's list. Now you can prove my sentence. But I'll give you an example of a *new* sentence—one that's unprovable even from your new, longer list of axioms. And my new sentence is also true."

How does Gödel know his new sentence is true? Because he proves it! This time he "cheats" by using yet another new axiom—call it the SuperDuperAxiom: *the expanded list of axioms—that is, the Peano axioms plus the SuperAxiom—is still consistent.*

The SuperDuperAxiom is true because all of the other axioms, including the SuperAxiom, are true. Gödel's new sentence is therefore true, because he can prove it using the SuperDuperAxiom. But *you* can't prove it, because the SuperDuperAxiom is not on your list.

To review: You started with the Peano axioms. Gödel gave you a true sentence you couldn't prove. But *he* proved it, using the SuperAxiom. You said: "Fine. I'll add the SuperAxiom to my list of axioms; now I can prove your sentence." Gödel said: "Fine. I'll give you a *new* sentence you can't prove—even using your new, liberalized rules of proof." He proves his new sentence using the SuperDuperAxiom.

Your next gambit, of course, is to add the SuperDuperAxiom to your list of axioms. Gödel's next gambit, of course, is to come up with a *new* sentence that you can't prove, using even the SuperDuperAxiom. He knows this sentence is true, because he's proved it using a SuperDoubleDuperAxiom. And on and on we go. (And Gödel did in fact prove that he can go on and on forever.)

No list of axioms can prove all the true sentences of arithmetic; this is half the content of Gödel's theorem.[4] That alone tells you that there's a difference between what's true and what's provable.

To recap: There are such things as true statements in arithmetic. "True" does not mean "provable." Instead it means *true* in the ordinary sense of the word. But to be true, these statements must be *about* something, and that something is the system of natural numbers. Moreover, these statements were true long before anybody thought about them, and would be true whether anybody ever thought about them or not. Therefore the natural numbers were around before anybody ever thought of them and would be around whether anybody ever thought of them or not. That observation was central to the arguments in Chapter 1 of this book.

---

4 If you are very clever, you might be tempted to take *all of the true sentences of arithmetic* as axioms. Then every true sentence has a one-line proof. How do you prove that the sum of two even numbers is even? Answer: That's an axiom! How do you prove that there is no largest prime number? Answer: That's an axiom! But this dodge won't do. The problem is that under this system, there's no way to tell what's an axiom and what isn't. Is it or is it not an axiom that every even number is a sum of two primes? Answer: It's an axiom if and only if it's true—but we have no way to tell whether it's true and hence no way to tell whether it's an axiom. The rules of the game are this: You can use any axioms you want *provided* there's a clear rule for determining what is and isn't an axiom. By this criterion, a list of all true sentences is not a list of axioms.

10 Unfinished Business

Hercules and the Hydra

> Nor could he effect anything by smashing its heads with his club, for as fast as one head was smashed there grew up two.
>
> —*Apollodorus*

In the preceding chapter, I promised you an example of a sentence that's true but not provable. You might expect that task to be very difficult, perhaps even Herculean. So let's start with Hercules.

Hercules, as you may know, killed his wife and children in a fit of rage. By way of penance, he agreed to perform a series of tasks assigned by his sworn enemy Eurystheus.

The first task was to slay the dreaded Nemean Lion; this Hercules accomplished with his bare hands. The second task was to take on the many-headed hydra. Ancient sources tell us that each time Hercules severed a head, two grew back to take its place.

In fact, the ancients had it wrong. The situation was far worse than that.

First, there were many hydras. Each had a slightly different shape, but here's one that's typical:

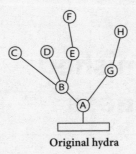

Original hydra

As you can see, this particular hydra has heads growing out of heads (each lettered circle is a head). Hercules can chop off any of the topmost heads: C, D, F, or H.

The hydra responds by reproducing the head's "father" and everything above it (not counting the chopped head). If Hercules chops C, the hydra reproduces B (C's father) and everything branching off above B (namely D, E, and F). Like so:

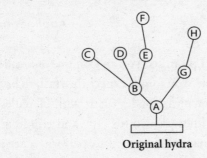

Original hydra

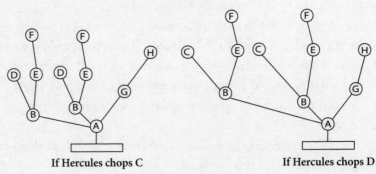

If Hercules chops C   If Hercules chops D

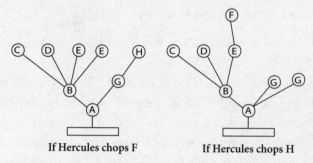

If Hercules chops F   If Hercules chops H

On the next round, Hercules can chop off any of the topmost heads—either one of the originals or one of the copies. This time, the hydra reproduces that head's father and everything above it—twice! (That is, it creates two full copies and adds them to itself.) If after chopping C, Hercules chops the first D, the hydra creates *two* new versions of the B-E-F branch:

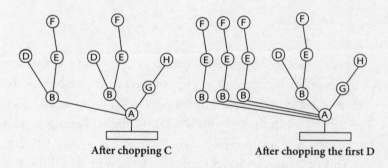

After chopping C   After chopping the first D

And so on. Hercules chops a head; the hydra creates *three* new versions of the corresponding branch. Hercules chops another head; the hydra creates *four* new versions of the corresponding branch . . .

Hercules wins if he kills the hydra by removing all its heads.

There are many hydras, of many shapes and sizes, and some are easier to kill than others. The question is: Can Hercules beat any hydra that comes his way? Actually, let's make that two questions:

- Can Hercules always win if he's smart?

- Can Hercules always win if he's stupid?

The answer to the first question is yes: If Hercules is smart (which means, roughly, that he chops the highest heads first), he always wins.

More surprisingly, the answer to the second question is also yes. *No matter how stupidly Hercules plays, he always wins eventually.* This is hardly obvious, but it's true.

Winning when you're stupid can take a really really really long time. By playing stupidly against even a simple five-headed hydra, Hercules can drag the game out for a number of steps that's bigger than the hundredth number in this sequence:

$$2 \quad 2^2 \quad 2^{2^2} \quad 2^{2^{2^2}} \quad 2^{2^{2^{2^2}}} \quad 2^{2^{2^{2^{2^2}}}} \quad \ldots$$

There is simply no way to begin to comprehend the vastness of this number, so let's look at some of the earlier numbers in the sequence instead. The first four are equal to 2, 4, 16, and 65,536. The fifth is a number of almost 20,000 digits. (Compare this to the famously enormous "googol," which has a mere 101 digits.) This fifth number has no name, so let's give it one: I'll call it a schnoogol.

The mathematician J. E. Littlewood once calculated the probability that a mouse could survive for one week on the surface of the sun. Obviously, this probability is effectively zero; Littlewood calculated it to be 1 in 10^{137} (that is, a 1 followed by 137 zeros)— in other words, effectively zero. Extrapolating from Littlewood's calculation, if you sent 144 mice to the surface of the sun, the odds against *every one of them* surviving for at least a week are about a schnoogol to one. That's how big a schnoogol is.

So much for the fifth number in the sequence. As for the sixth—call it a kanoogol—if you flip a schnoogol coins simultaneously, the odds against them all coming up heads are exactly a kanoogol to one. As for the seventh—I give up. There's just no way to talk meaningfully about numbers that big.

It's the *hundredth* number in this sequence that tells you how long a five-headed hydra can hold out against an exceptionally stupid Hercules. Nevertheless, Hercules does eventually win. It just takes a really really really really long time.

That's a mathematical fact; indeed, it's a fact about simple arithmetic, because the hydra game is really just an exercise in arithmetic. The pictures help to see what's going on, but they're not really necessary; the entire game can be recast as a game with numbers.

Now here's the even more remarkable fact: Although it's *true* that Hercules always wins, it is not *provable* that Hercules always wins. "Not provable" means "not provable using the standard axioms for arithmetic," where the standard axioms are the Peano axioms we met in the preceding chapter.

If Hercules' invincibility is not provable, how do we know it's true? Because it's been proven, of course—but the proof uses one extra axiom that's not on the usual list. That extra axiom is what I've called the SuperAxiom: *Arithmetic is consistent.* (That is, Peano's axioms cannot be used to derive a contradiction.)[1]

There's an even easier way to prove that Hercules always wins: Just adopt the Hercules Axiom, which says, "Hercules always wins." That makes the proof a one-liner: "Hercules always wins

---

1 The *known* proof uses the SuperAxiom. Might there be some other proof, not yet discovered, that does not use the SuperAxiom? No. Here's why: Not only does the SuperAxiom imply Hercules' invincibility, but the opposite is also true: Hercules' invincibility implies the SuperAxiom. But we know from Gödel that the Peano axioms do *not* imply the SuperAxiom. Therefore the Peano axioms cannot imply Hercules' invincibility.

because that's an axiom." Logically, that's rock solid, but it's never going to convince anybody of anything. Pulling an axiom out of the air doesn't make it true.

But there is such a thing as truth. Hercules either does or does not always win. And virtually everybody—well, virtually everybody who cares about such things, which is admittedly a pretty small subset of "everybody"—believes that in truth, he always wins. They believe this because there's a proof based not on the Hercules Axiom, but on the SuperAxiom, and the SuperAxiom is *not* just pulled out of the air. The SuperAxiom is self-evidently true.

What makes the SuperAxiom self-evident? One thing and one thing only—we recognize that the axioms of arithmetic are *about something*. A random list of axioms can easily be inconsistent, but the axioms of arithmetic are not random. They describe something real, namely the system of natural numbers. That's the one reason we know they're consistent; in other words, that's the one reason we know the SuperAxiom is true.

If someone someday discovers a hydra that Hercules can't beat, we'll know that the SuperAxiom is false, so we'll know that the axioms of arithmetic are inconsistent and the natural numbers don't exist. But the odds against that are about a kanoogol to one.

11 Incomplete Thinking

The question of the actual or potential reach of the human mind when it comes to proving theorems in arithmetic is not like the question how high it is possible for humans to jump, or how many hot dogs a human can eat in five minutes, or how many decimals of π it is possible for a human to memorize, or how far into space humanity can travel. It is more like the question of how many hot dogs a human can eat in five minutes without making a totally disgusting spectacle of himself, a question that will be answered differently at different times, in different societies, by different people.

—*Torkel Franzén*

Gödel's incompleteness theorem enjoys the distinction of inspiring two opposite and enduring fallacies. It's been invoked to "prove" that the human mind is both more and less limited than you might expect.

The first fallacy seems to be inspired primarily by an overbroad interpretation of the word *incompleteness;* something like

"Gödel proved that all forms of reasoning must be dreadfully inadequate."

Here is what Gödel actually proved: First, as we've seen, no matter what (true) axioms you adopt for arithmetic, there will always be (true) statements you can't prove. Second, arithmetic cannot be used to prove its own consistency.

These are significant limitations on the power of axiomatic systems. They are not significant limitations on the power of human thought, because human thought is not an axiomatic system. We think in analogies and metaphors; we are guided by intuition and instinct; we change the rules as we go along. Human thought is a haphazard farrago that leads us frequently into error, but for that very reason, it is immune from the constraints of the incompleteness theorem.

So much for the first fallacy. The second is more interesting.

The argument goes something like this: A computer, programmed with the axioms of arithmetic (the so-called Peano axioms), can never prove that Hercules beats the hydra.[1] But you and I, because we know full well that arithmetic is consistent, *know* that Hercules beats the hydra. Therefore you and I know something that no computer can ever prove. Therefore your mind and mine are more powerful than any computer.

When I was a child, I had an absolutely wonderful toy called a Digi-Comp I; I'm delighted to see that after an absence of several decades, it is back on the market. The Digi-Comp I was a completely mechanical computer; it ran on springs and rubber bands, and you built it yourself from a kit. You programmed it by putting little plastic cylinders (cut from drinking straws) on

---

1 I am using two facts about the Hercules/hydra game: 1) Using the Peano axioms alone, it's not possible to prove that Hercules beats the hydra. 2) If we add the SuperAxiom that says the Peano axioms are consistent, it *is* possible to prove that Hercules beats the hydra.

appropriate tabs, and you pushed a lever to run the program. The back of the computer was completely exposed, so you could watch the cylinders and the straws and the rubber bands push each other around. A child with a Digi-Comp I is a child with deep insight into what makes a computer work.

You could program the Digi-Comp I to play games, though not very complicated ones. It could count as high as eight. Personally, I can play chess (not terribly well) and I can think of occasions when I have counted accurately as high as three hundred. Does that prove that my mind is more powerful than any computer? No, it proves only that my mind is more powerful than a Digi-Comp I.

Likewise, the Hercules/hydra argument proves only that your mind and mine are more powerful than *some* computers, not that they're more powerful than *any* computer. A computer programmed only with the Peano axioms cannot discover that Hercules always beats the hydra. But a computer programmed with the Peano axioms *plus* the SuperAxiom that says arithmetic is consistent (or for that matter, the axiom that Hercules always beats the hydra!) can discover it easily.

If you want to make a Gödelian argument about human minds being more powerful than computers, you've got to do better than that. Here's an attempt: You and I can "just see" that once you've accepted the axioms of arithmetic, you might as well accept the SuperAxiom. No computer, it's claimed, can make that leap.

Unfortunately for the argument, it's easy to build a computer that can make that leap. First you program your computer with the Peano axioms for arithmetic. Then you put a big blue button on the side. When the button is pressed, a new axiom is added, saying that the store of existing axioms is consistent. Finally, you give your computer a robot arm so that whenever it gets stuck on a proof and needs a new axiom, it can push that big blue button.[2]

Now we have a computer that can "just see" that it's okay to add the SuperAxiom. And then if it needs to, it can push the button again and "just see" that it's okay to add the Super-DuperAxiom: *The expanded list of axioms (including the Super-Axiom) is consistent.* And so on. Just like a human.

Ah, but there's still something you and I can do that the computer can't: You and I can see that it's okay to add the Ultra-Axiom: *No matter how many times you push the blue button, your axioms are still consistent.* Does that make you and me more powerful than any computer? No, it only makes us more powerful than *this* computer. It doesn't make us more powerful than a computer with a big red button that, when pushed, adds the UltraAxiom.

And so on. You tell me what principles you apply to "just see" that it's okay to add certain axioms to your theories, and I'll build a computer with buttons that embody those principles.

This almost, but not quite, disposes of the second fallacy. Here's a last-ditch attempt to resurrect it: "Sure, if I tell you some of my principles for adding axioms, you can build a computer that embodies them. But there is *no limit* to my principles. I have a principle that says no matter how many times you push the big red button, your theory is still consistent. You can build that into a big green button, but I also have a principle that says no matter how many times you push the big green button, your theory is still consistent. No matter what computer you build, I've got a principle you didn't build into it. So no computer can be as powerful as I am."

The response to this is that as you go higher up the hierarchy

---

2 I am indebted for this image to the late lamented logician Torkel Franzén.

of principles, it becomes harder and harder to grasp exactly what each principle *means,* let alone to be sure it's correct. Are you really sure that no matter how many times you apply the principle that no matter how many times you apply the principle that no matter how many times you apply the principle that no matter how many times you apply the principle that pushing the blue button is okay, you'll still have a consistent theory? In the words of Torkel Franzén:

> As we continue to formulate stronger and more involved principles for extending a correct theory to a stronger theory that is still correct, we are confronted with a number of questions about what is or is not evident . . . questions to which different mathematicians and philosophers will give different answers, and where many would say that there is no definite answer. To program a robot to perfectly emulate human mathematicians, we would have to give it a similar range of responses to these questions. If we manage to do this . . . we will have no grounds for the claim that we as human mathematicians can prove anything not provable by the robot. We will have succeeded in programming a robot that becomes just as confused and uncertain as humans do when pondering ever more complicated or far-reaching ways of extending a correct theory to a stronger correct theory.

In other words, the principles you're really comfortable with are probably not unlimited, and if they're not unlimited, I can build them all into a computer. And nothing Gödel says can stop me.

12 The Rules of Logic and the Tale of the Potbellied Pig

The point of philosophy is to start with something so simple as not to seem worth stating and to end with something so paradoxical that no one will believe it.

—*Bertrand Russell*

Mathematicians are like lovers. Grant a mathematician the least principle, and he will draw from it a consequence which you must also grant him, and from this consequence another.

—*Bernard de Fontenelle*

The most famously counterintuitive theorem in all of mathematics is the celebrated Banach-Tarski theorem: Start with a ball of any size you want; say a soccer ball. Then it's always possible to divide this ball into five pieces, rearrange the pieces, and put them back together to form *two* solid balls of exactly the same size as the first. Now do it again, and you can have four solid balls; do it enough times and you'll have enough to fill the universe.

This sounds like a very useful theorem if you're not sure how many people are going to show up to your birthday party. Just bake a cake of any size you like (the theorem works even if it's not ball-shaped), cut it into five appropriately shaped pieces, fit them back together the right way, and now you've got two cakes.

Unfortunately, the Banach-Tarski theorem applies only to genuinely *solid* objects, and birthday cakes are not remotely solid. Neither is anything else in the real world, where everything is made of atoms and atoms are mostly empty space. Banach-Tarski shocks our intuitions partly because we have no experience of real solidity.

We know that Banach-Tarski is true not by evidence, and certainly not by intuition or insight, but by pure logic: There happens to be a proof, which any first-year graduate mathematics student can understand. The proof in turn rests on basic facts about arithmetic and set theory, which, as I've stressed, we know for extra-logical reasons. But taking those basic facts as given, Banach-Tarski follows logically.

The moral here is that some knowledge is accessible only through logic. This applies not just to mathematical knowledge; later in this chapter I'll give some examples from economics. But first just a little more math.

If you want a good example—in fact the best example I know—of a simple, beautiful, and powerful mathematical proof, turn back to pages 36–37. The argument there shows that no finite list of prime numbers can be complete (or, in other words, that there are infinitely many prime numbers). Like the Banach-

Tarski theorem, this is a result you could never have reached through pure insight, intuition, or ESP. It takes proof.

For a more startling example, what is the probability that a number chosen at random is not divisible by any square (other than 1)?[1] The answer is exactly $6/\pi^2$, or approximately 60.79 percent. That's the same π you remember from geometry class, the one that's approximately 3.14. There's nothing particularly interesting about a number like 60.79, but that π sort of jumps out at you. Why is the ratio of a circle's circumference to its diameter popping up in a problem about arithmetic?

Proving that $6/\pi^2$ is the correct ratio is a little harder than proving the infinitude of primes, and a little easier than proving the Banach-Tarski theorem. For those with an appetite for this sort of thing (and a good memory for college calculus), I've posted my version of the proof at www.the-big-questions.com /pi.pdf.

In mathematics, pure logic can reveal great truths. The same is true in other areas. For example, pure logic—unsupplemented by any kind of evidence—tells me that the world almost surely has too much air pollution. That's less obvious than it might sound. Granted, nobody likes pollution, but that doesn't prove we have too much of it. After all, nobody likes paying bills either, but that doesn't prove you pay too many bills. Pollution, like bill paying, is an unpleasant by-product of things we value (electric power, modern architecture, and air travel, to name a few). The right amount is not zero.

So if the right amount is not zero, how I can be sure we have too much, as opposed to too little or just the right amount? How can I know such a thing without even knowing the current level

---

1 If this were a math textbook, I'd spend some time here specifying the exact meaning of the phrase *at random*. Since it's not, I won't. By way of example, the number 104 is divisible by a square (namely 4); the number 105 is not.

of pollution or the amount of harm it causes? The answer begins with a potbellied pig.

I once had a graduate student with the same name as a professor of veterinary medicine. One day, she received the following (obviously misdirected) letter from a local farmer:

Dear Dr. Aldrich:

In October we purchased a potbellied pig from Astasia Kumpf of Longmont. Our vet says we need a health paper, especially for pseudorabies. We understand from Astasia that she takes her pigs to the university to have them treated. She also gave us your name. Also, could you please send information on the best way to blood-test a potbellied pig? Sure hope you can help us with this matter. Thanks.

John Wennekamp

She replied:

Dear Mr. Wennekamp:

Although I am not a specialist on blood-testing potbellied pigs, I am confident that the basic principles of economic theory, properly applied, can be employed to accomplish this task in the most efficient manner.

The blood of your potbellied pig should be tested until the marginal cost (MC) of testing is exactly equal to the marginal benefit (MB) of testing.[2]

Perhaps this diagram will illustrate my point:

---

2 The word *marginal* means, for example, that at quantity 3, the graph shows the additional cost and benefit from testing the third gallon of blood, after the first and second have already been tested.

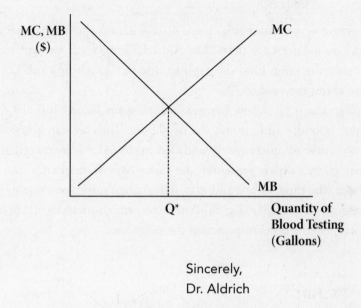

Sincerely,

Dr. Aldrich

At the risk of spoiling a good joke by explaining it, I'll observe that "Dr. Aldrich's" advice is both entirely correct and entirely useless. For the first, second, and third gallons of blood, the graph indicates that the benefit of testing (measured in dollars) exceeds the cost, so those gallons should be tested.[3] (It really would have been better to measure blood in some unit a little smaller than gallons.) The same is true for each gallon up to gallon number Q^*, where the costs and benefits are exactly equal. For all subsequent gallons, the cost of testing exceeds the benefit, so you should stop when you get to gallon Q^*.

A nice neat analysis. Unfortunately, we have no idea whether Q^* is equal to 4 or 8 or 17. How could we, when all "Dr. Aldrich" did was slap a few curves down on a piece of paper, without any particular knowledge of potbellied pigs? (That, of course, is the point of the joke.)

---

3 The graph shows *marginal* costs and benefits; that is, it shows the additional costs and benefits associated with each additional gallon.

How very remarkable, then, that with no greater expertise and no greater care than "Dr. Aldrich" employed, we can use exactly the same kind of graph to discover something substantive about the world.

Suppose that when Farmer Wennekamp bleeds his pig, it squeals loudly and annoys the neighbors. Then we can add one more curve to our graph. In addition to the old *private* marginal-cost curve, which measures the costs Mr. Wennekamp cares about (the time, effort, and materials that go into blood testing), we get a new *social* marginal-cost curve, which includes all these costs *plus* the costs imposed on the neighbors:

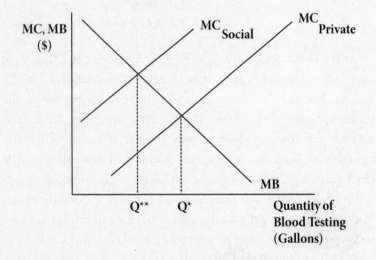

It still behooves Mr. Wennekamp to test exactly Q^* gallons of blood; the annoyance to the neighbors is no concern of his. On the other hand, if you care about his neighbors, and if you want to maximize the excess of *all* benefits over *all* costs (including the costs to the neighbors), you'll want him to test only Q^{**} gallons.

So there you have it: A selfish Mr. Wennekamp tests exactly Q^* gallons, whereas a socially conscious observer wants him to test exactly Q^{**} gallons. And as before, we have no idea what the values of Q^* and Q^{**} are. This looks every bit as useless as before.

Except . . . except for the fact that this time we've learned one substantive fact, and it's a profound one. Namely, Q^* is to the *right* of Q^{**}. In other words, when bleeding your pig annoys your neighbors, you'll bleed it *more* than you ought to. Ditto for any activity that annoys your neighbors—polluting the air, for example.

Here the phrase *ought to* has a very precise meaning. I'm going to say that you "ought to" do something if the total of all its benefits—to you and to everyone else—exceeds the total of all its costs. And the blood-testing graph illustrates an important general principle: *When the costs of your activities spill over onto your neighbors, you engage in more of those activities than you ought to.*

That's a bedrock principle of economics. It's also—at least in the case of bleeding potbellied pigs—completely untestable. It's untestable because in practice we can have no idea how *much* the bleeding annoys the neighbors, and hence no actual measure of the relevant costs and benefits. But even though the proposition is untestable, we still know it's true. As long as the social MC curve lies above the private MC curve, we know that Q^* lies to the right of Q^{**}. That's a consequence of pure geometry, and ever since Euclid, pure geometry has been a far more reliable guide to at least some kinds of truth than any observation.

A similar graph establishes the companion principle: *When the benefits of your activities spill over onto your neighbors, you engage in fewer of those activities than you ought to.*

You might think these principles are obvious, but their consequences are not. Consider, for example, the question of whether the world has too much or too little casual sex.[4]

Start with a thought experiment. Let's suppose that you (not necessarily the real-world you; some fictitious version of you) are a recklessly promiscuous person with a long list of past sexual partners. As a result, you're unusually likely to be infected with something horrible. Each time you have sex with a new partner, there's a chance you're passing that horrible virus along.

Now, that doesn't prove you should never have sex; it doesn't even prove you have too many partners. Like pollution, your recklessness has benefits that at least partly offset its costs. You're presumably making a lot of people happy with your licentious ways. So it's not immediately obvious whether you have too many partners or too few. But I am quite sure you have too many, for exactly the same reason I am quite sure the world has too much pollution—because the costs of your actions spill over onto the rest of us. We are all fishing for partners in the same pool, and every time you jump into that pool, you're polluting it. The potbellied pig principle tells me that you jump in too often. If you showed some restraint, the world would be a better place.

That, I think, is easy to understand and easy to believe. But now let's look at the flip side of that example, which is where all the surprises are.

Suppose, then, that you're the sort of cautious and sexually conservative person who has had very few partners and are therefore particularly *un*likely to be infected with anything horrible. When *you* jump into the partner pool, you magically leave it *less* polluted. The partner who goes home with you tonight is

---

4 What follows is a very brief introduction to the arguments you'll find, in much greater detail, in the first chapter of my book *More Sex Is Safer Sex: The Unconventional Wisdom of Economics.* Or, if you prefer video, you can view my lecture on this topic at www.the-big-questions.com/pueblatalk.html.

destined for a night of safe sex. They're getting even luckier than they realize.

This time it's not the *costs* of your actions that spill over, but the benefits. That probably means you have too *few* partners. Just as the polluters jump into the pool too often, you don't jump in enough. If we could get you to take on a few more partners, the world would be a safer and a happier place.

In fact, the world would be a better place for *two* reasons, of which I've mentioned only one: Your occasional partners get to have relatively safe sex. The second way you improve the world is a bit more macabre but probably also more empirically significant. Here it is: There are infected people out there, and if you go out looking for a partner tonight, you might go home with one of them. Then you might get infected yourself. Eventually you'll get sick and eventually you might even die. And as far as the rest of us are concerned, that's wonderful—because when you die, the virus dies with you. If somebody's going to get sick tonight, I want it to be you and not Promiscuous Pete, who would spread it to two dozen other people before dying.

Now, that argument is correct, but unfortunately you can't use it as a pickup line. You'll never get very far in the bars with a line like "Come home with me so I can infect you instead of someone else." The *whole point* is the disconnect between what's good for the individual decision maker and what's good for everyone else. Polluters don't care about the damage from their smokestacks; Promiscuous Pete doesn't care about the viruses he spreads, and you—the cautious sexual conservative—don't care about the people who will die because of your excessive chastity.

What should we do about that? Ideally, we'd find a way to encourage sexual conservatives to take on a few more partners. Not *too* many more partners—we don't want to turn them all into copies of Promiscuous Pete. Just a few more partners. How can we do that? I have no idea, though I suspect free condoms might be a small step in the right direction.

If we could somehow get those people to loosen up a bit, the world could be a better place—a place with fewer AIDS patients and more fond memories. Most remarkably, we can know this through pure logic, without any need for evidence.

How, exactly, would the world improve? First, your (presumably consensual) partners would have some fun. True, they'd risk getting sick, but they've already decided you're worth that risk—even without knowing how low the risk is. Second, you might actually slow down the spread of disease by increasing the fraction of safe encounters and/or stealing partners from Promiscuous Pete. On the other hand, you might also *speed up* the spread of disease—after all, we don't actually *know* that you're uninfected.

That's part good and part bad. Then there are secondary and tertiary effects on your partners' partners and your partners' partners' partners. Sorting out the pluses and minuses all the way down the line is a major research project. Fortunately, we know in advance how the accounting has to work out. On balance, increased promiscuity by the relatively cautious must be a good thing.[5]

If you find that conclusion surprising, keep in mind that it follows from *exactly the same reasoning* that tells us the world has too much pollution. If you believe the world has too much pollution, you must also believe it has too much chastity.

---

5 A more precise conclusion does require evidence, along with some knowledge of both economics (that is, the way people respond to incentives) and epidemiology (that is, the way viruses spread). Harvard's professor Michael Kremer, who is an expert in both fields, estimates that if we could take everyone who averages fewer than two and a quarter partners per year and bring them all up to two and a quarter, we'd substantially slow down the spread of AIDS.

Bear with me while I belabor the point: You don't have to know anything about potbellied pigs to know that if bleeding annoys the neighbors, there's too much of it. You don't have to know anything at all about actual pollution levels to know the world has too much pollution. You don't have to know anything at all about STD transmission rates to know that high-risk people have too many partners and that low-risk people have too few. All these things follow by pure logic. Sometimes that's all you need.

13 The Rules of Evidence

> If it is a Miracle, any sort of evidence will answer, but if it is a Fact, proof is necessary.
>
> —*Mark Twain*

Throughout the year 2004, the one million residents of Benares, India, went through about six hundred thousand condoms a day. Most of those condoms (provided free by the Indian government) were used not for family planning or disease prevention, but to lubricate the city's two hundred thousand looms. Weavers took the free condoms, rubbed them on the looms' shuttles, and discarded the latex.

If you'd known something about condoms, something about the Benares economy, something about Indian family-planning policy, and something about human nature, you might have predicted the broad outline of that story. But you'd never have predicted the exact numbers. Sometimes you need to gather some facts.

But facts alone are never enough. They've got to be supplemented by interpretation and a willingness to generalize. I believe you have an aorta not because I've seen it, but because I've heard that *other* people have been found to have aortas, so I'm guessing you do, too.

If you refuse to accept such reasoning, there's a home for you on the Internet. I recently had the honor of guest blogging on the Volokh Conspiracy, home to some of the best legal minds on the net, with, like all public blogs, visits from the occasional nutjob. There I made the (I thought) pedestrian observation that if houses came with free flood insurance, they'd be more expensive. I was immediately challenged to offer evidence for this apparently remarkable assertion. Well, there's plenty of evidence: A shave and a haircut costs more than a shave; a soup and a sandwich costs more than just soup; a washer and dryer costs more than a washer. And we understand why: When you throw in a free extra, you increase demand, and when you increase demand, prices are bid up. The same forces clearly exist in the housing market, so of course a house and insurance will cost more than a house.

My correspondents actually claimed (apparently seriously, but maybe they were just feeling ornery) that none of those examples is relevant because none of them concerns housing. Okay, then, a house with a fireplace costs more than the same house without a fireplace. Oh, but that's not an example of a house plus *insurance*! At some point I gave up.

The Volokh Conspiracy theorists wanted to stick to the facts, unsullied by theory. But that's not possible if you ever want to learn anything. Everything we know "based on evidence" is actually based on evidence together with appropriate theory. We know that grass is green partly because we've seen green grass and partly because we have a theory that allows us to generalize from one blade of grass to another. If you refuse to accept even a dollop of theory, then of course you can refuse to believe anything, no matter how evident it may be. If I had offered an example of an actual house in, say, Kansas City, that increased in price when the seller threw in a free insurance policy, I'm sure someone would have claimed that my evidence applied only to Kansas City, and only in months that contain the letter *R*.

This is, incidentally, no mere academic exercise; it has important policy implications. The federal government effectively provides free flood insurance when it adopts a policy of assisting flood victims. Because of that policy, houses on floodplains are made more expensive. That's no clear favor to the people (mostly poor people) who are trying to save money by buying cheap houses on floodplains. Paradoxically (at least to those who have never thought this through before), free flood insurance for poor people can make poor people considerably worse off.

Refusal to generalize is only one of several ways to bury your head in the sand. The Internet also provides a comfortable home for those who have trained themselves to bray "correlation does not imply causation" whenever they're confronted with evidence they prefer to ignore. It's true that correlation, by itself, does not imply causation. The mistake is to jump from this observation to the unwarranted conclusion that *nothing* implies causation.

Cigarette smoking is correlated with lung cancer. It would be easy to invent many theories consistent with that observation. Maybe smoking causes cancer. Maybe cancer causes smoking. (That is, maybe cancer typically sets in decades before it's detected, and the first symptom is a craving for tobacco.) Maybe a single gene causes both cancer and an addictive personality.

But there are ways to settle this. The gold standard for establishing causality is a controlled experiment. Randomly assign some people to smoke and others not to; monitor them to make sure they follow orders; track them for several decades, and see who gets sick. If the correlation holds up (and if your sample is large enough to rule out the likelihood of coincidence), you can be confident that smoking causes cancer. That's because you've ruled out the alternatives. "Cancer causes smoking" is not a viable theory when you know for a fact that the luck of the draw causes smoking.

It's unlikely any scientist will ever perform this experiment, but politicians have performed it repeatedly. Whenever the state of Pennsylvania raises its cigarette tax, some Pennsylvanians quit smoking—while their counterparts in New York go right on lighting up. That's a lot like a randomized trial where you're assigned to smoke if you happen to live in New York. If cancer rates decrease in Pennsylvania but not New York, you've got evidence that smoking causes cancer.[1]

That's an example of what economists call a "natural experiment" or (when we're talking jargon) an approach through "instrumental variables." (In this case the instrumental variable is the tax rate.) Economists are always on the lookout for good instrumental variables. For example: Across African countries, economic hard times tend to be accompanied by civil unrest and even civil war. The effect is quite large; a five-percentage-point drop in the rate of economic growth (the equivalent of a moderately severe recession) leads to a massive one-third increase in the probability of civil war.

Which way does the causality go? Do hard times cause dissatisfaction, leading to uprisings? Or do uprisings undermine productive activities, leading to hard times?

To answer that question, a trio of economists from Berkeley

---

1 Actually, the evidence shows a little less: It shows that smoking causes cancer *among the sort of people who are sensitive to tax hikes.* But it's a pretty safe bet that those people have pretty much the same biology as the rest of us, so you're probably comfortable drawing a more general conclusion. In other examples, this kind of generalization can be considerably more problematic. We'll see some of those examples later.

and NYU observed that a lot of hard times are caused by bad weather. And it turns out that even when hard times are clearly traceable to bad weather, they're associated with a far greater likelihood of civil war.

Once again we have an instrumental variable (namely the weather) and a natural experiment. The weather randomly assigns some countries to be (temporarily) poorer than others, and those countries have more wars. It appears, then, that economic difficulties *cause* wars.

Another example: States where people view a lot of pornography tend to have fewer reported rapes. What's the causality here? Do (some) potential rapists settle for pornography when it's easily available? Does good law enforcement drive potential rapists indoors? Do more enlightened attitudes toward sexuality lead simultaneously to more porn and less rape?

Here the rise of the Internet offers a gigantic natural experiment. Better yet, because Internet usage caught on at different times in different states, it offers fifty natural experiments.

The bottom line on these experiments is "More net access, less rape." A 10 percent increase in net access yields about a 7.3 percent decrease in reported rapes. States that adopted the Internet quickly saw the biggest declines. And, according to Clemson professor Todd Kendall, the effects remain even after you control for all of the obvious confounding variables, like alcohol consumption, police presence, poverty and unemployment rates, population density, and so forth.

That lets us conclude, at least tentatively, that *net access* reduces rape. But that's a far cry from proving that *porn* access reduces rape. Maybe rape is down because the rapists are all indoors vandalizing Wikipedia. But Professor Kendall points out that there is no similar effect of Internet access on homicide. It's hard to see how Wikipedia can deter rape without deterring other violent crimes at the same time. On the other hand, it's easy to imagine how porn might serve as a substitute for rape.

If not Wikipedia, what about Internet dating? Maybe rape is down because former rapists have found their true loves on match.com. But Professor Kendall points out that the effects are strongest among fifteen- to nineteen-year-old perpetrators—the group least likely to use those dating services.

Moreover, Professor Kendall argues that those teenagers are precisely the group that (presumably) relies most heavily on the Internet for access to porn. When you're living with your parents, it's a lot easier to close your browser in a hurry than to hide a stash of magazines. So the auxiliary evidence is all consistent with the hypothesis that net access reduces rape because net access makes it easy to find porn.

It's true that psychologists have found that male subjects, immediately after watching pornography, are more likely to express misogynistic attitudes. But as Professor Kendall points out, we need to be clear on what those experiments are testing: They are testing the effects of watching pornography in a controlled laboratory setting under the eyes of a researcher. The experience of viewing porn on the Internet, in the privacy of one's own room, typically culminates in a slightly messier but far more satisfying experience—an experience that could plausibly tamp down some of the same aggressions that the pornus interruptus of the laboratory tends to stir up.

When I wrote about Professor Kendall's research in *Slate,* I was deluged by e-mail from semieducated sea cucumbers who solemnly explained that this sort of knowledge is impossible because correlation does not imply causation and therefore it's *never* possible to establish causation. What must life be like for these people? Do they really pretend not to know that running out of gas *causes* their cars to halt? Do they live by their beliefs and drive to work every day on empty gas tanks, cursing the bad luck that strands them by the side of the road day after day? Or, somewhere in the deep recesses of their minds, do they admit, along with the rest of us, that knowledge is sometimes possible?

Still, the skeptics have one thing right: Even a good natural experiment proves almost nothing without a bit of accompanying theory, and if your theory is wrong, your conclusions can be tainted.

Take the cancer/smoking example. Pennsylvania raises its tobacco tax, Pennsylvanians cut back on smoking, Pennsylvania's cancer rate falls. Meanwhile, New York has a stable tax rate and a stable cancer rate. Does this prove that smoking causes cancer? Not quite. As I pointed out in the footnote on page 126 it proves at best that smoking causes cancer *among the sort of people who respond to tax hikes.* The more general conclusion requires a theory, in this case something along the lines of "The cancer/smoking link is biological and we all have the same relevant biology."

Of course nobody doubts that theory, so the general conclusion is certainly true. But we'll soon see that with other natural experiments, the relevant theory can be both elaborate and difficult to test.

Suppose you wanted to test the cancer/smoking theory. (I know, I know, you already believe the theory, so you don't see any need to test it. But bear with me. This will be instructive.) The first step is to learn enough about medicine so you can formulate the theory a little more precisely. Something like "Smoking causes lung damage and lung damage leads to cancer." The great thing about that formulation is that it's easily testable. It implies that if you measure the *correlation between smoking and lung damage,* and then measure the *correlation between lung damage and cancer,* and then multiply these two numbers together, you'll get the *correlation between smoking and cancer.* If that equation holds true (to a tolerable approximation), you have evidence to support your theory.

In economics, that sort of reasoning is called a "structural model." When there are more variables, structural models become more elaborate. High school dropouts are more likely than high school graduates to end up in jail. Does dropping out cause crime? Or do students who plan to be criminals drop out? Or does some other variable, like a low IQ or parental inattention, cause both? The causal relationships can run even deeper. Does a low IQ cause parental inattention? Does parental inattention cause a low IQ?

A structural model might take stands on all these questions, based on the researcher's understanding of the relevant science and economics. Once those stands are taken, you can derive complicated relationships among correlations (like "the ratio of correlation A to correlation B is equal to the sum of the ratio of correlation C to correlation D plus the ratio of correlation E to correlation F"). You can check to see if these equations hold, and if they do, you're entitled to have faith in the model.

Practical econometricians rely on both natural experiments and structural models to distinguish between causation and mere correlation. It's pretty well established, for example, that high school dropouts commit more crime *because* they are dropouts.

It's only through structural modeling that we know parachutes save lives. True, there is a high correlation between dying and not having a parachute, but of course correlation does not prove causation. Nobody has ever performed a controlled experiment in which ten randomly chosen subjects jumped from planes with parachutes and ten others jumped without. So why do all sane people believe parachutes actually *cause* survival? Answer: Because we have a structural model; that is, we have a story to tell about *how* parachutes save lives, and that story makes a variety of accurate predictions. It predicts that skydivers who die without parachutes are likely to be found with a lot of broken bones, and that those who land in treetops will have a higher survival rate than those who land on rocky beaches. The accuracy of those predictions bolsters our confidence that in this case correlation *does* derive from causality. This is exactly the kind of inference that economists draw all the time. It really is possible to know these things.

Here's an example that combines a natural experiment with structural modeling: We know that children who have attended preschool are more likely to graduate high school, more likely to avoid teen pregnancy, and more likely to stay off welfare. As adults, they earn higher wages than (apparently) similar children who skipped preschool. They hold jobs longer and they commit fewer crimes. Causality? Or mere correlation?

Here we have the advantage of actual controlled experiments, like the Perry preschool program for disadvantaged three-year-olds in Ypsilanti, Michigan, where eligibility was determined by a coin flip. Like other preschoolers, the Perry preschoolers led far more successful adult lives than their nonpreschooled neighbors.

Unfortunately, the experiment is not perfectly clean, because not all the winners chose to send their kids to preschool. Did Perry graduates succeed because they went to preschool, or because they had the kind of parents who sent them there?

This calls for structural modeling: We start with detailed theories about the interactions among variables like preschool attendance, IQ, parental attention, parental IQ, the skills learned in preschool, the contribution of those skills to skills learned later in life, and so forth. These theories predict complicated relationships among the correlations between different variables. You can test these relationships to see which theories hold up. Bottom line: It seems clear that preschool *causes* good outcomes. Based on his structural models, James Heckman, a Nobel laureate in economics and structural modeler par excellence, reckons that $15,000 spent on preschools prevents more crime than $80,000 spent on police departments.

It's not always that easy; the theory underlying the Perry preschool experiment is deep and difficult (with the accompanying peril that one theoretical error can jeopardize the entire enterprise). There's some healthy tension between economists who prefer to rely on natural experiments, keeping the explicit theory to a minimum, and those who prefer to rely on elaborate structural models.

I'll close with one more example: In the National Basketball Association, white referees are (very slightly) more likely to call fouls against black players, while black referees are (very slightly) more likely to call fouls against white players.

If you were listing all the possible explanations, here's one you might come up with: The NBA, for some reason, assigns white referees to games with rowdy black players and black referees to games with rowdy white players. That explanation would be wrong, because in fact referees are assigned randomly. So we have something like a natural experiment.

Does that experiment prove that white referees are tougher on black players? Not clearly at all; it might prove exactly the opposite! If white referees go particularly *easy* on black players, then black players will be more aggressive when the referee is white. So maybe, with a white referee, black players commit 20 percent more fouls but (because white referees go so easy on them), they only get called on an additional 1 percent. (And likewise with black and white reversed.)

You might find that theory implausible, but the point is that nothing in the numbers alone can reject it. To decide whether it's plausible, you've got to know something about how the game is played and how referees interact with players—just as, if you want to study the benefits of a preschool, you've got to know something about cognitive development. Theories make knowledge possible.

In fact, the theme of the past few chapters has been that knowledge is possible. This raises the question: Is it possible to know *everything*? You might have heard that modern physics is based on an *uncertainty principle* that declares full knowledge impossible. In the next chapter, I'll explain what the uncertainty principle is really about.

14 The Limits to Knowledge

The universe will not cooperate in a coverup.
—*Arthur C. Clarke*

A little inaccuracy sometimes saves a ton of
explanation.

—*H. H. Munro*

This chapter is full of lies. That's because I'll be explaining the
foundations of quantum mechanics, and I assume that if you
wanted a careful accounting of every detail, you'd be reading a
textbook. All of my lies will consist of oversimplifications that (I
hope) will make the chapter easy to follow without leaving out
anything really important.

I want to talk about quantum mechanics because we've been
talking about knowledge, and quantum mechanics is often said
to place fundamental limits on human knowledge, particularly
because of the famous (but often misunderstood) uncertainty
principle. So I think it's a good idea to explain what the uncertainty principle does and does not say.

Suppose, then, that you've caught an electron in a box. You can't see the electron (it's much too small) but you can imagine it moving around in there. If you actually went looking for it (say with a very powerful microscope), you might find it either in the left or the right half of the box.

But at this moment you're *not* looking. You're just idly wondering where the electron is. In most circumstances, quantum mechanics says that it's quite impossible for you to know the answer to that question.

Aha! A fundamental limitation on human knowledge, no? No. Here's why: Most of the time, the electron is *nowhere*. Asking "Where is the electron?" is akin to asking "What is the electron's favorite movie?" It's a nonsense question. The inability to answer nonsense questions is not a fundamental limitation on knowledge.

How can the electron be nowhere? Because electrons behave nothing at all like anything you're familiar with. Instead of a location, the electron has a *quantum state*. What's a quantum state? It's a point on a circle. Not a physical circle; a purely mathematical circle. Like this circle here (don't worry yet about what the labels mean):

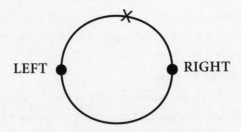

I've marked your electron's quantum state with an *X*. The electron "has" this quantum state in something like the same sense that you might "have" a thought. It's not something you can see or smell or weigh or touch; it has no color or location or any other physical attribute. It just *is*.

The quantum state travels around the circle, which is every bit as nonphysical as the quantum state itself. Along the way, it occasionally passes through the point marked "left"; at that instant, the electron is in the left half of the box. A little later, the quantum state passes through the point marked "right"; at that instant, the electron is in the right half of the box. The rest of the time, the electron is nowhere.

Now, suppose you go *looking* for the electron at a time when it's nowhere. Then something very odd happens: The quantum state jumps either to the "left" or the "right" point on the circle, so the electron will be someplace and you'll be able to find it.

How does the quantum state decide where to jump? Answer: More often than not, it jumps to whichever extreme is closest. The closer it is to that extreme, the more likely it is to choose it. Like so:

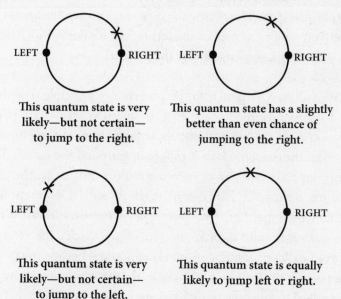

This quantum state is very likely—but not certain—to jump to the right.

This quantum state has a slightly better than even chance of jumping to the right.

This quantum state is very likely—but not certain—to jump to the left.

This quantum state is equally likely to jump left or right.

So what's the state of your knowledge? It depends on what question you ask:

- If you ask "Where is the electron?," you're asking a non-sense question (unless the quantum state just happens to be at the left or right point on the circle). The question is unanswerable, but only because it makes no sense.

- If you ask, "What is the electron's quantum state?," you can know the answer precisely. For example, if you looked at the electron an hour ago, and found it on the left side of the box, you know that the quantum state an hour ago was "left." If you also know how fast the quantum state moves around the circle (and basic physics does tell you this!), then you can easily compute what the quantum state is right now.

- If you ask, "Where will the electron be when I look for it?," you can't answer with certainty. This is a limitation on your ability to predict the future, but it's not a limitation on your knowledge about the present.

We still haven't gotten to the uncertainty principle. For that, we have to imagine asking another question: How fast is the electron moving? (This is entirely separate from the question of how fast the *quantum state* is proceeding around the circle!) This turns out to be another nonsense question; ordinarily, the electron has no speed. (That doesn't mean it's still; if it were still, it would have a speed of zero.) But there are two exceptions: When the quantum state is near the top of the circle, the electron moves fast (even though it's nowhere!), and when the quantum state is near the bottom of the circle, the electron moves slow. So it's natural to label the circle like this:

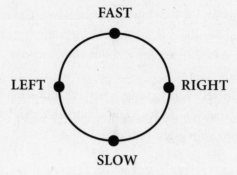

If you choose to *measure* the electron's speed, the quantum state jumps either to the top or bottom of the circle, whereupon you will discover the electron is moving either fast or slow. The closer the quantum state is to the top (or the bottom), the more likely it is to jump there.

Suppose, for example, that the quantum state is at the X in this picture:

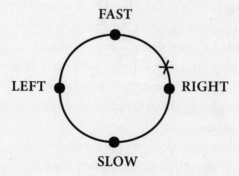

This X is much closer to the right than the left. Therefore if you measure the electron's position, you're very likely to find it on the right. The X is also slightly closer to the top than the bottom. Therefore if you measure the electron's speed, you're slightly more likely to find it moving fast than slow.[1] You've got a little uncertainty about the outcome of the location measurement and considerably more uncertainty about the outcome of the speed measurement.

Now I can tell you exactly what the uncertainty principle says. It is not mysterious. It's a fact about circles and you can easily explain it to your eight-year-old:

On the circle, points near the left or right are about midway between the top and bottom. Points near the top or bottom are about midway between the left and right.

Or to put this another way:

Whenever you're pretty certain of the outcome of a location measurement, you're pretty uncertain of the outcome of a speed measurement. And vice versa.

I want to stress this: The Heisenberg uncertainty principle is simply a fact—and not a very surprising fact—about the geometry of circles. In more complicated situations, quantum states travel not along circles but along more complicated geometric objects; still, the Heisenberg uncertainty principle remains nothing but a simple and straightforward observation about the geometry of those objects.

Does the uncertainty principle impose limits on human knowledge? It can't. The uncertainty principle is itself a bit of

---

1 What if you measure both the location and the speed simultaneously? There's no way to do that. Here's how we know: If you measure the location, the quantum state must jump either left or right; if you measure the speed, the quantum state must jump either up or down; and even in the weirdness that is quantum mechanics, a quantum state can't be two places at once.

knowledge about geometry that was easily understood long before anyone knew anything about quantum mechanics.[2]

You now understand the uncertainty principle. I've left just one bit of unfinished business: How do I know the electron is nowhere (at least most of the time) when you're not looking at it? Why can't it be somewhere unknown instead of nowhere at all? That's a story in itself. I'll deal with it in a separate chapter.

---

2 Does quantum mechanics—as opposed to just the uncertainty principle—impose limits on human knowledge? First, quantum states are fully knowable, so there is no limit on our ability to know the present. The question then becomes: Does quantum mechanics impose limits on our ability to predict the future? The answer depends on your belief about what happens when, say, a location measurement gets made. On one interpretation (the one I adopted above), the quantum state jumps either left or right, unpredictably. On an alternative interpretation, the Universe splits into several copies of itself, with the quantum state jumping left in some copies and right in others, all perfectly predictably. (Of course each Universe contains a copy of you, and some of those copies see only a leftward jump while others see only a rightward jump.)

15 Unfinished Business

Quantum Entanglement

Those who are not shocked when they first come across quantum mechanics cannot possibly have understood it.

—*Niels Bohr*

In this chapter I want to tell you about the results of four simple experiments. I expect you will find it almost impossible to believe that these experiments could turn out as they do. But trust me; I'm not lying, at least not in any way that matters. (I reserve the right to tell minor lies for the purpose of keeping things simple and easy to understand.)

After I've told you about the experiments, I'll talk a little about their profound implications for physics and their possible implications for economics. Along the way, I'll complete the unfinished business from the preceding chapter by explaining why I say that an electron is usually no place at all.

Imagine a machine that sits halfway between our houses. Every ten seconds, it somehow creates two tennis balls and hurls them in opposite directions, one through your living room window and one through mine.

Experiment One: We each sit on our living-room sofas for an hour, writing down the colors of the balls that come through the window. About half the balls are red and half are green, with no apparent pattern. My list, for example, might start off "Red, Red, Green, Green, Red . . ." Afterward, we get together and discover that our lists are identical. We repeat this experiment many times and your list is always the same as mine.

Based on this experiment, it's reasonable to believe that the machine always creates two identically colored balls, and then propels them in opposite directions.

Experiment Two: Just like Experiment One, except I wear my sunglasses. When we do this experiment, I still see about half reds and half greens, and so do you. When we compare notes, we discover that the lists are *almost* identical, but not quite. Out of, say, a thousand observations, we've recorded identical colors about 990 times but opposite colors the other ten times. We repeat this experiment many times and our lists always differ in about 1 percent of their entries.

Based on this experiment, it's reasonable to believe that my sunglasses lead me to make occasional errors—where "occasional" means "about 1 percent of the time." After all, Experiment One has already established that the balls are always the same color. If we're seeing opposite colors, *somebody* must be making a mistake, and the sunglasses are the obvious culprit.

Experiment Three: Just like Experiment Two, except you wear the sunglasses instead of me. Once again, our lists agree 99 percent of the time and disagree the other 1 percent.

Now it's reasonable to conclude that you see just about as badly with sunglasses as I do.

Experiment Four: This time we *both* wear sunglasses. What do you predict will happen?

Well, let's think about that. Our working hypotheses are first, that we always receive identically colored balls, and second, that sunglasses cause occasional errors. About 1 percent of the time *my* sunglasses will cause an error, and another 1 percent of the time *your* sunglasses cause an error. So between us, we should make mistakes about 2 percent of the time. The other 98 percent of the time, we should record identical colors. (Actually, we should do a little better than 98 percent, because occasionally we'll make simultaneous mistakes that cancel out.)

That's what you might expect. What actually happens is exactly the opposite. Our lists agree only 2 percent of the time, and disagree the other 98 percent.

Pause to think about that for a minute or two. The longer you ponder it, the more bizarre it will seem. No reasonable story can explain all four of these experimental results. Tennis balls could never behave this way. Electrons, however, do.

The machine that produces two electrons at once and propels them in opposite directions is an everyday bit of laboratory equipment called a Stern-Gerlach apparatus. Electrons have no colors, but they do have a property called "spin"; they can be either "spin up" or "spin down." The experimenters don't wear sunglasses; instead they tilt their measuring apparatus. But otherwise the results are the same.

I've exaggerated the percentages to emphasize how odd a result this is; with electrons (depending on how far the apparatus is tilted) we're talking about discrepancies on the order of 25 percent rather than 1 percent. But the real-world percentages are apparently self-contradictory in exactly the same way as my fictitious ones are. The story I've told you is in essence true.

So let's try to figure out what's really going on with those tennis balls. Here's an idea: Maybe the machine somehow senses our sunglasses before it paints the balls! If we've both got our sunglasses on, it switches from "paint most pairs identically" to "paint most pairs nonidentically."

That's a very odd theory—how could the machine possibly know about our sunglasses and why would it care about them?—but at least it would explain all four experiments. So let's test the theory with one more experiment: We won't decide whether to don our sunglasses till after the balls are in the air. Then the machine *can't* paint the balls according to whether we're wearing those sunglasses or not. When we do the new experiment, it turns out we get exactly the same results: With no sunglasses, we always agree; when one of us wears glasses, we almost always agree; when both of us wear glasses, we almost never agree. So much for that theory.

Okay, let's try again: Maybe the balls, on arrival in our living rooms, observe our sunglasses and send instant messages to each other: "Hey! My guy's wearing sunglasses! Is yours? If so, I'll turn red and you turn green!" This is a truly desperate theory but at least it seems to work. We can test it by positioning our houses so far apart that the instant message can't get there in time. (Even over the Internet, no message can travel faster than light.) And once again, the experimental results are unchanged. Another theory bites the dust.

Bizarre as it may sound, the *least* weird explanation is that the balls leave the machine uncolored, but with a commitment to *acquire* colors when we look at them, and to *coordinate* those colors in certain ways. The balls manage to carry out this commitment even though they have no way to communicate.

Albert Einstein found this explanation too bizarre to stomach, and derided it as a theory of "spooky action at a distance."

We now know, as Einstein did not, that any alternative explanation is even spookier. (This is essentially the content of "Bell's theorem," which was proved about ten years after Einstein died.) Einstein was thinking, essentially, about Experiments One, Two, and Three, and was convinced, not unreasonably, that there must be some more plausible explanation. But when John Stewart Bell pointed out that any explanation must account for Experiment Four as well, it became apparent that Einstein's optimism was impossible to defend.

In my little fiction about tennis balls, we study color. In the real-world version of the experiment, we study spin. But quantum mechanics tells us—and experiments confirm—that the same considerations govern every other observable property of the electron, including its location and its speed. Electrons have no spin—and no location—until you look at them.

Similar considerations, and similar experiments and thought experiments, tell us that electrons have no other properties until you look at them either. They *do* have quantum states, as we discussed in the preceding chapter. But they don't have conventional properties like location.

Now to the application: Suppose you and I play a game where we're put in separate booths, perhaps miles apart. We are not allowed to communicate in any way. A referee observes each of us through a webcam. Each of us has to name a color, either "red" or "green." We win if our colors match.

There's an easy way for us to beat this game: We agree in advance that we'll both always say "red."

But now let's complicate things by adding an element to the game. After we're in the booths, we each flip a coin before we name our colors. As before, we win by naming identical colors—*unless* both coins came up tails, in which case we win by naming the *opposite* colors.

If we stick to our strategy—we both always say "red"—we win three-fourths of our games. We lose only when both coins are tails, which happens only one-fourth of the time.

That's pretty good. Can we do better?

In a world governed by classical physics, we can't. The problem is that neither of us has any way of knowing when *both* coins are tails. We might as well stick to our strategy and be glad to win three-fourths of the time.

But if we happen to own one of those machines that tosses the weird quantum tennis balls, we can do better. First, we let it toss us each a ball. Then we slip those balls into our purses *without looking at them* and bring them with us into our game booths. Then we follow this strategy:

If your coin comes up heads, leave your sunglasses off. If your coin comes up tails, put your sunglasses on. Then look at your tennis ball and announce its color.

If both coins come up heads, that's Experiment One. We both leave off our sunglasses, the balls are guaranteed to be identically colored, and we're guaranteed to win. If my coin is tails and yours is heads, that's Experiment Two. I wear my sunglasses, the balls are 99 percent sure to be identically colored, and we're 99 percent sure to win. If your coin is heads and mine is tails, that's Experiment Three. Once again the balls are 99 percent sure to be identically colored, and we're 99 percent sure to win. And if both coins are tails, that's Experiment Four. Now we both wear our sunglasses, the balls are 98 percent sure to be *opposite* colors, which is exactly what it takes to win when both coins are tails. In the worst-case scenario, we're 98 percent sure of winning.

Did we cheat? No! The rules said "no communication," and neither we nor our tennis balls have communicated. Communication, after all, is the exchange of information, and no information has been exchanged. When I look at my tennis ball, I have no idea whether you're wearing your sunglasses and I have no idea what color you're seeing. All I know is what I knew when I walked into the booth—that we've got a really really good chance to win this game.

What if the referee changes the rules and says "no communication *and* no tennis balls"? Then, of course, we *are* cheating. But how's he going to catch us? Remember that in the real-world version of this story, we're talking about electrons, not tennis balls. There are approximately 10^{28} electrons in the human body. You can't direct a contestant not to bring any electrons into the game booth. And there's no way to identify the "special" electron that came from the Stern-Gerlach apparatus.

(On the other hand, you and I are going to have to figure out a way to keep our special electrons separate from the other 10^{28} electrons we're dragging around, and that's no minor problem.)

If, like so many undergraduates, you prefer to see a more "business-oriented" application, imagine that you and I are not game-show contestants but the presidents of American and United Airlines, and we're trying to set ticket prices. We'd like to coordinate our strategies, but the Justice Department has forbidden us from colluding. We've each got some partial information about demand conditions (analogous to our each having seen the outcome of one coin flip) and we've got to announce prices based on that partial information. It's not hard to concoct a story where we'd like to announce identical prices *unless* we've both received pessimistic information about demand, in which case we'd like to announce different prices (so that one of us can corner the high-price sector of the market while the other corners the low-price sector).

The information we've gotten about demand is like the outcome of a coin flip—instead of heads or tails, it's optimistic or pessimistic. Our goal is to announce identical prices unless we've both seen the pessimistic information, in which case we want to announce different prices. I trust you can see where this is going.

A contrived example? Certainly. Pure science fiction? Not entirely. Today you need a physics lab to harness quantum technology. A few decades from now, you might need nothing more than a $500 quantum computer.

Part

IV   Right and Wrong

Our instincts about morality, like everything else about us, must have evolved to enhance our reproductive fitness in a certain environment. But like our instincts about what to eat, our moral instincts aren't always well adapted for the modern world. For that reason—and also because reproductive fitness is not the only thing we care about—our instincts are worth reexamining and occasionally transcending. In today's world, it's usually best not to gorge on fat or fling feces at your enemies.

A moral philosophy is an attempt to identify common threads in our tangled web of intuitions, organize them in some sort of coherent way, and perhaps refine our instincts as a result of the exercise. Moral philosophies come in two flavors. There are the *deontological* philosophies—those that judge certain acts, like murder, to be wrong in an absolute sense; and then there are the *consequentialist* philosophies—those that judge actions by their consequences. In Chapter 16, I'll pose a few moral dilemmas designed to highlight this distinction.

Chapters 17 through 19 are about a moral philosophy I call the Economist's Golden Rule, which I hope to convince you is a pretty good guide to good behavior most of the time.

In these chapters, I'll mostly be talking about the standards we set for ourselves, which are not always the same as the standards we set for our friends or our governments. You might feel a strong moral compulsion to contribute to Oxfam, or to live a life of chastity, or to vote Republican, without requiring all good people to share your priorities. You can refuse to tolerate racist language without believing that all racist language should be outlawed. Although I'll concentrate on codes of personal morality, the discussion will spill over substantially into how we want our neighbors and our governments to behave.

In Chapters 20 and 21, I'll talk about fairness, which is not exactly the same thing as morality, but is surely closely related.

Along the way, we'll pause to discuss matters of life and death, the economics of counterfeiting, socially responsible career choices, the moral underpinnings of our policies on immigration, climate control and affirmative action, and the ancient mysteries of the Talmud.

16 Telling Right from Wrong

Good is better than evil cuz it's nicer.

—Pansy Yokum

How do we tell good from evil or right from wrong? Sometimes it's easy: Wanton murder is evil. Other times it's hard, or at least controversial: Is abortion evil? What about capital punishment, or racist language, or voting Republican? You might think some of the answers are obvious, but you've surely got neighbors who disagree.

What's needed is a moral philosophy—a criterion for deciding what counts as right and what counts as wrong.

Philosophers have long sought the One True Moral Philosophy, but I suspect those efforts are misguided. Like everything else about us, our moral instincts are evolutionary accidents; surely a society of hyperintelligent cats would have very different moral expectations than our own society of hyperintelligent apes. Given that, any search for the One True Moral Philosophy must be as futile as a search for the One True Digestive System.

Morality, then, is a biological accident. But that doesn't mean we shouldn't care about it. In fact, pretty much *everything* we care about is a biological accident. The color green, for example, is a biological accident. The grass on your lawn and the wool on your Christmas sweater reflect entirely different patterns of light; it's the human eye and brain that interpret those patterns as the "same color." If our eyes and brains were different, your lawn might be the same color as a fire truck and your sweater the same color as an egg yolk. Then we'd invent names for those colors, but neither of them would be the color we now call "green."

For that matter, time—or at least the rigorous distinction between time and space—is also a biological accident. The physicist Richard Feynman once invited his students to imagine a creature that perceives "width" and "depth" as fundamentally different. The creature simply cannot grasp what is so obvious to you and me—that the distinction between width and depth is a matter not of physics, but of perspective. When it comes to space and time, you and I are like that creature. We are blind to the fact that the distinction between space and time is largely a matter of perspective (and that time and space can be partly interchanged through high-speed travel, just as width and depth can be partly interchanged by walking partway around an object). Time is an artifact of the human brain.

Colors are biological phenomena, but that doesn't make us indifferent between brown and purple hair dye. Time is a biological phenomenon, but that doesn't mean you can be late for dinner. Morality is a biological phenomenon, but that doesn't make it okay to use your neighbors for target practice.

What it does mean is that moral truths are not to be found in some abstract realm that transcends human experience. The best we can do, probably, is to pull a few moral philosophies off the shelf and try them on for comfort. Personally, I'm shopping for something reasonably simple and internally consistent, but above all something that conforms to our most powerful moral instincts: A philosophy that says it's always okay to cut off the ears of small children is a bad philosophy.

The available philosophies come in two broad styles. There are the *consequentialist* philosophies that judge actions by their consequences, and the *deontological* philosophies that judge actions in their own right.

If that's too abstract, take a concrete example: A very battered and distraught-looking woman runs past you and ducks into an alleyway. Two minutes later, a very angry-looking man carrying an ax accosts you and asks, "Which way did she go?" Is it okay to lie? The extreme deontological position is that lying is wrong, period. The consequentialist position allows you to feel okay about saving a woman's life.

Not every deontologist believes that lying is always wrong, but every deontologist (by definition) believes that *some* things are always wrong. My problem with deontology is that I can't think of *anything* that's always wrong. I'd cheerfully cut off the ears of a small child to cure malaria.

Another example: We all know it's not okay to walk down the street firing a machine gun in random directions. Why not? A deontologist might say it's inherently *wrong* to violate other people's bodies nonconsensually. You sometimes hear principles like this expressed in slogans like "Do your own thing, but not on my back."

But as a guide to behavior, this will never do. Taken literally, it's a recipe for paralysis. What exactly are the limits of "not on my back"? Your hundred-watt desk lamp hurls about ten million billion photons per second through the body of the stranger walking past your window. You're not just on his back; you're in his organs.

We all agree that desk lamps are okay and serial murder is not. But where in that great gray area do we draw the line?[1]

The alternative to deontology is consequentialism: It's okay to lie when the consequences are good, and not okay when the consequences are bad. It's okay to propel photons through other people's bodies because they do very little harm; it's usually not okay to propel bullets through other people's bodies because the consequences are dire.

Philosophers use stylized moral dilemmas to separate the deontologists from the consequentialists. Here are two that have gotten a lot of recent attention:

The Trolley Problem, Version I. A trolley is hurtling out of control along a track, bearing down on five people who have been tied to the track by a mad philosopher. You can avert the disaster by flipping a switch that diverts the trolley to another track. Unfortunately, there is one man tied to that other track. Is it morally permissible (or for that matter morally mandatory) to flip the switch?

The Trolley Problem, Version II. A trolley is hurtling out of control along a track, bearing down on five people who have been tied to the track by a mad philosopher. You can stop the trolley by pushing a man in front of it. Is it morally permissible (or for that matter morally mandatory) to push the man in front of the trolley?[2]

---

1 You might be tempted to think there's an obvious answer: Photons, unlike bullets, are okay because nobody objects to them. But I don't think that's the answer at all—because if some crank passing by your window *did* object to your photons, I don't think you'd apologize and live in the dark.

2 In case you were planning to flaunt your moral superiority by jumping in front of the trolley yourself, let's suppose for the sake of argument that that's impossible; you're too small to stop the trolley.

According to surveys, most people would flip the switch in Version I but wouldn't push the man in Version II. To a deontologist, this might make perfect sense: Pushing people in front of trolleys is *wrong* and therefore you shouldn't do it, even to save lives. But to a consequentialist, it's troubling. Both actions have exactly the same consequences: Five lives saved, one life lost. If actions should be judged by their consequences, then flipping the switch and pushing the man should be equally good (or equally bad).

Interestingly, people with damage to a part of the brain called the ventromedial cortex are substantially more likely to answer like consequentialists: They pull the switch *and* they push the man. Perhaps I am one of those people, because when I first heard these problems, it seemed obvious to me that in either case, there's a moral obligation to sacrifice the one for the five. I was, in fact, quite surprised to learn that there was anyone—let alone a substantial majority—who believed otherwise.

Of course, if I were the man about to be pushed in front of the trolley, I might feel differently. But that's a matter of self-interest, not morality. The very essence of moral judgments is that they're divorced from self-interest.

In other words, your moral judgments are the judgments you'd make if you could somehow forget who you are and what you've got at stake. Is there a moral imperative to tax the rich and give to the poor? We're entitled to question the motives of both the rich man who says no and the poor man who says yes. The man to trust is the amnesiac who can't remember whether he's rich or poor.

This "amnesia principle" comes to us from John Harsanyi, a Nobel Prize–winning economist who, before turning to economics, had won a national mathematics competition in his native Hungary and then earned a Ph.D. in philosophy. Harsanyi was interested in questions like this: Would it be better for everyone to earn $50,000 a year, or for two-thirds of us to earn $60,000 while one-third earn $40,000? Of course the real question here is: What does "better" mean? According to Harsanyi, the better world is (by definition) the world you'd prefer to be born into, *without knowing* whether you'll be in the upper two-thirds or the lower third.

You can rephrase the question this way: In a world of three people (call them Manny, Moe, and Jack), is it better for everyone to earn $50,000 or for Manny and Moe to earn $60,000 while Jack earns $40,000? The answer, according to Harsanyi, is the answer you'd give in the amnesiac state where you're not sure who you are.

But amnesia is hard to imagine, so it's hard to trust people's answers to the "If you had amnesia . . ." question. The solution is to ignore what people *say* and observe what they *do*. Find, say, a salesperson who's been offered a choice between a salary of $50,000 a year, or a commission that has a two-thirds chance of being $60,000 and a one-third chance of being $40,000. His choice tells you which income distribution he prefers. And if you find many salesmen in similar situations all making similar choices, you are entitled to draw an inference about which world is better.

That's a pretty abstract example. In the real world, policy makers don't get to choose from a menu of income distributions. Instead, they have to do things like design tax systems and welfare programs, which then have indirect effects on how income is distributed. In 1996, the British economist Sir James Mirrlees and the Canadian-American economist William Vickrey were awarded the Nobel Prize partly for adapting Harsanyi's amnesia principle so that it can be applied to real-world policy questions.

I want to apply the amnesia principle to the trolley problem. In the first version, five people are tied to one track and one person to the other. If I've somehow forgotten who I am, I at least know this: I am five times as likely to be one of the five as to be the one alone. My death is therefore five times more likely if you fail to pull the switch. I hope you pull it.

In the second version, five people are tied to the track and one man is in jeopardy of being pushed in front of the train. I, the amnesia victim, know that I am five times more likely to be tied to the track. My death is therefore five times more likely if you fail to push the man. I hope you push him.

In one sense these calculations are entirely self-interested, but in another they're the very opposite. As long as I don't know who I am (and as long as I think I'm equally likely to be any given person as another), my "self-interest" accounts for *everyone's* interests. That's what a moral judgment ought to do, and that's why I believe it's morally imperative both to pull the switch and to push the man.

Now, the philosophers in the audience, if they're doing their job, will do their best to make me uncomfortable by pushing my reasoning to its limit. The philosopher Judith Jarvis Thompson, for example, poses this problem:

The Doctor Problem. A brilliant transplant surgeon has five patients, each in need of a different organ, each of whom will die without that organ. Unfortunately, there are no organs available to perform any of these five transplant operations. A healthy young traveler, just passing through the city the doctor works in, comes in for a routine checkup. In the course of doing the checkup, the doctor discovers that the traveler's organs are compatible with all five of his dying patients. . . .

As stated, this problem is too easy. Nobody would want to live in a world where doctors routinely harvest healthy organs from random travelers, and it's easy to explain why. First, there'd be far less incentive to take care of yourself; why watch your cholesterol in a world where healthy hearts are treated as communal resources? Second, there'd be a lot less travel. I'd cheerfully skip the next annual meeting of the American Economic Association rather than risk falling prey to a physician with a recreational interest in philosophy.

So to make the problem interesting, we should rewrite it in a way that fails to penalize good health and makes clear that this is a onetime event with no implications for future travelers. My colleague Romans Pancs suggests something like the following:

> *The Doctor Problem, Revised.* A mad philosopher has apprehended six travelers and has removed and discarded a different vital organ from each of the first five. He is about to remove a vital organ from the sixth traveler when he is frightened by a burst of lightning. Exit the philosopher. Enter the prodigal surgeon.
>
> In the absence of a healthy transplant, each of the first five travelers will die within the hour. The only source of healthy organs is the sixth traveler.

Should the doctor kill the one to save the five? The amnesia principle seems to say so, but your ventromedial cortex probably disagrees. This problem seems to bring out the deontologist in almost everyone. We think it's *wrong* to kill people without permission, regardless of the consequences.

On the other hand . . . in exactly what relevant way does harvesting the sixth traveler's organs differ from throwing the trolley switch? I don't have a good answer to that. Perhaps in this case, our gut moral instincts are just *wrong*. Perhaps the doctor *should* kill the sixth traveler.

For the most part, I trust my moral instincts, just as I trust my eyes. But sometimes my eyes deceive me. There are even optical illusions that deceive pretty much *everyone's* eyes. What I'm suggesting here is that Professor Thompson's doctor problem might be a "moral illusion" that leads pretty much everyone astray. The purpose of moral philosophy is to shatter moral illusions.

In this, economists might be more advanced (or perhaps more ventromedially challenged) than many philosophers. I recently stumbled on a paper, written by a distinguished philosopher, that posed this scenario:

> *The Headache Problem.* A billion people are experiencing fairly minor headaches, which will continue for another hour unless an innocent person is killed, in which case they will cease immediately. Is it okay to kill that innocent person?

I didn't actually understand why this was a dilemma; the answer is yes, for reasons that would be immediately obvious to any economist. The philosopher reached the same conclusion for the same reasons, but took forty pages to get there and then declared the result "counterintuitive."

Here's how an economist sees the question: First, virtually nobody will pay a dollar to avoid a one-in-a-billion chance of death. (We know this, for example, from studies of willingness to pay for auto safety devices.) Second, most people—at least in the developed world, where I will assume all of this is taking place—would happily pay a dollar to cure a headache. (I don't actually know this, but it seems probable.) Third, this tells me that most people think a headache is worse than a one-in-a-billion chance of death. So if I can replace your headache with a one-in-a-billion chance of death, I've done you a favor. And I can do precisely this by killing a headache sufferer at random.

The philosopher who found this conclusion bizarre and counterintuitive (though nevertheless compelling) must have very little experience living in the real world, where we all agree to kill random people all the time. We drive, install swimming pools, use drain cleaners, and drink tequila, knowing with certainty that some number of other people will die as a result. People have died so that other people can drive to the opera. Why shouldn't they die to cure other people's headaches?

17 The Economist's Golden Rule

> Regard your neighbor's gain as your own gain, and your neighbor's loss as your own loss.
>
> —T'ai-Shang Kan-Ying P'ien

Trolley tracks, mad philosophers, mass headaches curable through random assassinations—I believe we learn a lot from thinking about extreme hypotheticals. But sooner or later we have to translate those lessons into practical guides for everyday behavior.

All moral codes come down to variations on a single theme: "Don't treat other people too badly." But nobody—or almost nobody—thinks you're required to treat others as well as you'd treat yourself. If you're walking around with two kidneys, you've chosen to ignore the plights of thousands of dialysis patients who could make excellent use of your spare. Some of us are vaguely disturbed by that thought, but few of us are disturbed enough to act on it. By and large, we think it's okay to let strangers suffer while we take care of ourselves, our friends, and our family.

On the other hand, almost nobody thinks it's okay to *steal* from strangers, at least in ordinary circumstances. That's a little odd when you think about it. How can it be okay to let a man die of kidney disease but not to take a dime from his dresser?

The deontological answer is that stealing is *wrong*. I have a lot of sympathy for that answer, but I also have some problems with it. What makes stealing wrong? Is it because we all have the right to control our own property? If that's it, then why is it okay for me to turn on my desk lamp and bombard your property (not to mention your body) with photons?

A more nuanced—and more consequentialist—answer is that stealing is wrong because it's destructive. A well-executed theft takes time and energy, which could have been used productively. If I spend an hour stealing your bicycle, we still have only one bicycle between us; if I spend that same hour building (or earning) a bicycle, we have two. By diverting productive resources from useful activities, theft leaves the world an unnecessarily poorer place.

There are good consequentialist reasons for wanting the world to be as wealthy as possible, and therefore there are good consequentialist reasons for disapproving of theft. And likewise, there can be good consequentialist reasons for respecting property rights more generally, and for treating people fairly and with dignity. In other words, there are good consequentialist reasons for adopting positions that appear deontological on the surface.

That, I think, accounts for many of our notions of fairness and good behavior. We subscribe to principles that sound deontological, but are ultimately justified by their consequences.

I have a favorite consequentialist rule of thumb for good behavior. It's a rule that I think captures most of our moral intuitions. Roughly, the rule is "Don't leave the world worse off than you found it." A corollary is "Don't spend valuable time and energy in nonproductive ways."

Productivity is to be understood quite broadly here; if you're producing something of value (to anyone, including you), then you're productive. Idling away the afternoon over a crossword puzzle is entirely productive, as long as you enjoy doing crossword puzzles. You're productive when the benefits of your actions (to everyone, including you) exceed the costs (to everyone, including you).

I call my rule of thumb the Economist's Golden Rule, or EGR for short. Like more traditional versions of the Golden Rule, it enjoins you to love your neighbor as yourself. A cost is a cost and a benefit is a benefit, whether they're felt by you, your neighbor, or a stranger in Timbuktu.[1]

Economists measure costs and benefits in dollars, for reasons I hope to make clear. The benefit of driving to the grocery store is the maximum amount you'd be willing to pay for the privilege; the cost is the maximum amount the rest of us would be willing to pay to avert your carbon emissions.

Why should costs and benefits be measured in dollars instead of some other way? Bear with me; I promise to return to that question.

If you live by the EGR, you're unlikely to play loud music at night in an apartment with thin walls. That's because the dollar value (to you) of hearing music rarely exceeds the dollar value (to your neighbor) of a good night's sleep—or, if you've got ten neighbors, of ten nights' sleep. If each neighbor loses $50 worth of peace and quiet, your music had better be worth at least $500, where "worth $500" means that you'd honestly be willing to pay $500 for the privilege of hearing it.

Even if you really really love your music—even if you love it

---

1 In Chapter 12, when we talked about the right amount of pollution (or the right quantity of blood to draw from a pig), I was essentially using the Economist's Golden Rule to define the notion of a "better" outcome.

$500 worth—you still can't justify blaring your loudspeakers unless that's worth at least $500 *more* than listening through earphones—and $500 more than waiting till morning when the neighbors have gone to work.

You might object that it's *never* okay to wake your neighbors against their will, but that's probably because you haven't fully digested the spirit of the example. The EGR allows you to wake the neighbors only if hearing your music—and hearing it now, and without headphones—is quite extraordinarily important to you. This is the kind of exception we grant all the time. Normally, weaving in and out of traffic makes you a jerk. But if you're rushing your child to the emergency room—or even rushing to a key business appointment—a reasonable person might cut you some slack. The EGR tells you when to cut yourself some slack—and when not to.

My students sometimes object that the EGR is a bad criterion because it allows the rich to run roughshod over the poor. Bill Gates's investment income exceeds a million dollars a day. If he wants to crank his volume up, he might happily pay $10,000 for the privilege and never miss a penny of it. If his ten neighbors are very poor, they might be willing to cough up only $10 apiece to stop him, even though the music makes them extremely unhappy. Do we really want to conclude that it's okay for Bill to keep the neighbors up all night? What kind of crazy tunnel-visioned economist would look at those raw numbers and conclude that Bill cares more about this issue than the neighbors do?

The answer goes to the heart of why we measure costs and benefits in dollars. It's not a terribly complicated answer, but it's as widely misunderstood as anything in economics. Let me do my bit to combat that misunderstanding.

Here, then, is the answer: *Nobody—not even the crazy tunnel-*

visioned economist—claims that dollar values represent "degrees of caring." The economist is thinking something else entirely.

He's thinking this: For Bill to turn off his music represents a ten thousand dollar sacrifice. If we're prepared to ask for that kind of sacrifice, wouldn't it make a whole lot more sense to ask him for ten thousand dollars? Surely the neighbors would prefer the cash to one night of peace and quiet.

Bill is perfectly free to hand out cash to his neighbors anytime he wants to. For better or worse, he's chosen not to do that, and we've chosen not to force him to. If he won't give up ten thousand dollars cash in order to give the rest of us ten thousand dollars cash, why should he give up ten thousand dollars' worth of music to give us a hundred dollars' worth of sleep?

The EGR takes no stand on whether Bill should give us money, either voluntarily or involuntarily (say through the tax system). It says only this: If Bill *does* make a ten thousand dollar sacrifice, he should do it not by turning down his volume but by giving us ten thousand dollars.

Should rich guys like Bill make sacrifices for middle-class guys like you and me? Some say no, some say yes. If you say no, then don't ask Bill for any favors. If you say yes, then ask him for money. Either way, it's crazy to ask for a night of quiet that Bill will miss just as much as he'd miss the money and that you'll value a whole lot less. *The EGR uses dollar values to rule out that kind of craziness.*[2]

Charity is neither productive nor destructive; it takes wealth

---

2 There's (at least) one problem with this reasoning, and that's figuring out exactly what it means to say your quiet is "worth" a hundred dollars to you. Is that *the price you'd pay to eliminate the stereo,* or *the price you'd accept to put up with it*? Those numbers need not be equal, and when they differ substantially it can render my argument incoherent and make it harder to justify the EGR. Fortunately, economic theory provides good reasons to believe that the two numbers are usually very close. Unfortunately, "usually" is not the same as "always."

from one person's pocket and moves it to another's. The EGR, therefore, takes no stand on how much charitable giving is appropriate. It allows us each to make that call for ourselves. If there's a moral imperative to be charitable, then the EGR is indeed an insufficient moral philosophy. But the way to fix that is to supplement the EGR with a requirement to be charitable, not to abandon it altogether.

In other words, if you're willing to insist that Bill give up his music, you should change your focus and insist that he give up his money instead. Your real beef is not with the EGR; it's with the fact that Bill is rich.

So I think it's morally okay for Bill to crank up the volume. But I still don't think the law should allow it. That's because we have only Bill's word for the fact that the music's worth ten thousand dollars to him, and he could very well be lying. A law that prohibits waking your neighbors is an imperfect law, but it's probably a law that will get things right more often than it gets them wrong.

I'm pretty well convinced that the EGR is a good guide to personal morality. You might want to supplement it with a requirement to be charitable. This raises the question: Exactly how charitable do you feel obligated to be? Different people have very different answers to that question, and I have no idea how to arbitrate among them. I'll therefore skip over the question of charity, not because it's unimportant but because I don't know what to say.

The EGR does a pretty good job of capturing what most people mean by social responsibility. If you're trying to lower your carbon footprint but still own a car, you're in the spirit of the EGR: driving when the benefits are high (like getting your kid to school) but refraining when the benefits are low.

I've devoted the next chapter to a catalog of ethical dilemmas, together with the EGR's answers and the reasons behind them. For the most part, the EGR will tell you to keep right on doing what you're doing. You don't need the EGR to tell you not to steal. But occasionally, as you'll see, it tells you to do something surprising. Maybe that's because the EGR is the wrong moral philosophy. Or maybe it's because you're sometimes careless in your moral judgments. In the latter case, a little rethinking might be worth your while.

18 How to Be Socially Responsible

A User's Guide to the Economist's Golden Rule

Philosophy must be of some use and we must take it
seriously; it must clear our thoughts and so our actions.
——*Frank Plumpton Ramsey*

Questions and answers for those who would live by the Economist's Golden Rule:

IS IT OKAY TO STEAL? Certainly not, and I've already told you why: The time and effort you spend stealing things is time and effort you could spend producing things instead. Theft leaves the world poorer than it could have been.

IS IT OKAY TO COUNTERFEIT? Certainly not, because counterfeiting is stealing. The time and effort you spend producing a phony dollar bill entitles you to a Hostess cupcake or a bus ride or a Blockbuster video rental without adding anything to the world's stock of food, transportation, or entertainment. The cupcake you eat is made of flour and sugar that someone else could have eaten.

It's worth understanding exactly who you're stealing from. When you print and spend that bogus bill, you (ever so slightly) expand the supply of money, which (ever so slightly) pushes up the prices of everything from birdseed to locomotives, which (ever so slightly) erodes the value of the dollars in your countrymen's pockets. This nearly imperceptible loss to each of your countrymen, times 300 million countrymen, works out to a total loss of exactly a dollar.

I know this because at the end of the day, you've got an extra dollar's worth of goodies on your plate, and those goodies had to come from somewhere. So the total damage you've done must add up to just that dollar.

If you'd spent the same time and effort *baking* a cupcake instead of (essentially) stealing one, the world would have one additional cupcake. If you'd spent the same time and effort washing a window so you could earn real money to *buy* a cupcake, the world would have one more clean window. By counterfeiting, you've left the world poorer than it might have been. Just like a thief.

HOW MUCH SHOULD I GIVE TO CHARITY? That's entirely up to you. When you give a hundred dollars to, say, CARE, the cost is a hundred dollars (to you) and the benefit is a hundred dollars (to the recipient). The EGR shrugs its shoulders and says, "Give what you feel like giving."

If you feel like giving generously, that's great. If your neighbor gives less, or not at all, the EGR says that's okay, too.

SO IN YOUR OPINION IT'S OKAY TO BE COMPLETELY UN-CHARITABLE? My opinion is not the issue. The EGR is meant to express a moral principle we pretty much all agree on. We don't all agree on the appropriate level of charity, so it's fitting and proper that the EGR is silent on the matter.

IS IT OKAY TO LITTER? Not unless the benefit to you exceeds the total cost to everyone who has to see, smell, or navigate around your litter. In other words, probably not.

IS IT OKAY TO BURN CARBON-BASED FUELS? Yes, when and only when the benefits exceed the total cost (to you and your neighbors). In an ideal world, you'd pay a fair price for your carbon emissions, just as you pay a fair price for oranges. (*Fair* here means "reflective of the costs you're imposing on other people.") In our less than ideal world, the EGR tells you to curb your pollution *as if* you were paying a fair price. It's been estimated that you cause about 50 cents' worth of environmental damage for every gallon of gas you burn. If you believe that estimate, and if you currently pay $3 a gallon for gas, pretend you're paying about $3.50 and adjust your driving habits accordingly.

SHOULD I BUY A MORE FUEL-EFFICIENT CAR? MAYBE ONE OF THOSE HYBRIDS? Careful. Hybrid cars are subsidized by the government, which is to say that they're subsidized by your fellow taxpayers. Since when is it socially responsible to spend other people's money on yourself?

The EGR says: Act as if you were feeling the full costs of your actions. In other words, buy that Prius only if you'd have been willing to pay full price in the subsidy's absence—probably about $500 more than you're actually paying.

IS IT OKAY TO DRIVE INTO NEW YORK CITY? When you drive into New York, the social cost of your carbon emissions is dwarfed by your contribution to congestion on the bridges and tunnels. If you delay each of the thousand cars behind you by just fifteen seconds, you've easily caused hundreds of dollars' worth of damage. Was your trip really worth that much?

In your defense, though, the line is likely to have been just as long without you. If your very presence deterred someone else from entering, then on balance you've added *nothing* to the line length.

Now, you might think that adding fifteen seconds to a forty-five-minute wait is very unlikely to deter anyone from entering, and you'd be right. The chance you'll make a difference is maybe one in a thousand. Which means that of the thousand or so cars in line, you'll deter exactly one.

That might sound like I'm just guessing, but in fact a little economic analysis (of the sort that requires a blackboard, a diagram, and a few minutes of hard thought) reveals that under quite general conditions, your presence *does* deter exactly one entrant. The congestion problem is therefore no worse with you than without you.

You *can't* make that argument for pollution. Sure, your car's emissions are only a tiny fraction of the global problem, but that's not what's relevant. A dollar's worth of harm is a dollar's worth of harm, and you have it in your power to avoid that harm. With power comes responsibility.

But congestion is different, because every time you make the problem worse (by joining the line), you also make it better (by discouraging other entrants).

In the Philadelphia neighborhood where I grew up, Halloween was preceded by Soap Night on October 28th, Chalk Night on the 29th, and Mischief Night on the 30th. (I was stunned when I moved to upstate New York and learned that these were not national holidays.) On Soap Night, you marked things (sidewalks, windshields, mailboxes) with soap and on Chalk Night you marked them with chalk. (Using chalk on Soap Night would have been as inappropriate as trimming a tree for Halloween.)

Each year on Soap Night, my mother issued me a bar of soap and carefully instructed me to draw only on sidewalks and not on private property. Each year, I argued that if I didn't soap the neighbor's windshield, some other kid surely would. Each year, my mother was unimpressed with that argument. Even if something bad is bound to happen, she said, let it be someone else's doing.

If you agree with my mother, avoid long tollbooth lines— except, of course, when your trips are unusually important. (Of course you *already* avoid long lines, because you hate waiting. But the point is that you should avoid them even more, accounting for not just your own waiting time but everyone else's.) If you agree with my nine-year-old self, go ahead and enter those lines guilt-free.

WHAT CAREER SHOULD I PURSUE? A socially productive one, of course. By and large, the best way to be sure you're doing something useful is that somebody's willing to pay you to do it. If you're a doctor, an architect, or a circus clown, your compensation is probably a pretty good measure of your social contribution.

CAN I BE A LAWYER? It depends. A lot of lawyers devote a lot of effort to transferring wealth around without creating any; the plaintiff's gain is the defendant's loss. Better to do something that *creates* wealth than something that merely transfers it. On the other hand, lawsuits deter a lot of unproductive behavior, which is good. On the first hand, lawsuits also deter a lot of *productive* behavior, which is bad. So I guess it depends on what kind of lawyer you want to be.

IS IT REALLY OKAY TO BE A CIRCUS CLOWN? Sure. Circus clowns produce entertainment, which is every bit as legitimate a commodity as food and clothing.

IS IT OKAY TO BE AN OLYMPIC ATHLETE? Get serious. You really think it's fitting for an ambitious hardworking twenty-three-year-old to devote his life to volleyball? You'd be more productive wandering down to the grocery store and returning stray carts from the parking lot.

WAIT A MINUTE. AREN'T THE OLYMPICS A FORM OF EN-TERTAINMENT? AND DIDN'T YOU JUST SAY ENTERTAINMENT IS SOCIALLY VALUABLE? Yes and yes. There's huge social value in the Olympics.

THEN WHY SHOULDN'T I PARTICIPATE? Because the question isn't whether the Olympics have value. It's whether you *add* to that value.

If you build a table, the world has one more table. If you bake a cupcake, the world has one more cupcake. If you become a circus clown, the world has one more squirt of seltzer down someone's pants. But if you win an Olympic gold medal, the world will not have one more Olympic gold medalist. It will just have you instead of someone else.

YES, AND IF I BECOME A CLOWN AT BARNUM & BAILEY, BARNUM & BAILEY WON'T HAVE ONE MORE CLOWN. IT WILL JUST HAVE ME INSTEAD OF SOMEONE ELSE. WHAT'S THE DIFFERENCE? The clown you displace from Barnum & Bailey will go do something else. Maybe he'll be a clown at Carson & Barnes; maybe he'll go to welding school. But the swimmer you beat in the hundred-meter butterfly will still have spent years training for the hundred-meter butterfly. Instead of turning him into a welder, you've merely turned him into a loser.

HRMPH. BUT IF ONLY TEN PEOPLE TRIED OUT FOR THE OLYMPICS, THE COMPETITION WOULD BE LAUGHABLE. DON'T MORE ATHLETES ADD TO THE QUALITY? Yes. And if only ten people tried out for the Olympics, you'd make a great social contribution by becoming the eleventh. But *given* the tens of thousands who are already competing, your contribution is tiny.

We wouldn't want to eliminate 90 percent of the competitors, but we might well want to eliminate half. If you could set half the Olympic swimmers to driving taxicabs, the winning times would be slightly slower and the spectators' experience would be (just slightly) worse. Meanwhile, it would be a whole lot easier to get a cab.

The same is true for professional athletes. Would the world really suffer so much if the fastest pitch in Major League Baseball were ninety-four miles an hour instead of ninety-six (with a commensurate reduction in the batter's skill)? For that matter, the same is true of *any* tournament—including the competition to write bestselling books. If this book sells a million copies, they'll be read by a million people who would otherwise have been reading some other book that's probably almost as good. My financial reward will be huge; my social contribution might be neglible.

The key difference is that, at any given time, a circus clown can entertain only a few thousand people and a doctor can operate on only one patient. Therefore we can always use more clowns and doctors, and their wages are a good measure of how much we need them. But a single athlete or a single author can entertain the entire world. Along the way, they capture a lot of income that would otherwise have gone to their competitors. That income represents a transfer of wealth, not a social contribution.

IS IT OKAY TO BE A CORPORATE EXECUTIVE? For the most part, sure. An executive's job is to maximize profit, and usually the best way to do that is to produce goods and services that people value. Unfortunately, some executives seek profits by lobbying for subsidies, tariff protection, and import quotas, all of which are socially destructive. If you're that kind of corporate executive, I hope you're ashamed of yourself.

You could argue, of course, that those corporate executives are merely doing the jobs they were hired to do. You could argue the same for a professional hit man.

ALL RIGHT, SO I SHOULDN'T LOBBY FOR IMPORT QUOTAS. BUT IF THE QUOTAS ALREADY EXIST, IS IT OKAY TO PROFIT FROM THEM? Oh, yes. It's even admirable. The quota on Chinese silk shirts props up the price of American shirts by creating an artificial shortage. To profit from that quota, you've got to supply shirts, which helps alleviate the shortage. For that you deserve a reward, and I'm glad you're earning one.

AND THE SAME GOES FOR TARIFFS, I ASSUME? AS LONG AS I DON'T LOBBY FOR THEM, IT'S OKAY TO PROFIT FROM THEM? Nope. Imported plywood is taxed at about 40 percent, which props up the price of American plywood. If that's the only reason you're selling plywood, you're basically a leech.

That's perhaps not obvious. At least I hope it's not, because it took me a good twenty minutes (and the help of two colleagues) to get it right. But here's the accounting: A foreign sheet of plywood is available for (say) $5 plus $2 tax. Therefore American suppliers can get $7 a sheet, and they do. If you can produce plywood at $6 a sheet, you make a $1 profit—but only by costing the U.S. Treasury (and ultimately the U.S. taxpayers) $2 worth of revenue. Your $1 profit comes at a $2 cost to your neighbors. That's a no-no.

Even without working through the details, it should be obvious that your plywood business is socially destructive. You are using up $6 worth of resources to produce a sheet of plywood someone in Canada could have produced for $5. That can't be good.

Like house fires, both quotas and tariffs are destructive. If you're in business because of a quota, you're pouring water on the fire; if you're in business because of a tariff, you're pouring gasoline.

IF I FIND AN IPOD ON A DESERTED SIDEWALK, CAN I PICK IT UP AND KEEP IT? Sure.

IF I FIND A HUNDRED-DOLLAR BILL ON A DESERTED SIDE-WALK, CAN I PICK IT UP AND KEEP IT? Nope.

HUH? WHAT'S THE DIFFERENCE? I'm assuming in both cases that you have no idea how to locate the rightful owner, and if you don't claim these items, nobody else will. (Maybe they're about to be washed away by a thunderstorm.)

Here's the difference: If you pick up the iPod, you gain an iPod and nobody else loses anything. That's a clear net gain for society. But if you pick up the $100 bill, you're eventually going to spend it, which is going to drive up prices, which is going to cost the rest of us exactly $100, just as if you'd counterfeited. The final accounting: You gain about $99.98 ($100 minus about two cents' worth of effort bending over to pick up the bill); the rest of us lose $100. Your two cents' worth of effort is wasted. That's social destruction. Not a lot of social destruction, but social destruction nonetheless.

BE HONEST. IF YOU SEE A HUNDRED-DOLLAR BILL ON THE STREET, DO YOU REALLY JUST WALK AWAY? Nope. I pick it up.

BUT I THOUGHT YOU JUST SAID . . . I answered two different questions. First I told you what the EGR requires. Then I told you what I'd do.

SO YOU DON'T BUY THE EGR AFTER ALL? I didn't say that exactly. The EGR accurately captures what I (and I suspect you) mean by social responsibility. And I usually try to be socially responsible. Just not always.

WHY NOT? The EGR adds up all costs and benefits, no matter who feels them. It tells me to treat myself, my friends, and my family exactly as I'd treat a stranger in Timbuktu. I don't do that. I do care about strangers in Timbuktu, but I care about my loved ones more.

SO IF YOU FEEL PERFECTLY FREE TO IGNORE THE EGR, WHAT GOOD IS IT? It's an excellent guide for behavior most of the time and a good approximation the rest of the time. I'm sometimes okay with imposing $100 worth of costs on strangers for a $99.98 gain to myself, but decidedly not okay with imposing $100 worth of costs on strangers for a $25 gain to myself.

SO EXACTLY HOW MUCH IS IT OKAY TO FAVOR YOURSELF AND YOUR LOVED ONES OVER STRANGERS? I'm not sure I can give you an exact answer to this, but I'll have a lot to say about it in the next chapter.

IS THAT EVERYTHING YOU HAVE TO SAY ON THE MATTER? Not quite. We often feel moral obligations to treat other people with fairness and dignity, regardless of the EGR. If I find an iPod on the street, I'm willing to spend ten dollars locating the rightful owner, even though the EGR suggests I shouldn't.[1] Perhaps that's because I'm a bit of a deontologist after all. Or perhaps it's because I think that *acting* like a deontologist—for example, going out of my way to respect other people's property rights—has good consequences in the long run.

OR MAYBE IT'S BECAUSE YOU GET MORE THAN $10 WORTH OF PLEASURE OUT OF KNOWING YOU'VE DONE THE RIGHT THING. That kind of reasoning won't get you anywhere, since the whole problem here is to figure out what "the right thing" is in the first place. But fairness is important, even if I can't quite reconcile it with the EGR. In fact, it's important enough to merit some serious thought about what fairness really entails. I'll get to that in Chapter 20.

---

1 My ten dollars' worth of effort merely transfers an existing iPod from me to the owner without creating anything and is therefore socially wasted.

19 On Not Being a Jerk

> The propagandist's purpose is to make one set of people forget that certain other sets of people are human.
>
> —*Aldous Huxley*

A jerk is someone who weaves in and out of traffic, talks in movie theaters, dumps trash in Central Park, or denies a life preserver to a drowning man. You're a jerk, in other words, if you impose large costs on others to achieve smaller benefits for yourself. A jerk is someone who violates the Economist's Golden Rule.

That still gives you plenty of latitude. Ignoring the plight of a tsunami victim in Malaysia does not make you a jerk. Chances are, the very best thing you can do for that tsunami victim is send money; a dollar of cost for a dollar of benefit. If you're inclined to give, by all means give, but the EGR doesn't dictate the amount.

If your parents were diligent about your dental hygiene, you probably remember Goofus, the quintessential jerk from the

"Goofus and Gallant" cartoons in *Highlights for Children*.[1] Each cartoon contrasts Goofus's selfishness with Gallant's kindness and generosity, summarized in single-sentence captions. Goofus takes the last apple. Gallant shares his orange. Goofus makes his friends wait. Gallant is ready on time. Goofus erects a border fence. Gallant says, "Send these, the homeless, tempest-tossed, to me."

Goofus, being a jerk, would consign millions of unskilled Mexicans to lives of desperate poverty because—well, because he doesn't think they count for very much.

Goofus responds that as an American, it's only natural for him to care more about his fellow citizens than a bunch of foreigners. Granting him that for the moment, we are entitled to ask: How *much* more? Surely there is some limit. Not even Goofus thinks that Americans should be allowed to hunt Mexicans for sport. So my question for Goofus is: Exactly how much are you willing to hurt a foreigner to help an American? Is a foreigner's well-being worth three-quarters as much as an American's, or half as much, or one-quarter as much—or what? In other words, just how big a jerk are you?[2]

Let's do the math: When we admit an unskilled Mexican immigrant, his wage typically rises from about $2 an hour to $9 an hour—call it a $7-per-hour gain. To justify keeping him out, we'll have to weigh that gain against the harm he does to Americans.

Right away, our calculation runs into a problem, because on balance immigrants don't harm Americans; virtually all econo-mists agree that immigration makes us richer, not poorer. Every

---

1 *Highlights for Children* has been the primary reading material in pediatric dental waiting rooms for more than sixty years.

2 I'm grateful to the anonymous proprietor of the YouNotSneaky blog for for-mulating the question this way.

immigrant is a potential trading partner, a potential employee, and a potential customer. He bids down wages, but that's a two-edged sword: It's bad for his fellow workers, but it's good for employers and good for consumers.

In the very short run, most of the gains go to employers, and a substantial fraction of those gains probably go to people named Walton. In the somewhat longer run, all that excess profit gets competed away and shows up in the form of lower prices for consumer goods. At that point, even the workers who took pay cuts can come out ahead: If your wage falls by 10 percent while prices fall by 20 percent, you're a winner.

But let's ignore all that. In order to make the best possible anti-immigrant case, let's ignore all the benefits of immigration and focus strictly on the costs to American workers, i.e., falling wages.

Since we're talking about a single immigrant, wages fall infinitesimally—but you've got to multiply that infinitesimal drop by millions of American workers. A high-end estimate is that 100 million Americans experience wage reductions of about $.00000003 per hour. Multiply that out and you have a $3-per-hour loss.[3] This estimate comes from the labor-economics literature, and it really applies only in the very short run, because in the long run, falling wages attract new businesses, which partly bid wages right back up again. But let's ignore all that, too, and assume a worst-case scenario, where the short-run effects are somehow never ameliorated.

Bottom line: When the immigrant crosses the border, 100 million Americans lose a total of $3 (per hour of work), and the individual immigrant gains $7 (again per hour of work). To op-

---

3 Note to econogeeks: I assumed a wage rate of $10 an hour and an elasticity of wages with respect to labor of 0.3.

pose that, you'd have to count an immigrant as less than three-sevenths of an American.

Goofus deviates pretty severely from the Economist's Golden Rule, which says that a $7 gain beats a $3 loss, regardless of who gains and loses. Well, Goofus isn't alone; you and I deviate from the EGR, too. We care more about ourselves, our friends, and our neighbors than we do about strangers. But unlike me (and I hope unlike you) Goofus also cares more about strangers in the American city of San Antonio than about strangers in the Mexican city of Juárez. That strikes me as unappealing, just as if he cared more about strangers who happen to share his skin color.

Moreover, Goofus appears to care about those strangers in San Antonio more than *twice as much* as the strangers in Juárez (because seven is more than twice three). That's an unsettlingly large ratio.

Indeed, if you're going to deviate from the EGR, most of us think you ought to deviate in the *opposite* direction, by putting more weight on the needs of the desperately poor. In this case, we're weighing a $7 gain to a $2-an-hour immigrant versus a total of $3 in losses to a bunch of $10-an-hour Americans.

When economists think about income distributions, there's a range of standard assumptions about how to value a poor man's dollar against a rich man's. The most conservative of those assumptions—that is, the one most biased *against* the conclusion I'm aiming for—is that the value of an extra dollar is inversely proportional to your income, so an extra dollar is worth five times as much to a $2-an-hour Mexican as it is to a $10-an-hour American. The immigrant's second dollar is worth a little less, and the third a little less than that.

Accounting for all that, it turns out that the immigrant's $7 gain is worth about five times the Americans' collective $3 loss. By that calculation, to justify keeping the immigrant out, you'd have to say he's worth less than one-fifth of an American citizen. In other words, you'd have to be a pretty enormous jerk.

Here's where Goofus points out that not even Gallant allows the world's desperate poor to bunk in Gallant's living room, so perhaps Gallant's just a big jerk, too. That's because Goofus has thoroughly misunderstood (or pretended to misunderstand) the argument. Let's break it down for him:

First, the EGR does not require Gallant to open up his living room. In fact, it tells him not to. If Gallant wants to help the poor, it's far more effective to send them money. How much he sends is his choice to make.[4]

Second, while sending money is far more effective than opening your living room, opening the borders is far more effective than sending money. If you send \$3 to a Mexican, he gains \$3. If you sacrifice \$3 to an open-border policy, that same Mexican gains \$7. That's why Goofus's demand for a border fence is far jerkier than Gallant's presumed unwillingness to send money.[5]

There's no getting around the fact that Goofus prefers to see \$3 in the hands of a (relatively) rich American than to see \$7 in the hands of an extremely poor Mexican. That's pretty jerky.

Once again, I do not fault Goofus for deviating from the

---

4   To fill in the gaps: José, being very poor, would much rather have a few dollars than a spot in Gallant's living room; Gallant, being much richer, would rather have his privacy than have a few more dollars. In other words, Gallant values his privacy more than José values a spot in Gallant's living room; therefore, according to the EGR, Gallant should retain his privacy. In still other words, the EGR recognizes that Gallant does more good by giving money than by opening up his living room. That's what I like about the EGR.

5   One might also observe that Gallant, in restricting access to his living room, is exercising a property right, whereas Goofus, by denying American landlords the opportunity to rent to José, is *violating* a property right (not to mention the rights of all those Americans who want to hire José, or sell him groceries). I've omitted this argument from the main text because I'm trying to prove that Goofus is wrong *even if you ignore the interests of all those other Americans*. The observations in this footnote, by contrast, show that Goofus is wrong *even if you ignore the interests of José himself.*

EGR; I fault him for deviating from it by so very much and in such an unappetizing way. We all care more about some people than others. Usually we care about our loved ones more than strangers, and to some extent we care more about the poor than the rich; I'd rather help my daughter than help yours, and I'd rather help a starving Bangladeshi than a Microsoft vice president. But Goofus favors neither his loved ones nor poor people; he favors relatively rich American strangers over relatively poor Mexicans. Moreover, he favors them by at least a seven-to-three ratio, which is huge. If it were seven to six, I'd cut him more slack.

Goofus has one more argument up his sleeve. He challenges the arithmetic. "You left out the cost of welfare! What about the illegal immigrants who come not to work, but to exploit our welfare system?"

I might have a little more sympathy for that argument if there weren't so many Goofuses looking to put illegal aliens out of work by prosecuting their employers. If your complaint is that illegals exploit our welfare system, why screw up the lives of those who are *working*?

Today it's a crime to hire illegals. Tomorrow, I fear, it will be a crime to date them. Or to smile at them. Or to walk past them and fail to punch them in the nose.

Goofus is swept into the Senate on a tidal wave of xenophobia. Gallant sadly shakes his head.

————

Having talked about strangers who are distant in space, let's talk about strangers who are distant in time—in other words, let's talk about what we owe to future generations. The more we consume, the less our grandchildren will inherit. The more carbon we burn, the warmer their world is likely to be. How much should we care?

The Economist's Golden Rule says: Count your grandchildren's interests as equal to your own. Unfortunately, that's a recipe for total paralysis. Is it okay to spend a dollar on a Hershey bar? Sorry; that same dollar, deposited in a bank account, could toss off a few cents' interest for your children, and then a few cents for your grandchildren, and then a few cents for your great-grandchildren . . . and so on until the sun burns out. Your craving for chocolate, no matter how great, will always be outweighed by that effectively *infinite* stream of benefits.

If you applied the EGR to cross-generational issues, you'd never buy a candy bar. You'd never do much of anything else, either, except work yourself into the grave building up the largest possible bequest. No matter how much you hate your job as a peep-show janitor—no matter how much you want to retire—your desire is swamped by the infinite stream of interest an extra dollar of income can throw off for your heirs.

So for cross-generational issues, the EGR will never do.[6] The alternative is to somehow "discount" the interests of future generations so they don't run roughshod over us.

The less we discount, the more we'll save and the more we'll worry about global warming. If your discount factor is very low, you'll want to encourage saving (best bets: eliminate taxes on capital income and pare back the Social Security system) and

---

6 You might reasonably ask: If we can't trust the EGR for cross-generational comparisons, why should we *ever* trust it? I might reasonably answer: Remember how we justified the EGR in the first place (in the discussion of Bill Gates and his stereo). Whenever we violate the EGR, we've missed an opportunity to make *everyone* better off by transferring income instead. But that argument doesn't apply across generations, because income can't be transferred from the future to the present.

discourage carbon emissions (best bet: a carbon tax, of course). If your discount factor is very high, you'll want to live (and encourage others to live) a little more riotously, spending more freely and burning more fossil fuels.

One argument for a big discount factor is that future generations are likely to be unfathomably wealthy. If you expect economic growth to continue at the average annual rate of 2.3 percent, to which we've grown accustomed, then in four hundred years, the average American will have an income of more than $1 million per day—and that's in the equivalent of today's dollars (i.e., after correcting for inflation). How much should you and I sacrifice to improve the quality of life for those future gazillionaires?

We should discount further for the fact that those future generations might never materialize. If you think life on Earth will be destroyed by an asteroid in two hundred years, it makes little sense to worry about the climate three hundred years from now. If you think Earth *might* be destroyed by an asteroid, it makes sense to worry at least slightly less about the climate.

The standard line among economists is that those are the only good reasons to discount, and aside from these corrections, all generations should count equally; you and I should care exactly as much about a stranger born a thousand years hence as we do about a stranger who's alive today. But even economists are sometimes wrong. Few of us feel morally bound to churn out as many children as we possibly can, which means we think nothing of denying future generations the gift of life. If it's okay to deny them their very lives, shouldn't it be okay to deny them a temperate climate?

I want to make that argument explicit:

Step One: Your grandchildren would rather be born with no inheritance than not be born at all. As a good consequentialist, I infer that leaving no inheritance is better than having no grand-children.

Step Two: I feel quite sure that it's morally okay to have no children (and therefore no grandchildren!).

Conclusion: Leaving no inheritance beats having no grand-children; having no grandchildren is okay; therefore leaving no inheritance is okay.

So feel free to squander your grandchildren's inheritance—including the quality of their air and water. Feel free, in other words, to trash the Earth (just not the part I'm living on)!

That doesn't mean you should *want* to trash the Earth. Maybe you care very much about your grandchildren. And then, of course, I should act as if I care about them, too—not because I owe anything to your unborn grandchildren, but because I owe something to your very much alive and present self. Only a jerk would believe otherwise.

20 The Economist on the Playground[1]

All I really need to know I learned in kindergarten.
—*Robert Fulghum*

Fairness, like morality, is something we can't seem to help caring about. It's therefore worth thinking hard about what fairness does and doesn't mean.

Every time a child cries, "That's not fair!", a parent is forced to confront an issue of economic justice. Kids come to us for guidance on whether it's okay to change the rules of checkers in the middle of a game, or what to do when one child lays claim to a quarter of the communal sandbox. Teaching our kids to play fair is a big part of our jobs. When it comes to distinguishing good from bad behavior on the playground, every parent is an expert.

That expertise, though, does not always carry over to the marketplace or the voting booth. Your kids look to you for guidance, while your congressman looks to you only for votes. So, quite sensibly, you think a lot harder and more clearly about

---

1 Portions of this chapter are adapted from my earlier book *Fair Play*.

what you'll tolerate from your kids than what you'll tolerate from your congressman.

I believe that the best way to become an expert on fairness in general is to pay close attention to what you already know about fairness on the playground. In that spirit, here are some principles that are obvious to every parent, and some thoughts about their implications in the world of adults.

1. *Don't take things that aren't yours.* Whenever a politician proposes to make the tax code more progressive, we hear rhetoric about how the rich have too much, the poor have too little, it's only fair to spread the wealth more equally, and so forth. To me, the interesting thing about that rhetoric is that nobody believes it. Of this I am certain, because in all the years I took my daughter to the playground, I never once heard another parent tell a child that if some kids have more toys than you do, that makes it okay to take some of them away. Nor did I ever hear a parent tell a child that if some kids have more toys than others, that makes it okay to form a government and *vote* to take some of those toys away.

Of course we encourage sharing, and we try to make our children feel remorse when they are very selfish. But at the same time, we tell them that if other children are being selfish, you must cope with that in some way short of a forcible expropriation. You can cajole, bargain, or ostracize, but you cannot simply steal. Nor is there any such thing as a legitimate government with the authority to do your stealing for you.

That's simple. The adult world is more complex. Adults face issues that don't arise on the playground. We have to tax ourselves to provide government services. That leaves room for a lot of legitimate disagreement about who should pay how much for what, with no playground experience to guide us. Should the rich contribute more to national defense than the poor? Probably. How much more? I don't know.

But taxation *for the sole purpose of redistributing income* is closely parallel to behavior that we admonish on the playground all the time. If we don't accept this from our kids, I'm not sure why we should accept it from our congressmen. There might or might not be good reasons to shift the tax burden more heavily to the rich (and I'll mention some in Chapter 22). Basic fairness is not one of them.

2. *Live with your choices.* I once took two children to dinner. Each had a choice: ice cream now or bubble gum later. Alix chose the ice cream; Cayley chose the bubble gum.

After Alix had finished her ice cream, we went off to get Cayley's gum. Cayley got the gum, Alix got nothing, and Alix cried foul. To any adult outsider, it would have been clear that Alix had no case; she'd been given the same choices as Cayley and taken her rewards up front.

The same issues arise in adult life. Peter and Paul face the same opportunities early in life. Peter chooses to work forty hours a week for a guaranteed wage; Paul works around the clock to create a new enterprise with uncertain rewards. Thirty years later, when Peter is poor and Paul is rich, Peter cries foul and assaults the system that fosters such inequality.

I wouldn't want to argue that Paul's choice is intrinsically more admirable than Peter's, any more than I would want to argue that a taste for gum is intrinsically more admirable than a taste for ice cream. But I do want to argue with Peter's reasoning about the *consequences* of that choice. A good test is to ask whether any adult would take it seriously in a dispute between first graders. Peter's griping fails that test.

3. *Don't be envious.* If you've ever served cake to more than one child at a time, you've heard the refrain "No fair! My piece is smaller!" And if you were feeling very patient at the time, you might have tried to explain that a child who can enjoy his cake without regard to what's on his sister's plate can expect a lot more happiness in life than a child who is constantly distracted by the need to make comparisons. Because we want our children to be happy, we tell them that when somebody gives you a piece of cake, you have occasion to rejoice, and that if another child has more, you might remember that the world is also full of children who have less. Remember that the next time your coworker gets an undeserved promotion.

4. *Two wrongs don't make a right.* If you live in the average American household, the Corporation for Public Broadcasting lifts about five dollars a year from your wallet to fund projects like National Public Radio. NPR apologists, adults all, are wont to dismiss that small predation by pointing to others that are much larger; by some estimates, the government spends almost two hundred times as much on corporate welfare. Perhaps those apologists are aiming their appeals at childless voters. What parent would accept an excuse like "Sure, I stole the cookies, but I know another kid who stole a bicycle"?

5. *Don't butt in where you're not wanted.* More than two hundred years ago, Adam Smith founded the new science of economics on human beings' natural propensity to truck, barter, and exchange one thing for another. By the age of eight or so, this propensity is fully realized in the schoolyard markets for decals, trading cards, and bottle caps.

   Sometimes a child—call her Lucyann—wants to trade with her classmate Liz, but finds that Liz prefers to trade with

Emily, from the other third-grade class. Disappointing as that may be, we expect Lucyann to realize that she can't force Liz to trade with her—and more importantly, that it would be wrong to try. Only a very demanding child would even imagine asking her teacher to intervene and prevent Liz from trading with "foreigners."

Protectionist politicians see the U.S. Congress as the great national teacher, maintaining order on the school yard, ensuring a "level playing field" by making sure that all the children play the way the teachers' special pets—or special industries—want them to play. As any eight-year-old could tell you, that stinks.[2]

6. *Stand up to bullies.* Princeton Professor Alan Blinder has recently estimated that 30 to 40 million Americans face the prospect of losing their jobs to lower-paid foreign competitors. Or in other words, all Americans face the prospect of lower prices for the output of 30 to 40 million workers. That's good, though of course 60 to 80 million would be better.

All economists, including Professor Blinder, know that when American jobs are outsourced, Americans in toto are net winners—what we lose through lower wages is more than offset by what we gain through lower prices. In other words, the winners can more than afford to compensate the losers. Does that mean they ought to? Does it create a moral mandate for, say, taxpayer-subsidized retraining programs?

Let's start by observing that there is almost surely no such thing as a net loser from free trade. (I owe this observation to

---

2 The argument from fairness is a deontological argument for free trade, which is quite independent of the consequentialist argument we met in Chapter 5. Sometimes deontology and consequentialism clash; sometimes, as here, they lead to the same conclusion by different routes.

George Mason University professor Don Boudreaux.) I doubt there's a human being on earth who hasn't benefited from the opportunity to trade freely with his neighbors. Imagine what your life would be like if you had to grow your own food, make your own clothes, and rely on your grandmother's home remedies for health care. Access to a trained physician might reduce the demand for Grandma's chicken soup, but—especially at her age—she's still got plenty of reason to be thankful for it.

Even if you've just lost your job, there's something fundamentally churlish about blaming the very phenomenon that's elevated you above the subsistence level since the day you were born. If the world owes you compensation for enduring the downside of trade, what do you owe the world for enjoying the upside?

But let's sweep that observation under the table and pretend it somehow makes sense to morally isolate the effects of a single new trading opportunity or free-trade agreement. Surely we have fellow citizens who are hurt by those agreements, at least in the limited sense that they'd be better off in a world where trade flourishes, except in this one instance. What do we owe those fellow citizens?

One way to think about that is to ask what your moral instincts tell you in analogous situations. Suppose, after years of buying shampoo at your local pharmacy, you discover you can get the same shampoo cheaper on the Web. Do you have an obligation to compensate your pharmacist? If you move to a cheaper apartment, should you compensate your landlord? When you eat at McDonald's, should you compensate the owners of the diner next door?

Perhaps there's some arcane moral philosophy that answers

yes to those questions, but I think that would be a tough philosophy to buy into. Public policy should not be designed to advance moral instincts that we all reject every day of our lives.

In what morally relevant way, then, might displaced workers differ from displaced pharmacists or displaced landlords? You might argue that pharmacists and landlords have always faced cutthroat competition and knew what they were getting into, whereas decades of tariffs and quotas have led, say, manufacturing workers to expect a modicum of protection. That expectation led them to develop certain skill sets, and now it's unfair to pull the rug out from under them.

Once again, let's ask how that instinct meshes with our everyday instincts in analogous situations. For many decades, schoolyard bullying has been a profitable occupation, and all across America, bullies have built up skill sets so they can take advantage of that opportunity. If we toughen the rules to make bullying unprofitable, must we compensate the bullies?

Bullying and protectionism have a lot in common. They both use force (either directly or through the power of the law) to enrich someone else at your involuntary expense. If you're forced to pay a $20-an-hour American for goods you could have bought from a $5-an-hour Mexican, you're being extorted. When a free-trade agreement allows you buy from the Mexican after all, rejoice in your liberation. To compensate your former exploiters is to succumb to Stockholm syndrome.

7. *Tolerate intolerance.* Every child has felt the pain of exclusion, and every child eventually understands that such pain is part of the price we pay for freedom. You won't get invited to every

birthday party. And if someone excludes you out of sheer meanness, you've got a right to feel hurt but no right to crash the party.

Adults manage to remember and forget this principle all at the same time. Take a stylized example: Mary owns a vacant apartment. Joe is looking for a place to live. If Joe disapproves of Mary's race or religion or lifestyle—even if he disapproves out of sheer meanness—he's free to shop elsewhere. But if Mary disapproves of Joe's race or religion or lifestyle, the law requires her to swallow her misgivings and rent the apartment to Joe.

Or: Bert wants to hire an office manager and Ernie wants to manage an office. The law allows Ernie to refuse any job for any reason. If he doesn't like Albanians, he doesn't have to work for one. Bert is held to a higher standard: If he lets it be known that no Albanians need apply, he'd better have a damned good lawyer.

These asymmetries grate against the most fundamental requirement of fairness—that people should be treated equally, in the sense that their rights and responsibilities should not change because of irrelevant external circumstances. Mary and Joe—or Bert and Ernie—are looking to enter two sides of a business relationship. Why should they have asymmetric duties under the antidiscrimination laws?

There are two good reasons to be concerned about this kind of hypocrisy. One is principled: Asymmetric burdens are unfair. The second is practical: A system that restricts your neighbors' freedom today can expand to restrict yours tomorrow. Today, the authorities tell Mary how to choose her tenants; tomorrow, they could tell Joe how to choose an apartment. Today they tell Bert how to choose an office manager; tomorrow they could tell Ernie how to choose a job. If Ernie rejects a job offer from an Albanian employer, will he have to prove that his decision was not based on national origin?

And why stop there? If the principles of affirmative action are applied consistently, they'll eventually govern every aspect of the housing market, the job market, and for that matter the marriage market. In that surreal future, it will be illegal to consider ethnicity in your choice of lovers. Justice Department statisticians will scrutinize your dating patterns to make sure you're sampling a reasonable cross section of the community. When you finally settle down, you'll have to prove that the spouse you chose is objectively more qualified than any other applicant. Once the system is in place, it can be expanded (as affirmative action has) to cover gender as well as ethnicity: Mary will be hauled into court for marrying a man when a more experienced woman was available.

If that vision sounds implausible, remember that affirmative action in its present form would have seemed equally implausible not so many years ago. If it sounds like a nightmare, remember that it's already a nightmare come true for Mary and Bert.

Affirmative action has been called unfair to white male job applicants, unfair to business owners who are innocent but presumed guilty of discrimination, and unfair even to its own intended beneficiaries. All or any part of that might or might not be correct, but none of it has anything to do with the issue I'm trying to raise. I am arguing that affirmative action is unfair to *bigots,* and that even bigots have a right to be treated fairly. Even the kid who excludes you from his party out of pure meanness has a right to exclude you from his party.

You and I disapprove of bigotry. But the private virtue of *tolerance* and the public virtue of *pluralism* require us to countenance things of which we do not approve. The idea of tolerating intolerance sounds suspiciously paradoxical, but so do a lot of other good ideas—like freedom of speech for the advocates of censorship. In fact, freedom of speech has a lot in common with tolerance: Neither of them means a thing unless it applies equally to those we applaud and those who offend us most viscerally.

8. *Don't punish the innocent.* Racial set-asides and affirmative-action programs are defended, in part, as fair compensation for the legacy of slavery. Unfortunately, the costs of these programs are borne largely by white ethnics whose ancestors arrived in the United States long after slavery had been abolished. Racial preferences are not a way to erase the lingering effects of slavery; they're simply a way to transfer those effects from one innocent party to another.

When I made this argument to a roomful of undergraduates at Duke University, one thoughtfully observed that the oppression of American blacks did not end with slavery. He argued that even an immigrant family arriving in the twentieth century might have benefited (at the expense of black Americans) from the next several decades of segregation and Jim Crow.

But Jim Crow was (among other things) a barrier to trade between the races, and economists know that barriers to trade are generally detrimental *to both* populations. Whites who were discouraged from serving black customers, or patronizing black businesses, or hiring black workers, or working for black employers, were *victims* of Jim Crow, just as their counterparts were.

To argue otherwise would be bad economics. It would also be racist. Jim Crow prevented blacks from dealing with whites, and it also prevented whites from dealing with blacks. Who would want to argue that being denied the right to trade with white people is a form of oppression but being denied the right to trade with black people is no big deal?

It's true of course that the Jim Crow laws were enacted by a white electorate, so one might be tempted to conclude that they were generally beneficial to whites. But that logic would require a theory of democracy that is at odds with all experience. Sugar subsidies, tobacco subsidies, and oil subsidies have all been enacted by the American electorate, and no sane person believes that any of those programs is generally beneficial to Americans. Instead, they benefit small special-interest groups with the political clout to exploit someone.

It's true also that Jim Crow was about a lot more than trade barriers; it was about indignities large and small, from segregated water fountains to separate and unequal public schools. There's therefore little question that it imposed a far greater burden on blacks than on whites. But that's a far cry from saying that whites were its *beneficiaries* and are therefore in debt for the privilege of living under the reign of Jim Crow.

Here we have a political controversy that would not be controversial at all if we applied the standards of the playground. There, when Johnny steals Mary's sand bucket, nobody thinks of ordering the innocent Bobby to make it up to her.

9. *Don't demand a mile from those who volunteer an inch.* When lettuce is expensive at the grocery store, shoppers curse the grocer, but they don't curse their friends and neighbors who won't sell them lettuce at all. Nor do we often find the grumblers offering to set up their own grocery stores and offer lower prices. The grocer is called upon to go an extra mile by those who haven't yet taken a first step.

Likewise, workers curse the employer who offers low wages without stopping to curse the many other employers (and nonemployers) who offer them no wages at all. This is not only morally senseless; it's also bad economics. The employer who hires anyone—even at low wages—takes a few workers off the market and forces other employers to compete among themselves for the workers who remain—which drives wages *up*, not down. If you're looking for a high-wage job, then a low-wage employer is part of the solution, not the problem.

Or consider again Mary the landlord, who won't rent to people she dislikes. Maybe you're one of those people. Nevertheless, when Mary constructs an apartment building and excludes you from it, she's still done you a small amount of good: By taking in tenants, she creates vacancies in other buildings and takes a little pressure off the housing market. Compare that to the amount of good *I'm* likely to do you. I have no plans to get involved in real estate. I won't rent to you any more than Mary will; I won't even acquire any property that I *could* rent to you. But according to the law, Mary's done you some positive harm, while I'm entirely innocent. That's crazy.

Resenting the grocer, employer, or the landlord, while giving a free pass to everyone else in the world who has failed to offer you cheap lettuce or a good job, is at least a relatively harmless kind of moral inconsistency. But the same morally confused instinct arises elsewhere, and it's not always so benign. Every six months or so, you'll see news stories about amoral profiteers who charge seven dollars a gallon for water, or some other outrageous price for some other critical necessity, following a natural disaster that cuts some community off from its usual resources. The news anchors and politicians are always in high dudgeon about this stuff, but I never see *them* trucking in any water, at seven dollars a gallon or any other price. If the amoral profiteers have an obligation to sell water at less than seven dollars a gallon, why don't the news anchors?

Likewise, small-business owners are required to hire the handicapped. If that's based on some moral obligation— if, in other words, there's a moral responsibility to hire the handicapped—then the rest of us should be required to start small businesses so we can hire the handicapped, too. After all, moral responsibilities, when they exist, are universal: They apply to everyone or they apply to no one.

Occasionally—not too often, but occasionally—a child on the playground decides to clean up some litter. We do not usually respond by ordering that child to police the entire playground. The grocer who sells you lettuce, but only at a high price; the landlord who rents to others but not to you; the business owner who improves your employment prospects by hiring your neighbors but who won't hire you directly—all these people have done you small bits of good, like the kid who picks up a few candy wrappers. It's fine to wish they'd do more, but it's churlish to demand it.

21 Unfinished Business

Let the Rabbi Split the Pie

It's a Jewish thing. If you've got a little time, I'll explain it to you.

—*Nancy Lebovitz*

Parents may be the world's greatest experts on fairness, but they're not the only experts. There's a class of economists called "axiomatic bargaining theorists" who think about fairness by writing down some simple axioms (along the lines of "everyone should be treated symmetrically") and then prove theorems about when it is and is not possible to live by all those axioms simultaneously. When you've written down a few axioms that look incontrovertible and discover that they're mutually incompatible, you're forced to think hard about what's essential and what you're willing to jettison.

The Babylonian Talmud, roughly ninety volumes' worth of commentary on Jewish law compiled in about the fifth century A.D., also addresses issues of fairness, usually from a very different perspective. So it's a little eerie that on at least one occasion, the Talmudists seem to have anticipated the economists by about fifteen hundred years.

Both economists and Talmudists love stylized ethical puzzles like this one: A man dies, leaving more debts than assets. How should the estate be divided among his creditors? The sages of the Babylonian Talmud addressed this question in a mysterious way—by offering a series of numerical examples, with no hint of the general underlying principle.

For concreteness, suppose the three creditors are owed $100, $200, and $300 respectively—a total of $600 in debts—but there is less than $600 to distribute. Who gets how much? The Talmud (Kethubot 93a) makes the following prescriptions:

1. If there is $100 to distribute, then everyone gets an equal share; that is, everyone gets $33.33.

2. If there is $200 to distribute, then the first creditor gets $50, while the other two get $75 each.

3. If there is $300 to distribute, then the first creditor gets $50, the second gets $100, and the third gets $150—the payouts are proportional to the original claims.

Where do these numbers come from, and what should we do if there is, say, $400 or $500 to distribute? The Talmud does not tell us. But certain patterns are evident.

Apparently the rabbis reasoned that nobody can legitimately claim more than the entire estate. Thus when the estate contains only $100, the claims to $100, $200, and $300 are treated as equal. When the estate contains only $200, the claims to $200 and $300 are treated as equal (but superior to the claim of $100).

Another clue can be found elsewhere in the Talmud (Baba Metzia 2a): "Two hold a garment; one claims all, the other claims half. Then the one is awarded ¾, the other ¼." The rabbinical reasoning seems to have gone something like this: "Both claim half the garment, while only one claims the other half. So we'll split the disputed half equally and give the undisputed half to its undisputed owner." Elsewhere in the Talmud, the rabbis apply similar reasoning to settle a case where one claims all and the other claims a third.

Now we have two principles: First, claims cannot exceed 100 percent of the estate, and second, we should follow the contested garment rule. When there are just two creditors, these principles suffice to prescribe the division of any bankrupt estate. Here are a few examples:

Example 1: The estate consists of $125. Moe and Larry claim $100 and $200. By the first principle, Larry's $200 claim is immediately reduced to $125. Now there is $100 in dispute and $25 undisputed. According to the contested garment principle, the disputed $100 is divided equally. Therefore Moe gets $50 and Larry gets the remaining $75.

Example 2: The estate consists of $125. Moe and Curly claim $100 and $300. Curly's $300 claim is reduced to $125, and from there on, everything is just as in Example 1. Moe gets $50 and Curly gets $75.

Example 3: The estate consists of $150. Larry and Curly claim $200 and $300. Both claims are reduced to $150, leaving the entire $150 estate in dispute. So Larry and Curly get $75 each.

Now what if there are *three* creditors—in other words, what if Moe, Larry, and Curly make claims of $100, $200, and $300 against an estate of $200? We've already seen that the Talmud prescribes a split of $50, $75, and $75. What justifies these numbers?

Professors Robert Aumann and Michael Maschler, of the Hebrew University of Jerusalem, were the first to observe that there's something very special about these numbers: They are *consistent,* in the following sense: Each pair of creditors divides their collective share according to the principles we've already enunciated.

Moe and Larry, for example, receive a collective share of $50 + $75 = $125, and they split it 50/75, just as Example 1 prescribes. Moe and Curly receive a collective share of $125, divided as Example 2 prescribes. Larry and Curly receive a collective share of $150, divided per Example 3.

Among all possible consistent divisions, why settle on this one? That turns out to be the wrong question. There *are* no other consistent divisions. (In other words, with any division other than 50/75/75, some pair of creditors would have its collective share divided incorrectly.) In fact, Aumann and Maschler have proved more generally that every bankruptcy problem has *exactly one* consistent solution.

Now the striking part: In every Talmudic example, the given solution is consistent. (You can, if you like, check this for the examples on page 207.) Somehow, the rabbis managed to discover the one and only consistent solution to each problem they considered.

How did they manage this? Perhaps they used trial and error, guessing at various divisions until they found a consistent one. Or perhaps they had a more systematic procedure. But that seems unlikely, because every known systematic procedure is pretty complicated. I'll describe one of those procedures so you can see for yourself. Bear with me (or give up); I'm convinced there's no way to make this simpler.

Step 1: Build (or at least draw) a "Talmudic jug" to represent the claims:

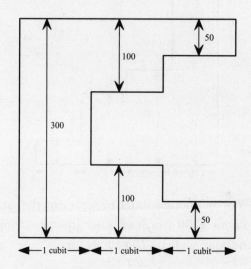

This particular jug represents Moe, Larry, and Curly's claims of $100, $200, and $300, reading from right to left (in good Talmudic fashion). Each compartment is one cubit wide. The combined height of the two right-most compartments is 100 cubits, the combined height of the two middle compartments is 200 cubits, and the height of the left-most compartment is 300 cubits. If your ruler doesn't show cubits, feel free to use inches or millimeters. It's important for all claims except the largest to be split into top and bottom compartments of equal size.

Here's a different jug, representing claims of $100, $300, $400, and $600:

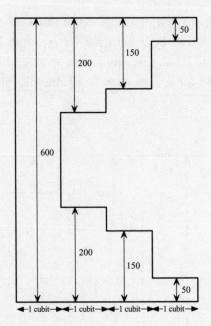

Step 2: Pour in enough water to represent the estate. Here's the first jug with $200 worth of water (that is, enough to fill a container one cubit wide by 200 cubits high):

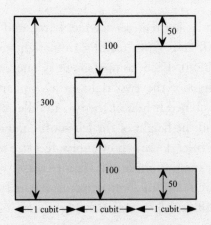

Step 3: Read off the payouts (again from right to left) according to the height of the water. In this case, Moe gets $50, because there are fifty cubits of water in the right-most part of the jug. Larry gets $75, because there are seventy-five cubits in the middle part of the jug. Curly gets $75, because the water reaches a height of seventy-five cubits in the left-most part of the jug.

So, according to the Talmudic jug, a split of 50/75/75 is the one and only consistent solution to this particular bankruptcy problem (that is, the problem of dividing a $200 estate among creditors with claims of $100, $200, and $300).

What if Moe, Larry, and Curly had laid their $100, $200, and $300 claims against an estate of $400? We could discover the consistent solution by filling the Talmudic jug with $400 worth of water:

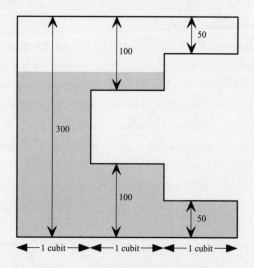

Reading off the payouts from right to left, Moe gets $50, because there are 50 cubits of water in the right-most part of the jug. Larry gets $125, because there are 125 cubits in the middle part of the jug (100 on the bottom and 25 at the top). Curly gets $225, because the water reaches a height of 225 cubits in the leftmost part of the jug.

If you're feeling obsessive, you might want to check that this solution is really consistent. For example, Moe and Larry have a collective share of $175, to which they lay claims of $100 and $200. The $200 claim is reduced to $175. Moe and Larry split the $100 that's in dispute and Larry takes the remaining $75. This gives Moe $50 and Larry a total of $125, just as the jug prescribes. Feel free to check consistency for the pairs Moe/Curly and Larry/Curly.

Although the ancient rabbis failed to consider this particular example (a $400 estate with claims of $100, $200, and $300), Aumann and Maschler express confidence that if they *had* considered it, they would have somehow discovered and endorsed this unique consistent solution.

Exactly *how* they'd have discovered it remains a mystery. The Talmudic jug is a thoroughly modern invention (in fact, it was invented by a *Slate* reader named Jayaraman Ramachandran to replace a less comprehensible presentation in one of my columns). It seems unlikely the rabbis could have known about it.

But whatever method the rabbis used, they appear to have used it (pardon the pun) consistently. It's not hard to check that every one of the Talmudic examples satisfies the consistency principle, which means that in every example they considered, the ancient Talmudists found the same answers as the modern jug-fillers. And the consistency principle gives a complete explanation for each example, in the sense that, in each case, only one consistent solution is possible, and we can imagine that the rabbis kept trying until they found it.

The consistency principle is both universally applicable (because a consistent solution can always be found) and universally unambiguous (because there is never more than one consistent solution).

Why is the consistent solution the right solution? Aumann and Maschler argue that consistency appeals to our intrinsic sense of fairness. But, in the Talmudic tradition, if you don't like that argument, Aumann and Maschler have another.

Imagine that all the creditors are put in a room and told to agree among themselves on a division of the estate; if they can't agree, nobody gets anything. Suppose also that any creditor who is offered 100 percent of his claim (by a consensus of the others) is required to accept it and leave the room. What would the bargaining process look like and what would the outcome be?

Modern-day axiomatic bargaining theorists try to answer such questions; unfortunately, the answers turn out to depend rather heavily on auxiliary assumptions. But Aumann and Maschler have proven that in the case of the bankruptcy negotiation, it follows from reasonable assumptions that the creditors would eventually agree to divide the estate in accordance with the consistency principle. Thus, according to Aumann and Maschler, all of the Talmudic prescriptions coincide with what the creditors themselves would have agreed to, given appropriate bargaining rules and sufficient time.

Part

V The Life of the Mind

Finally, a few words on how to think and what to study. Chapter 22 is a farrago of observations on the general theme of thinking clearly and avoiding fallacies; Chapter 23 is directed particularly at college students thinking about what to study. We'll also meet Frank Ramsey, the Cambridge scholar whose work overlapped substantially with the themes of this book.

Along the way, we'll revisit such issues as the biological basis of mind, protectionism, income redistribution, environmentalism, the fragility of belief, the basis of knowledge, the difference between truth and provability, and the nature of our obligations to future generations.

22 **How to Think**

> They are ill discoverers who think there is no land, when they can see nothing but sea.
>
> —*Sir Francis Bacon*

Sometimes I play solitaire. That's bad enough, but I have a bigger confession to make. When I have a choice between moving, say, either of two black eights onto a red nine, I follow the rule of thumb my mother taught me when I was six years old: Move the (face-up) card with the larger number of (face-down) cards buried beneath it, unless you need a space for a king, in which case do the opposite.

For all its intuitive appeal, I have no idea whether this rule is optimal. And though I've applied the rule my entire life, I've never applied it without feeling a twinge of guilt for not stopping to figure it out. I'm not sure I *could* figure it out, but the sad truth is that I've never tried.

You could argue that this is entirely sensible behavior because, after all, it's only solitaire. Of course, if solitaire matters so little, you're entitled to ask why I'm playing it in the first place. Anyway, the guilt has never sufficed to goad me into action.

As I've said several times in this book, there's a lot we don't stop to think about, and often for good reason. But when we cultivate good habits of thought, we lower the cost of thinking and therefore choose to do more of it. That's often a profitable venture.

In this chapter, I'll catalog (in pretty much random order) some habits of thought that strike me as useful, particularly for thinking about economic matters. None of them will improve your solitaire game, but some of them might improve the way you see the world.

THINGS MUST ADD UP

Sometimes, when you see the world as an economist, you lose all track of what it's like to see through the eyes of a normal person.

I was waiting my turn in an insanely crowded delicatessen—one of those "take-a-number" places—when the lady with ticket number 37 gave up and walked out, randomly handing her ticket to number 45. "How nice of her to do that instead of just throwing her ticket away!" said someone in front of me, and several people nodded, glad to see that a valuable resource had been preserved rather than callously discarded.

At that moment, I found myself entirely unsure whether it takes the equivalent of a Ph.D. in economics to see that moving someone eight places forward means moving eight people one place back—without changing the only thing that matters, which is the number of people served per minute. I ran home, checked with my noneconomist friends, and learned, to my reassurance, that it's obvious to pretty much everyone except the patrons of that particular deli.

But the underlying fallacy—the failure to notice that things must add up—is, in my experience, the single greatest source of economic error. Politicians routinely promise to make medical care or housing or college educations more widely available by controlling their prices; economists routinely scratch their heads and ask where the extra doctors or houses or classrooms are going to come from. You can no more speed up the line for medical care by lowering prices than you can speed up the deli line by handing out tickets.

The same fallacy is father to the prejudice that the accumulation of great financial fortunes somehow impoverishes the rest of us. In fact the exact opposite is true. The tycoon who hoards wealth in the form of stocks, bonds, and currency instead of splurging on goods and services is leaving more goods and services for you and me. If more people grasped this simple point, there might be less enthusiasm for "economic stimulus" packages that promise to fill our bellies by encouraging others to grab ever larger shares of the communal pie.

Vernon Smith, the 2002 Nobel laureate in economics, and his colleague James Cox have performed a series of experiments that seem to me to highlight the underlying fallacy. First, a subject is put in an isolation booth, handed ten one-dollar bills, and invited to hand some of those dollar bills over to the stranger in the next booth.

The result: About two-thirds of the subjects keep all the money for themselves. In other words, people don't like giving money to total strangers. So far, so good. Giving away money seems like a nice thing to do, but why give it to a stranger who might already be very rich or very lucky, or for that matter very nasty, when you could give it to, say, one of those starving-children's funds instead?

In the next experiment, the subject is told that any funds

passed to the stranger will be tripled by the experimenter. Give up a dollar and the stranger gets three; give up two and the stranger gets six.

Now all of a sudden a lot of money gets passed. The average subject hands over $3.63 (out of the initial $10), so the stranger receives $10.89.

At first blush, this seems to make sense. People like to do good. They won't pay a dollar to give someone else a dollar, but they *will* pay a dollar to give someone else *three* dollars. It's the Economist's Golden Rule!

Except it's not.[1] Passing dollar bills from one room to another is not a productive activity. No wealth is created in the process. Every dollar passed to the stranger comes from somebody—in this case, probably from the taxpayer who's funding the experiment.

The naive reading is that subjects will pay a dollar to create an extra two dollars' worth of wealth. The correct reading is that subjects will pay a dollar for the privilege of forcing one total stranger (the taxpayer) to give two dollars to another total stranger.

But in the absence of any information about these total strangers, why would you care what direction the money moves? Maybe people just love moving other people's money around.

More likely, the subjects are under the delusion that wealth can appear out of thin air, even in the absence of any productive activity. They've forgotten, in other words, that things have to add up. It's a little sobering to realize that these people are allowed to vote.

---

1 Professor Smith, a man of whom I am very fond, profoundly disagrees with the analysis to follow. I have tried very hard to understand his objections, and I have failed.

TAKE METAPHORS SERIOUSLY

I love metaphors. I think they clarify a lot of issues. But once you've bought into a metaphor, you must be willing to follow it wherever it leads you.

Political philosophers frequently use metaphors to defend the redistribution of income. Our welfare system, they say, is "like an insurance contract" where we all pay premiums (i.e., taxes) to ensure ourselves against bad fortune. That's a powerful metaphor and potentially the basis of an excellent argument. But because I'm an economist and not a philosopher, I prefer to think about the argument a little more deeply.

Welfare ensures you in large part against bad stuff that happens before you're even born. You get handed the wrong genes or the wrong parents or get born into the wrong school district and therefore end up short of marketable skills. So if welfare is like an insurance plan, it's a plan you'd buy into pre-birth. More precisely, it's a plan you *would* buy into pre-birth if the insurance salesmen had figured out how to reach you.

Given that we'd have bought into this contract *if we could have,* there's a reasonable case for enforcing it. Courts frequently enforce the contracts that they believe litigants would have signed if only they had thought to do so, and economists generally applaud such rulings. If we enforce the contracts people *forgot* to write, why shouldn't we enforce the contracts people were *unable* to write simply because of the inconvenient fact that they weren't yet born?

So far so good. But you can't enforce a contract unless you know its terms, so we're forced to ask just how *much* insurance an unborn soul would want to buy. At this point, the political philosophers are reduced to guessing. But there's no need to guess. We have data on the variance of genetic and environmental factors that affect earning power, so we have a pretty good idea how much risk you faced when God was handing out the brains and good fortune. We also have data on the amount of insurance people choose in the face of various risk levels. Putting this all together, we can *calculate* how much insurance the unborn would choose, and therefore how big the welfare system ought to be.

To complete the calculation we need one more piece of information: the *price* of the insurance. When insurance is more expensive, people buy less of it. The price of the welfare system is that it creates disincentive effects, leading to lower productivity and lower incomes across the board. So our answer is going to depend on the size of those disincentive effects.

That in turn depends on the fine structure of the welfare system; an earned-income tax credit works very differently than, say, a food-stamp program. But based on a quick back-of-the-napkin calculation done over the lunch table, I can give you some bounds: If you can construct a welfare system with no disincentive effects at all, you'll want something like 23 percent of the population permanently unemployed and on welfare—a far bigger social safety net than any Western country has ever contemplated. If you have no control at all over disincentive effects, you'll want about six-tenths of 1 percent of the population receiving welfare—probably a far smaller safety net than has ever been seriously contemplated.

From six-tenths of one percent at one extreme to 23 percent at the other; that's a pretty enormous range. But what do you expect from a quick back-of-the-napkin calculation? With a few years of hard work, you could get much tighter estimates. If we're really going to justify the insurance system with an insurance metaphor, somebody's got to do that work.

As an aside, the best way to minimize disincentive effects is to transfer income not to the poor, but to groups of people who are poor on average—like blacks, women, and midgets. Subsidizing the poor creates an incentive to loaf, but subsidizing midgets does not create an incentive to shrink (though I suppose it could give children an excuse not to eat their spinach). Midgets on average earn substantially less than the rest of us (typically, an extra inch of height is worth about an extra thousand dollars a year in wages), so you'd still, on average, be transferring income in the correct direction. And of course you can do the same for blacks, women, and for that matter ugly people, who also suffer in the labor market. (This is, of course, an argument in favor of affirmative action, though it's a stronger argument in favor of direct transfers to these groups.)

The other metaphor that comes up in discussions of income redistribution is the family metaphor: Society is "like a family," and families don't allow one member to struggle while another prospers. This is a hard metaphor to defend, because in point of fact families *do* allow one member to struggle while another prospers. We have data on this! In the vast majority of cases, parents split their bequests equally among their children—even when one of those children is very rich and another very poor. A bequest is your final opportunity to redistribute income among the people you love the most, and people by and large reject that opportunity. So if you honestly believe society should be more like a family, you should be lobbying for less income redistribution, not more.

EXPAND YOUR IMAGINATION

In Chapter 1, I described a wine-tasting machine that enjoys a velvety Pinot just as you do. (Personally, I prefer Diet Coke.) The machine's sense of enjoyment comes from its mechanical reproduction of the pattern of neuron firings in your brain. I said there (echoing Daniel Dennett) that if you find this impossible to imagine, it's likely because you're not imagining hard enough. Probably you've envisioned a system of dozens or hundreds of interacting neurons, which bears no useful resemblance to a system of billions.

It's impossible to imagine a billion of anything, so sometimes we settle for imagining a hundred. But a hundred can be a poor proxy for a billion. That, I think, is why so many people recoil from the headache problem of pages 161 to 162, where we sacrifice one life to cure a billion headaches. They imagine something like a hundred headaches instead, and overlook just how much suffering a billion headaches can add up to.

Likewise, if you find it difficult to imagine that a decentralized economy can allocate resources better than any central planner, it's probably because you've been led astray by irrelevant visions. You imagine organizing a birthday party or a small business and conclude that someone's got to be in charge. But the economy is complex in ways that a party or a business is not.

When I organize a party, I tell people how they can be most helpful. If you asked me to organize an economy, I'd be paralyzed. The economy is too big and too complex—and your talents are too varied and too unobservable—for me to have any idea how you can be most helpful. I need you to figure that out for yourself. For that, you've got to know which goods are in high demand. And for that, you need prices.

Amazingly, that's *all* you need. Goods are efficiently produced and delivered through interaction among billions of individual decisions coordinated by prices, just as mental experiences arise from interaction among billions of neurons. Economists understand one process better than neuroscientists understand the other, but there's every hope that the neuroscientists will catch up someday.

It takes a lot of study to grasp fully the workings of the price system, but fortunately it requires only a few paragraphs to convey the basic idea. There are thousands of plausible ways to transport an orange from Florida to Maine (because, for starters, there are thousands of trucks leaving Florida each day) and no plausible basis for a central planner to choose among them. The miracle of the marketplace begins with the fact that the low-cost transporter is also the high-profit transporter, and therefore the first to volunteer.

And it gets even better: When the world price of wheat is, say, five dollars a bushel, Farmer Jones plants the field where his costs are four dollars a bushel but not the (somewhat rockier) field where his costs are six dollars a bushel. Worldwide, all the under-five-dollar fields are planted and all the over-five-dollar fields are put to other uses. The result: The world's ten-billion-bushel wheat supply is produced at the lowest possible cost, maximizing the resources left over for the production of corn, soybeans, textiles, and locomotives.

That works because (and only because) all farmers face the same price. Otherwise we get bad outcomes. Suppose, for example, that Farmer Jones sells his wheat for five dollars a bushel while Farmer Brown sells for ten. Then Jones's six-dollar-a-bushel field sits idle while Brown's eight-dollar-a-bushel field gets planted, driving up the total cost of the world's wheat supply.

I want to repeat that: The key to efficient production is not just that we face prices, but that we all face the *same* prices. If you understand why, you've taken the first and biggest step toward understanding the breathtaking efficiency of the competitive price system.

Without prices, complex systems can't be efficient. There is, for example, no clear analogue of the price system in the world of biology. Animals face *costs;* they risk death in the claws of predators every time they dart out to retrieve a morsel of food. But a cost is not the same thing as a world price; there is no resource for which cows from Maine to Singapore face identical prices. Unlike economies, ecological systems are complex in a way that carries no guarantee (or even expectation) of desirable outcomes. A herd of cattle with a limited food supply will overgraze until everyone starves; they lack the price system that would give them an incentive to conserve.

Think about that the next time someone tells you we have to preserve our wetlands or our rain forests because the ecology is a delicate interconnected system that ought not be lightly disrupted—especially if it's coming from someone who has no qualms about disrupting our delicate interconnected economy with price controls, minimum wages, equal-pay legislation, and fuel-efficiency standards. To be simultaneously an ecological preservationist and an economic interventionist tends to require a substantial ignorance of economics. Nothing in biology suggests that deviations from the status quo are in any sense always bad, whereas in economics, we know that deviations from an unfettered competitive price system are invariably disimprovements.

"I cannot imagine that" is a poor counterargument. If you cannot imagine consciousness arising from a pattern of neuron firings, perhaps all you've demonstrated is a failure of imagination. If you cannot imagine efficient resource allocation arising from a pattern of prices, you've demonstrated a far more spectacular failure of imagination—because in this case there is a fully fleshed-out theory detailing how you get from the pattern to the desired outcome.

A COST IS NOT A SIN

In March 2008, the Catholic Church announced that pollution is now a sin, thereby advancing the good Catholic principle that sin is everywhere. If you breathe in oxygen and breathe out carbon dioxide, you're now a sinner.

I'd thought the word *sin* was reserved for the intolerable. Pollution is something we all tolerate in limited quantities, and something we all *should* tolerate in limited quantities, and something we all *realize* we should tolerate in limited quantities. The right questions are: What quantities, and how can we best achieve them?

The answers are already implicit in Chapter 12 of this book: The world has too much pollution because polluters don't feel all the consequences of their actions. The solution is to *make* them feel those consequences by taxing them commensurately. If burning a gallon of gasoline causes seventy-five cents' worth of ecological damage, then let's have a tax of seventy-five cents per gallon of gasoline.

When things are priced correctly, there's no need to moralize about them. Every time you eat an orange, you leave the world one orange poorer. But nobody thinks it's sinful to eat an orange, because the orange eater *pays* for the privilege—and thereby reimburses the rest of us for the damage done.

Under the right tax system, emitting small amounts of additional pollution would be as unobjectionable as eating an orange. Pete the Polluter causes ten dollars' worth of damage to our lungs; he reimburses us with a ten-dollar contribution to the Treasury (which the government can use to provide us ten dollars' worth of services, or to reduce our taxes by ten dollars), and at the end of the day, he's done us no net harm.

So why don't we have such taxes? I suspect it's at least partly because in a world with rational taxation, there would be fewer jobs for priests. Solve a social problem and there's no evil left to rail against.

Evolution has endowed us with a drive to identify, decry, and sometimes slaughter the "bad guys" who don't share our obviously superior values. Too often, we'd rather assign blame than solve a problem. The instincts that were useful for our ancestors back on the savannah are not always useful for us today.

SEE THE BIG PICTURE

On average, nonagenarians are in worse health than the rest of us. That doesn't make them unlucky. I hope very much to be one of them someday.

More generally, it's a mistake to judge someone's good or ill fortune by looking at facts in isolation. In the past few decades, the income gap between rich and poor has expanded, probably because new technology has increased the return to skills and education. But it's important to see such facts in a broader context.

While the income gap has grown in one direction, the leisure gap has grown in the other. In 1965, leisure was pretty much equally distributed across classes. People of the same age, sex, and family size tended to have about the same amount of leisure, regardless of their socioeconomic status. But since then, two things have happened. First, leisure (like income) has increased dramatically across the board. Second, though everyone's a winner, the biggest winners are at the bottom of the socioeconomic ladder.

In 1965, the average man spent forty-two hours a week working at the office or the factory; throw in coffee breaks, lunch breaks, and commuting time, and you're up to fifty-one hours.

Today, instead of spending forty-two and fifty-one hours, he spends thirty-six and forty. What's he doing with all that extra time? He spends a little on shopping, a little on housework, and a lot on watching TV, reading the newspaper, going to parties, relaxing, going to bars, playing golf, surfing the Web, visiting friends, and having sex. Overall, depending on exactly what you count, he's got an extra six to eight hours a week of leisure—call it the equivalent of nine extra weeks of vacation per year.

For women, time spent on the job is up from seventeen hours a week to twenty-four. With breaks and commuting thrown in, it's up from twenty hours to twenty-six. But time spent on household chores is down from thirty-five hours a week to twenty-two, for a net leisure gain of four to six hours. Call it five extra vacation weeks. A small part of those gains is because of demographic change. The average American is older now and has fewer children, so it's not surprising that he or she works less. But even when you compare modern Americans to their 1965 counterparts—people with the same family size, age, and education—the gains are still on the order of four to eight hours a week, or something like seven extra weeks of leisure per year.

But not for everyone. About 10 percent of us are stuck in 1965, leisurewise. At the opposite extreme, 10 percent of us have gained a staggering fourteen hours a week or more. (Once again, your gains are measured in comparison to a person who, in 1965, had the same characteristics that you have today.) By and large, the biggest leisure gains have gone precisely to those with the most stagnant incomes—that is, the least skilled and the least educated. And conversely, the smallest leisure gains have been concentrated among the most educated, the same group that's had the biggest gains in income.

Man does not live by bread alone. Our happiness depends partly on our incomes, but also on the time we spend with our friends, our hobbies, and our favorite TV shows. So, it's a good exercise in perspective to remember that by and large, the big winners in the income derby have been the small winners in the leisure derby, and vice versa.

IDEAS MATTER

Both in this book (Chapter 16) and elsewhere, I've written on questions of life and death. When is it okay to push someone in front of a trolley, or to harvest a healthy man's organs, or to turn off a ventilator?

I have argued, for example, that it is crazy to provide ventilator support for uninsured poor people. This isn't because I want to punish poor people; it's because ventilators are expensive, and I believe that if we're going to spend that kind of money helping poor people, there are better ways to spend it—helping with the grocery bills, for example. (And it's no use saying we should do both; if you want to spend a billion a year helping the poor with ventilators and another billion helping with groceries, I'm going to suggest that you'd do better spending the whole two billion on groceries.)

Whenever I write about such matters, I'm deluged with e-mail suggesting that this kind of cost-benefit analysis is all well and good for thinking about policy issues of little consequence, but surely not for matters of life and death. What a curious notion: Economists have useful ways of thinking about trade-offs, and we should heed those ideas—except when something important is on the line. It's like saying that science is all very useful for designing household appliances, but when it comes to something really important like curing cancer, we'd better resort to witchcraft.

Sometimes witchcraft is disguised to look like science, but

it's still witchcraft. My e-mail is also rife with complaints that my cost-benefit analysis fails to distinguish "identified lives" from "statistical lives"—that is, the lives of total strangers whose names I either do or do not happen to know.

The objection is curious because I don't recall ever having made an argument where this distinction would make a difference. Nor can I imagine any remotely reasonable argument that could *cause* it to make a difference.

Take for concreteness the headache problem from Chapter 16: We know that people will pay a dollar to cure a headache, but not to avoid a one-in-a-billion chance of death. Therefore, if you approach a billion headache sufferers and offer to cure their headaches by randomly choosing and killing one of them, you've done them all a favor. It's good to do favors. So go for it. At no point in that argument does the name of the chosen victim play a role.

I recently had several rounds of e-mail with Professor Mark Kleiman of UCLA, who had raised this objection on his blog (in response to a column I'd written about ventilators). Professor Kleiman's objection is that once you choose the victim, his life switches over from "statistical" to "identified," negating all previous reasoning. But nothing has changed. We knew all along we were going to kill one person; we're still going to kill one person; if it was a good idea before, it's still a good idea.

By Professor Kleiman's "reasoning," everyone who's ever chosen a risky path and had it turn out badly should get a mulligan. We all agree that it's a good thing to let unpopular restaurants fail. But as soon as a *particular* restaurant goes under, it switches from "statistical" to "identified," so I suppose we have to offer the owners a bailout.

Let's try a thought experiment to see where the Kleiman philosophy would lead us. A mad philosopher has captured five people—people whose names you know, so their lives count as "identified"—and plans to kill them unless you allow him to kill six random strangers instead. Presumably, Professor Kleiman would sacrifice the six to save the five. (I'm assuming here that six statistical lives are worth less than five identified lives; if Professor Kleiman has some other ratio in mind, we can change the numbers to ten and eleven, or whatever makes him happy.) The six are selected, and just before they're about to die, their names are revealed. At this point, Professor Kleiman is willing to sacrifice seven random strangers to save the six. The seven are chosen, their names are revealed . . . and eventually the professor sacrifices the entire world population.

Or maybe not. Professor Kleiman's blog posts and e-mails were imprecise enough that I could never tell what he was really arguing for. For example, he often flirted with incoherence by blurring the key distinction between "How much would I have to pay you to risk death?" and "How much would you pay me to rescue you from a risk of death?" So to get back on firmer ground, I finally translated my argument into a few lines of math and asked him to tell me which line he disagreed with.[2] At this point he stopped e-mailing and repeated his assertions on his blog, where they seemed no clearer to me than before.

The lesson is that throwing words around—even four-syllable words like *statistical* and *identified*—is a poor substitute for analysis. If you're objecting to a logical argument, try asking yourself exactly which line in that argument you're objecting to. If you can't identify the locus of your disagreement, you're probably just blathering. Which brings us to:

---

2 You can see these lines at www.the-big-questions.com/lives.html.

DON'T BLATHER

In particular, don't be Al Gore. In his movie *An Inconvenient Truth,* Gore insults the intelligence of his audience by casting the debate over climate policy as a trade-off between climate control and "gold bars." "Mmmm-mmmm," he says sarcastically. "Don't those gold bars look good?"

But gold bars, as everybody over the age of eight is aware, are not what's at stake here. Instead, those gold bars are used to *measure* the value of the very real sacrifices that must be made if we choose to limit our carbon emissions. They stand for food, lighting, and transportation.

It would be just as honest to replace the gold bars with enough food to feed the continent of Africa and the Earth with a picture of a thermometer. Mmmm-mmmm. Doesn't that thermometer look good?

To speak sensibly about climate control, you must confront roughly a half-dozen difficult questions. What are the harmful effects of climate change? What are the costs of avoiding those effects (say by moving New York City inland)? What are the offsetting benefits (an Alaskan wheat crop)? How likely is the Earth to suffer some other disaster—an asteroid strike?—that will make our carbon emissions irrelevant? What do we owe to future generations? How risk averse are we?

(Risk aversion matters not just because of uncertainty about the effects of climate change but because it affects the way future generations want us to behave. Imagine yourself as a disembodied soul, waiting in line to be born—possibly next year, possibly a hundred years hence. If you have little tolerance for risk, you'll want us to pursue policies that make life about equally good for all generations; if you're willing to roll the dice, you might prefer a policy that allows some generations to live riotously at the expense of others.)

Serious students of climate change—like the authors of the Stern Report to the British government—have been admirable in their willingness to confront these thorny questions of philosophy, science, and economics. To trivialize the entire matter with phony metaphors designed to obscure these deep and difficult issues is to merit a Nobel Prize in anti-intellectualism.

REALLY. DON'T BLATHER.

Words are no substitute for ideas. Here are a few of the words I've recently heard thoughtless people say:

> *Life begins at conception because the fertilized egg contains all the information necessary to create an adult human being.*

Well. All the genetic information in a fertilized egg fits comfortably on a DVD. If I burn that information to a disk, is the disk alive?

> *We should strive less to make money and more to touch the lives of our fellow human beings.*

Fine, but how are you supposed to know when you've touched the lives of other human beings? Usually, it's because they're willing to pay you.

Some of us, of course—teachers, for example—are fortunate enough to get direct feedback from the people whose lives we touch. But what about, say, the assembly-line worker or the corporative executive whose work improves the lives of thousands they will never meet? Touching many lives in a small way can do as much good as touching a few lives in a big way. Often the best way to be sure you're doing good is to look at your paycheck.

First, do no harm.

Taken literally, this means "never take any action," because any action runs the risk of doing harm. Nobody means this, so why do they say it?

Every vote should count. If an election is close, we should keep recounting until we're sure who's won.

Maybe the people who say this have some argument in mind, but I can't imagine what it is. The theory of democracy (stripped down to bare essentials and omitting all sorts of important caveats) is that on average, the guy with more votes is the better candidate. Surely, then, it should follow that the guy with only slightly more votes is only the slightly better candidate. And if one guy's only slightly better than the other, than a miscount is no great tragedy. Given the costs of recounting, it's often far more sensible just to flip a coin.

DELIGHT IN LOSING ARGUMENTS

Argue passionately for your beliefs; listen intently to your adversaries, and root for yourself to lose. When you lose, you've learned something.

23 What to Study

Some Advice to College Students

> To create a healthy philosophy, you should renounce
> metaphysics but be a good mathematician.
>
> —*Bertrand Russell*

When I was in college, I took a course on Shakespeare. It was taught by a man I'll call Professor N. I hadn't much appreciated Shakespeare in high school, but Professor N. brought the plays to life for me. After classes were over, I stopped by his office to thank him for changing my life in a small but significant way. He smiled and said he was particularly grateful for the kind words, as he was just getting over the shock of having been fired that morning.

Many years later, I googled Professor N. and found that he's now teaching at a small community college where students complain that he's dull and overly demanding. Among them, perhaps, are a happy few who appreciate their good fortune.

I'm very glad I took that course, more so than most of my college courses. But I don't understand why I was allowed to take it for academic credit. True, it enriched my life profoundly. But so did sex and drugs, and nobody gave me credit for them.

I love Shakespeare; I also love *The Simpsons*. Professor N. turned me on to one; my daughter (at age three!) turned me on to the other. I'm grateful for both, but neither strikes me as suitable fodder for a college class. An optional series of lectures, sure. College should offer lots of optional life-enriching experiences, like intramural basketball and a place to sunbathe. But reading books, like basketball or sunbathing, is a leisure activity, neither more nor less admirable than any other, and colleges should not pretend otherwise.

Be that as it may, getting students to read books is the more benign of the English department's twin missions. The other is teaching students to write, and that's where the real harm is done.

The bane of a college professor's existence is the student who has been taught in a writing course that there is such a thing as good writing, independent of having something to say. Students turn in well-organized grammatically correct prose, with the occasional stylistic flourish in lieu of any logical argument, and don't understand why they've earned grades of zero.

In the other direction, if your writing is murky, it's usually because your thinking is murky, too. The cure for that is not a series of writing exercises; it's to master your subject matter.

In my decades of writing for magazines and newspapers, I've written some pretty strong columns and some pretty weak ones. In nearly every case, the weak ones were weak because I hadn't nailed down the logical structure of my argument. A good column comes, almost always, from translating a logical argument into mathematics, filling a pad of paper with calculations to ensure that the argument is solid, burning the mathematics, and translating my understanding into prose. The translation to prose is the easy part. Prose flows easily when you understand what you're saying. If you're struggling to "craft" your prose, you're probably confused.

So I generally advise college students to avoid the English department. If you like to read, read. You don't need to take classes. Grateful as I am to Professor N., the fact remains that if I hadn't spent so much of my adult life rereading *Richard III,* I'd have been reading and rereading something else, maybe not quite as good, but who knows? And if you don't like to read, play tennis or something instead. One hobby is as good as another.

If you want to take a literature course or two, I won't begrudge you; just don't let them get in the way of your education. But for God's sake, avoid the writing courses. If you want to write, spend a couple of years studying, say, cognitive science. Take an idea that fascinates you, spend a lot of time thinking hard about the fine structure of the idea, and then explain it to your friends. You won't have trouble finding words. Now put those words down on paper.

So what *should* you study? The cliché is true, and has some good economics behind it: You must study something you love. No matter what career you pursue, you're sure to be competing with people who love it, and their passion will feed their stamina. If you don't share that passion, you'll never keep up.

I think philosophy is a lovely subject that addresses important questions in useful ways. I also have some qualms about the way it's usually taught. An undergraduate philosophy major will usually take a course or two on Aristotle or Kant or some other long-dead white guy. Aristotle wrote on many subjects besides philosophy: biology, physics, politics, and music among others. But no student of biology or physics is asked to read Aristotle. Aristotle's thinking was remarkable for its time, but in the intervening 2,400 years, people have found better ways of thinking.

Only the philosophers, apparently, are so insecure about the progress of their own subject that they still offer courses mired in antiquity.

To my mind, there is no subject more beautiful—or healthier for the brain—than mathematics, the study of what is possible. As you already know (unless you're reading this book from back to front), I am enamored, too, of economics and physics, subjects that extract logical order from apparent chaos. But there's no reason to be bound by my tastes—or your perception of your own. I came to college thinking I'd major in history, political science, or (yes) English. Thank God I shopped around.[1]

If you enjoy mathematics, and have a knack for it, you cannot go wrong by taking math courses no matter where you think you're eventually headed. Top-ranked economics Ph.D. programs almost always prefer to admit students with strong math backgrounds over students with strong economics backgrounds; I'm told the same is true in biology and I suspect it's the same way in many other disciplines. In the economics department where I teach, we frequently admit math majors with few (or even zero!) economics courses on their transcripts; we would never admit an economics major with inadequate math training.

Partly that's because we believe that if you can do math, you can think clearly, and clear thinking is what economics (or pretty much anything worth doing) is all about. Partly it's because mathematics is the study of patterns in general, and is therefore applicable to pretty much anything of intellectual substance.

Once, at Cambridge University in England, there was a math

---

1 Not that there's anything wrong with history or political science. But for me, they'd have been the wrong choices.

major named Frank Plumpton Ramsey. His interests ranged over all the topics I've touched on in this book, and many others. He loved philosophy and literature, and was extremely well-read (without any help from the English department!). As much as he loved good books, he loved good company. He was easygoing, likable, and known for his modesty, his honesty, and his "spontaneous gurgling laugh." After he graduated and became a math teacher, his best buddies were Ludwig Wittgenstein, one of the world's most important philosophers, and Piero Sraffa, a leading economic theorist.

I'll pause to tell you a (quite irrelevant) little story about Sraffa: His major work was a book called *The Production of Commodities by Means of Commodities,* an attempt to resolve some deep paradoxes in the theory of how interest rates and productivity are determined. The book is highly technical and very difficult.

One day a Cambridge graduate student came rushing into the economics department lounge and collared Luigi Pasinetti, a colleague of Sraffa's and also a prominent economic theorist. The breathless student declared, "Professor Pasinetti! I've been studying Professor Sraffa's book for months now, and I think I finally understand it! I see exactly what he means! Let me explain it to you!" They sat down on a couch and Pasinetti listened patiently while the student reeled off fifteen minutes of complex and esoteric reasoning and then asked, "So have I got it? Is that it? Have I got the point?" Pasinetti replied, "Why don't you ask Sraffa? He's sitting right next to you."

The student turned around and to his horror and delight found that Sraffa had indeed been sitting next to him the entire time—with his head leaning on the back of the sofa, his eyes closed and pointed toward the ceiling. The student gingerly re-

Frank Plumpton Ramsey

peated his question: "Professor Sraffa? Was I correct? Was that what you meant to say in your book?" Sraffa, without opening his eyes, replied: "I'll never tell."

Ramsey was fascinated by beliefs and the boundary area between beliefs and knowledge. He observed that while people are capable of believing the most outlandish things, it's far more difficult for them to believe certain outlandish *combinations* of things. Nobody believes both that the Yankees are almost sure to beat the Red Sox tonight *and* the Red Sox are almost sure to beat the Yankees tonight. A gambler with both those beliefs would go bankrupt very quickly. He'd be willing to bet two dollars against one dollar on the Yankees, and also two dollars against one dollar on the Red Sox. No matter how the game comes out, he loses two dollars and gains one.

Ramsey posited that a combination of beliefs is impossible if it allows a con man to take all your money through a cleverly structured combination of bets. Then he figured out how to tell exactly which combinations of beliefs are ruled out by this criterion. This work forms part of the foundation for modern game theory.

We believe some things more certainly than others, and Ramsey's theory accounts for these *degrees* of belief as well as the beliefs themselves. If you tell me that you believe in the resurrection of the soul, how am I supposed to estimate your degree of belief? Ramsey's answer is to observe not what you say, but what you do. I plan my day around the assumption that my car will start; therefore you can infer that I have a pretty strong belief in that assumption. If your religion has no apparent effect on your behavior, I'm entitled to assume that your degree of belief is small, no matter how much you protest.

Now, how do we progress from beliefs to knowledge? Here Ramsey developed another extensive and influential theory, stressing the role of *reliable processes,* including mathematical insight, logical analysis, and the accumulation of evidence.

In mathematics, Ramsey was struck by a curious fact: At any party with six guests, there must be either three mutual friends or three mutual nonfriends. This is not so obvious, but it's also not terribly difficult to prove.[2] He asked the natural follow-up question: How many guests would I have to invite to ensure that there are either *four* mutual friends or four mutual nonfriends?

---

2 Here's the proof: Imagine yourself as a guest at a six-person party. Suppose for the moment that you've got three friends at this party. If any two of them are friends, then they plus you make up a trio of mutual friends; if none of them are friends, then they make up a trio of mutual nonfriends. On the other hand, suppose you *don't* have three friends at the party. Then, because there are six people altogether, you must have at least three nonfriends. If any two of them are nonfriends, then they plus you make up a trio of nonfriends; if all three of them are friends, then they make up a trio of friends. That covers all the bases.

It's not immediately obvious that this question has an answer! Perhaps parties can get arbitrarily large without *ever* having four mutual friends or four mutual nonfriends. But it turns out both that the answer exists (which Ramsey proved) and the answer is eighteen (which Ramsey died without knowing). A seventeen-person party can avoid having any mutually friendly or non-friendly foursomes, but an eighteen-person party can't.

Now what about fivesomes? Again, Ramsey died without knowing the answer—and so might you and I. All that's currently known is that the answer is somewhere between forty-three and forty-nine. But again, it was Ramsey who proved there *is* an answer.

For sixsomes, the answer is known to be somewhere between 102 and 165; for sevensomes, between 205 and 540; for eightsomes, between 282 and 1870. For nineteensomes, all we know is that the answer lies somewhere between 17,885 and 9,075,135,299. But Ramsey proved that no matter how high you go, there's always an answer.

In fact, he proved far more. For example, suppose we expand the range of relationships beyond "friends" and "nonfriends." Suppose any pair of people can be either friends, lovers, enemies, or strangers. Then how big a party must be to ensure that there's either a foursome of mutual friends, a fivesome of mutual lovers, a threesome of mutual enemies, or a tensome of mutual strangers? I haven't the foggiest idea, but once again, Ramsey's theorem tells me that the question has an answer.

In some vague sense, Ramsey's theorem says that within sufficiently great chaos, there is also always order. A nineteensome of mutual friends (or nonfriends) is a highly ordered structure, and I'm sure to find one amid the chaos of 9,075,135,299 party guests chosen at random.

There's now a whole branch of mathematics called Ramsey

Theory that deals with such questions. Ramsey Theory is a rich source of statements that are true but not provable—like the statement that Hercules always beats the hydra. Gödel was the first to give an example of such a statement, but that statement suffered from being almost incomprehensible. Ramsey Theory provided the first examples accessible to the average mathematician.

In fact, Ramsey was interested in the party puzzles not for their own sake but as a testing ground for his program to derive mathematical truths from purely logical principles. The program was only a partial success, but it was highly influential.

In economics, Ramsey made immortal contributions, motivated perhaps partly by his friendship with Piero Sraffa and certainly by his association with the economist John Maynard Keynes. Indeed, Ramsey's name comes up so often in the economics literature that most economists assume he was a full-time economist himself. They're often surprised when I tell them that economics was Ramsey's tertiary interest, after math and philosophy.

One problem Ramsey posed was "How much should people save?" The answer, of course, depends at least partly on how much we care about future generations. Ramsey's answer was that of course we should care about strangers born in the far future exactly as much as we care about strangers born today. Anything else, he said, would be "ethically indefensible." I wonder what he'd have made of my argument to the contrary on pages 188–89 of this book.

Having taken his ethical stand, Ramsey still faced formal technical problems. Okay, we choose to care about all generations equally. How do we get from that to a concrete answer like "We should save 7 percent of our income"? The "Ramsey Growth Model" that he devised to solve this problem is now standard fare for every first-year graduate student in economics. So is the "Ramsey Pricing Model," an analysis of how regulated monopolies should set prices for the greatest social good.

In part, Ramsey was able to take economics further than the economists could because of his thorough grounding in the related mathematics and philosophy. As John Maynard Keynes put it, "When he descended from his accustomed stony heights, he still lived without effort in a rarer atmosphere than most economists care to breathe."

Keynes meant what he said. He himself had embarked on a years-long research project to rewrite the foundations of probability theory, and had already produced a dense book on the subject, but abandoned the project when the nineteen-year-old Ramsey convinced him he was on the wrong track. Eminent philosophers from Bertrand Russell to Ludwig Wittgenstein drastically curtailed or revamped their own research agendas in response to Ramsey's criticism. And according to the eminent philosopher R. B. Braithwaite:

> I almost always felt, with regard to any subject which we discussed, that he understood it much better than I did, and where (as was often the case) he failed to convince me, I generally thought the probability was that he was right and I was wrong, and that my failure to agree with him was due to lack of mental power on my part.

In his willingness to subordinate his own opinions to Ramsey's, perhaps Braithwaite was one of those all-too-rare honest truthseekers we contemplated in Chapter 8! Anyone who works in academia has occasionally wasted a few weeks (or not uncommonly a few years!) on a project that, in retrospect, was ill-conceived from the beginning. Ramsey was no exception. He worked for a short while on this question: You've got to make a decision—say, whether to live in New York or Chicago. There's some information that might be relevant to your decision—say, the state of the job market in Chicago, or the annual rainfall. Question: Is it better to learn this information before or after you make your decision?

The answer, obviously, is "before." But what's obvious is not always true, and Ramsey, admirably, wanted to think things through from first principles. His first, entirely sensible, step was to translate the question into mathematics. Unfortunately, he translated it into unnecessarily complicated mathematics, which in turn required him to make a series of auxiliary technical assumptions. In the end, he found the right answer (which is, after all, "before"), but only after doing far too much work. Worse yet, because of those extra technical assumptions, his proof was not universally applicable. A far simpler argument would have proved far more.

At some point, Ramsey must have realized he was on the wrong track; he took his two pages of notes, stuffed them in a drawer, and as far as I know, never looked at them again. But many years later, long after Ramsey's death, the pages were discovered and published in the *British Journal for the Philosophy of Science,* together with an editor's note touting their profundity.[3] It's this kind of thing that sometimes makes me squeamish about the judgment of philosophers. But in the editor's defense, I know of no mathematician, economist, or physicist (myself included) who would want to be judged by the most foolish thing he'd ever said in print.

As with much else in this book, I've rambled on about Frank

---

3 The *British Journal for the Philosophy of Science* is considered highly prestigious by philosophers, and I've had the honor of being published there myself.

Plumpton Ramsey not to make any particular point but because it seemed to fit in and I think it's interesting. If there's a lesson to be learned, perhaps it's this: Don't be too constrained by traditional boundaries between subjects. Let your mind run free.

Or perhaps the lesson is: Make the most of your youth. Frank Plumpton Ramsey, the father of two daughters, good and hearty friend to Wittgenstein, Sraffa, and Keynes, and author of roughly fifteen immortal papers in philosophy, logic, mathematics, and economics, died of chronic liver disease on January 19, 1930. He was twenty-six years old.

Appendix

If I have seen farther than other men, it is because I have stood on the shoulders of giants.

—*Sir Isaac Newton*

If I have not seen as far as other men, it is because midgets are standing on my shoulders.

—*Anonymous*

A few further thoughts, and some pointers to thinkers I admire:

INTRODUCTION: THE BEGINNING OF THE JOURNEY

N. David Mermin's *Space and Time in Special Relativity* appeared in 1968. In 2005, Professor Mermin wrote a new book on special relativity called *It's About Time*. Professor Mermin believes the newer book is much better. I agree that the newer book is very good, but I still prefer the earlier one, and not only because it reminds me of my youth.

CHAPTER 1: ON WHAT THERE IS

I've asserted in the chapter that mathematical objects exist independently of the human beings who study them. This is certainly a mainstream belief, and possibly the only mainstream belief, among working mathematicians. Here are quotes from two of the most influential mathematicians of the past century; it would be easy to provide dozens more:

> I believe that numbers and functions of Analysis are not the arbitrary result of our minds; I think that they exist outside of us, with the same character of necessity as the things of objective reality, and we meet them or discover them, and study them, as do the physicists, the chemists and the zoologists.
>
> —*David Hilbert*

> I believe that mathematical reality lies outside us, that our function is to discover or observe it, and that the theorems which we prove, and which we describe grandiloquently as our "creations," are simply the notes of our observations.
>
> —*G. H. Hardy*

(Of course I've gone much further than Hilbert and Hardy in asserting that mathematical objects are not just real, but the fabric of the Universe.)

CHAPTER 4: DAYDREAM BELIEVERS

The physics of ripples is a complicated matter.

Here again is what I said in Chapter 4: Disturbances in odd-dimensional media (such as the three-dimensional air around us) propagate without ripples. By contrast, disturbances in even-dimensional media (such as a pond surface) must propagate *with* ripples.[1]

But here's what I didn't say: A pond is a complicated object, and the ripples you see on its surface can be considerably more complicated (and considerably larger and considerably longer-lived) than the ripples that must appear in any two-dimensional medium. To a considerable extent, pond ripples are driven not by the general physics of two-dimensional media but by the specific physics of ponds.[2]

None of this changes the main point: Ponds ripple; sounds don't. Yet when I was told that "sound is a wave," I accepted it without question—despite the fact that sound is obviously nothing at all like the other waves I was familiar with.

---

1 For readers who care, I've put the (highly technical) proofs of these facts on the Web at www.the-big-questions.com/ripples.html.

2 More precisely (for those with a tolerance for this sort of jargon), it is true that the wave equation always predicts ripples in two dimensions, but it is also true that pond ripples are at least partly nonlinear phenomena, and therefore not entirely governed by the wave equation.

CHAPTER 8: DIOGENES' NIGHTMARE

Aumann's proof that we can't agree to disagree appeared in the *Annals of Statistics* in 1976. The Geanakoplos/Polemarchakis proof that we can't go on arguing forever appeared in the *Journal of Economic Theory* (1982). Scott Aaronson's proof that we can reach agreement in a reasonable amount of time appeared in the *Proceedings of the Thirty-seventh Annual ACM Symposium* on the theory of computing.

There have been dozens of papers extending the scope of Aumann's result, pointing out potential loopholes, and then sewing them shut. As noted in the text, one potential loophole is that not all of our beliefs stem from logic and evidence; Robin Hanson analyzed and closed this loophole in the journal *Theory and Decision* (2006).

A few years earlier, in the journal *Economics Letters,* Hanson made the delightful observation that when honest truthseekers argue, their opinions should fluctuate quite unpredictably. Agent 86 says, "I'm pretty sure it's Curly." Agent 99 says, "I'm pretty sure it's Shemp." What does 86 say next? Maybe he says "Well, I still think it's Curly, but I'm less sure now." Or maybe he says: "By God, you're right! It's *got* to be Shemp!," *surpassing* 99's degree of certainty! Hanson proves that in a world of honest truthseekers, 99 should have no idea which reaction to expect.

For a reasonably thorough and exceptionally readable overview of this entire literature, see the paper "Are Disagreements Honest?" by Tyler Cowen and Robin Hanson, in the *Journal of Economic Methodology* (2009).

CHAPTER 9: KNOWING YOUR MATH

For a wonderfully clear and readable exposition of Gödel's argument, I enthusiastically recommend a little book called *Gödel's Proof* by Ernest Nagel and James R. Newman. I read it in my youth and have loved mathematical logic ever since.

Gödel, incidentally, endorses the view that mathematical knowledge comes to us through extrasensory perception, as opposed to logic or evidence:

But, despite their remoteness from sense experience, we do have something like a perception also of the objects of set theory, as is seen from the fact that the axioms force themselves upon us as being true. I don't see any reason why we should have less confidence in this kind of perception, i.e., in mathematical intuition, than in sense perception . . . they, too, may represent an aspect of objective reality, but, as opposed to the sensations, their presence in us may be due to another kind of relationship between ourselves and reality.

CHAPTER 10: UNFINISHED BUSINESS: HERCULES AND THE HYDRA

The inventors of the Hercules/hydra game are Laurie Kirby (of Baruch College) and Jeff Paris (of the University of Manchester). Their 1982 paper in the *Bulletin* of the London Math Society establishes both that Hercules always beats the hydra and that this statement is not provable from the axioms of arithmetic. In fact, something even more astonishing is true: The hydra of Chapter 10 reproduces 2 branches on its second turn, 3 on its third, and so on. Its far more ferocious cousin reproduces 2^2 (that is, 4) branches on its second turn, 3^{33} (that is, 19,683) on its third, 4^{444} (that is, 340, 282, 366, 920, 938, 463, 463, 374, 607, 431, 768, 211, 456) on its fourth, and so on. Nevertheless, even playing against this ferocious cousin, Hercules is still guaranteed to win no matter how stupidly he plays. This, too, is true but not provable. And likewise for even *more* ferocious hydras—in fact, for pretty much any hydra that can be described in words.

CHAPTER 13: THE RULES OF EVIDENCE

The study on economic hard times and civil unrest is by Professors Edward Miguel of Berkeley, and Shanker Satyanath and Ernest Sergenti of NYU. Their paper appeared in the *Journal of Political Economy* in 2008.

For the causality between education (or the lack thereof) and crime, see Lance Lochner's paper "Education, Work and Crime" (*International Economic Review,* 2004), or Lochner and Enrico Moretti's "The Effect of Education on Crime" in the *American Economic Review* of the same year.

A recent article in the *British Medical Journal* by Gordon C. S. Smith and Jill P. Pell reviewed the evidence that parachutes save lives and concluded that it fails to meet the standards of a medical community that fetishizes controlled experiments.

CHAPTER 14: THE LIMITS TO KNOWLEDGE

Knowledgeable readers will immediately recognize that I've cheated by drawing the electron's state space as a one-dimensional circle rather than a two-dimensional sphere; I trust those same readers will see that nothing of importance is lost in the translation.

However, those same readers might be confused as to how the points "left" and "right" ended up a full half-circle apart, rather than the expected quarter-circle. The answer (which will be comprehensible only to those who might have asked the question) is that this circle is not the unit circle S^1, but the real projective space P^1; the antipodal points of the circle have already been identified.

CHAPTER 16: TELLING RIGHT FROM WRONG

The trolley problem derives from some more or less equivalent dilemmas posed by the British philosopher Philippa Foot in her book *Virtues and Vices*. Professor Foot used these scenarios to illuminate the debate over abortion, but I (and others) have adopted them to illuminate the distinction between deontology and consequentialism.

For an exceptionally lively and thoughtful discussion of the trade-offs between deontology (especially in the form of elevating "respect for individual rights" to a moral absolute) and consequentialism, see David Friedman's classic work *The Machinery of Freedom*.

CHAPTER 17: THE ECONOMIST'S GOLDEN RULE

My friend David Levine, who labors mightily at the sometimes thankless task of keeping me honest, insists that I confront the Economist's Golden Rule with a particularly stark version of the trolley problem from the previous chapter. To satisfy David, then, let's consider the following problem:

> *The Trolley Problem, Golden Edition. A trolley is hurtling along a track, bearing down on one of the one hundred orphans who forage in the vicinity for scraps. A very rich man can avert the disaster by throwing his $300,000 gold watch in front of the train. Is he obligated to do so?*

Answer: It depends. An alternative use of that watch is to sell it and give $3,000 to each orphan. Which would the *orphans themselves* have preferred to receive if you'd asked them yesterday: $3,000 cash per orphan, or a guarantee that the rich man will save them from the occasional hurtling trolley car?

The EGR says at least this: If you are going to spend $300,000 helping orphans, you should spend it in the way that the orphans prefer. Therefore, *if* we assume that the orphans prefer the cash, and *if* we don't think the rich man has any obligation to hand out cash, we can conclude that the rich man has no obligation to stop the trolley car.

That's a shocking conclusion but it's not a morally blind one; it's based not on mindless arithmetic but on substantive moral reasoning. If the rich man didn't feel compelled to hand out $3,000 checks yesterday, why should he feel compelled to hand out something that is *less valuable in the orphans' own opinion* today?

Now maybe your answer is that the rich man indeed *should* have been handing out money all along. If that's your position, the EGR does not disagree; it is quite silent on the question of how much charity we owe. In other words, if you want to know how much charity we owe, you've got to supplement the EGR with some additional moral principle. The EGR never claimed to be the be-all and end-all of morality.

It's worth remembering, too, that we sacrifice poor people's lives for rich people's luxuries *all the time*. Every road without a guardrail is a potential death trap, and over time it's essentially certain that people will die on those roads. We could avert those deaths by taxing the rich and building guardrails. We choose not to do that. The poor routinely die so the rich can have caviar.

Perhaps we should never tolerate such income discrepancies in the first place. But in fact we do tolerate such discrepancies, and they don't seem to bother us, at least not nearly as much as this version of the trolley problem does.

So perhaps the moral of this exercise is that I should be less complacent about the income distribution. Or perhaps it's that I should be *more* complacent about letting orphans die on train tracks. Like David, I recoil from the latter option. But more so, I think, than David, I am willing to countenance the possibility that that's because the exercise is trying to teach me something.

CHAPTER 21: UNFINISHED BUSINESS: LET THE RABBI SPLIT THE PIE

The Aumann/Maschler theorem appeared in the *Journal of Economic Theory* in 1985.

CHAPTER 22: HOW TO THINK

The experiments of Vernon Smith and James C. Cox are reported in Cox's University of Arizona working paper called "On the Economics of Reciprocity."

The back-of-the-napkin estimate for the appropriate size of an insurance-metaphor-justified welfare system comes from my former colleagues James Kahn and Hugo Hopenhayn; a far more sophisticated calculation in the same spirit (but focused more on the design of the tax sytem than of the welfare system) earned Sir James Mirrlees the Nobel Memorial Prize in economics.

Greg Mankiw and Matthew Weinzierl explored the optimal taxation of height in a 2007 Harvard working paper.

In the section "A Cost Is Not a Sin," I've lamented the evolutionary legacy that drives us to identify, condemn, and persecute those we've defined as "bad guys." The philosopher David Livingstone Smith has emphasized (quite rightly I am sure) that the long history of human warfare (and violence more generally) is best understood in this evolutionary context, of which he gives a compelling account in his tour de force *The Most Dangerous Animal,* a remarkable fusion of biology, history, sociology, and philosophy. I've long believed evolutionary biology goes a long way toward explaining our xenophobic trade and immigration policies; Smith's work convinces me that the same observation applies to defense and foreign policy as well.

The data on time allocation come from a paper called "Measuring Trends in Leisure: The Allocation of Time over Five Decades" by Professors Mark Aguiar and Erik Hurst. See also their book *The Increase in Leisure Inequality: 1965–2005.*

CHAPTER 23: WHAT TO STUDY:
SOME ADVICE TO COLLEGE STUDENTS

You can learn more about Ramsey's philosophical work at Professor Nils-Eric Sahlin's Web site www.fil.lu.se/sahlin/ramsey or by reading Professor Sahlin's book *The Philosophy of F. P. Ramsey.*

Want more answers? Have some to share?
Join the discussion at www.the-big-questions.com.

Acknowledgments

I and my readers are much in debt to the many friends and colleagues who have offered suggestions, comments, encouragement, and criticism. Special thanks to Mark Aguiar, Mark Bils, Christy Birtcher, Elizabeth Boskey, Kathryn Campbell-Kibler, Bryan Caplan, Kate Charles, Barbara Farabaugh, Dan Grayson, David Grayson, Paul Grayson, Robin Hanson, Bennett Haselton, James A. Kahn, David I. Levine, Aaron Mandel, Dee McCloskey, David Mermin, my mom, Romans Pancs, Jesse Raymond, Michael Rizzo, David Livingstone Smith, Alan Stockman, Alex Tabarrok, Ellis Tallman, Lisa Talpey, Ronald Tansky, Gabor Virag, Michael Wolkoff, and the several others I will eventually kick myself for forgetting to mention.

And thank you Mrs. Rosenberg.

> Lately it occurs to me
> What a long strange trip it's been.
> —*The Grateful Dead*

Index

About the Author

Steven E. Landsburg is a professor of economics at the University of Rochester. He is the author of *The Armchair Economist, Fair Play, More Sex Is Safer Sex,* two textbooks in economics, a forthcoming textbook on general relativity and cosmology, and more than thirty journal articles in mathematics, economics, and philosophy. He has written regularly for Slate and *Forbes* and occasionally for *The New York Times, The Wall Street Journal,* and several other major publications.

ASSESSMENT AS LEARNING

USING CLASSROOM ASSESSMENT TO MAXIMIZE STUDENT LEARNING

LORNA M. EARL

EXPERTS IN ASSESSMENT™

SERIES EDITORS
THOMAS R. GUSKEY AND ROBERT J. MARZANO

CORWIN PRESS, INC.
A Sage Publications Company
Thousand Oaks, California

For information:

Corwin Press, Inc.
A Sage Publications Company
2455 Teller Road
Thousand Oaks, California 91320
www.corwinpress.com

Sage Publications Ltd.
6 Bonhill Street
London EC2A 4PU
United Kingdom

Sage Publications India Pvt. Ltd.
B-42, Panchsheel Enclave
Post Box 4109
New Delhi 110 017 India

Printed in the United States of America

Library of Congress Cataloging-in-Publication Data

Earl, Lorna M. (Lorna Maxine), 1948-
Assessment as learning: Using classroom assessment to maximize student learning / Lorna M. Earl.
    p. cm. — (Experts in assessment series)
Includes bibliographical references and index.
ISBN 978-0-7619-4625-0 (cloth) — ISBN 978-0-7619-4626-7 (pbk.)
    1. Educational tests and measurements. 2. Learning. I. Title. II. Experts in assessment.
LB3051.E19 2003
371.26'4—dc21

                                        2003002364

08   09   10   11   10 9 8 7 6 5

Acquisitions Editor:	Rachel Livsey
Editorial Assistant:	Phyllis Cappello
Production Editor:	Melanie Birdsall
Copy Editor:	Liann Lech
Typesetter:	C&M Digitals (P) Ltd.
Proofreader:	Teresa Herlinger
Indexer:	Kathy Paparchontis
Cover Designer:	Tracy E. Miller

Contents

Series Editors' Introduction

Standards, assessment, accountability, and grading—these are the issues that dominated discussions of education in the 1990s. Today, they are at the center of every modern education reform effort. As educators turn to the task of implementing these reforms, they face a complex array of questions and concerns that little in their background or previous experience has prepared them to address. This series is designed to help in that challenging task.

In selecting the authors, we went to individuals recognized as true experts in the field. The ideas of these scholar-practitioners have already helped shape current discussions of standards, assessment, accountability, and grading. But equally important, their work reflects a deep understanding of the complexities involved in implementation. As they developed their books for this series, we asked them to extend their thinking, push the edge, and present new perspectives on what should be done and how to do it. That is precisely what they did. The books they crafted provide not only cutting-edge perspectives but also practical guidelines for successful implementation.

We have several goals for this series. First, that it be used by teachers, school leaders, policymakers, government officials, and all those concerned with these crucial aspects of education reform. Second, that it helps broaden understanding of the complex issues involved in standards, assessment, accountability, and grading. Third, that it leads to more thoughtful policies and programs. Fourth, and most important, that it helps accomplish the basic goal for which all reform initiatives are intended—namely, to enable all students to learn excellently and to gain the many positive benefits of that success.

Thomas R. Guskey
Robert J. Marzano
Series Editors

Preface

Why This Book?

For almost 30 years, I have been working with teachers and administrators in schools and districts in the province of Ontario, Canada, as a colleague, researcher, and "critical friend." My work has taken me into classrooms and staff rooms, marking sessions and student-led conferences, professional development sessions and teacher discussion groups.

From my unique vantage point of researcher, observer, and colleague in many classrooms, I was struck by the way assessment always came at the end, not only in the unit of work but also in teachers' planning. And even in the planning, assessment received little attention. After columns of objectives and teaching strategies and resources in the planning grid, the assessment column would sit ominously stark, with cryptic entries such as "test" or "worksheet" or "project." Assessment was almost an afterthought. At the same time, it often seemed as though too much time was being dedicated to testing that didn't go anywhere.

I routinely heard that "assessment is the hardest part." As a young researcher working in a school district, I was intrigued by the tensions and challenges that assessment created for teachers. I became a student of the ways and means of classroom assessment, sometimes informally, sometimes more formally. Although the recent preoccupation with assessment as a lever for educational reform has brought the discussion to the foreground, teachers have always expressed concern about their roles as assessors. In some recent research, middle years teachers told us that they are being caught between competing purposes of classroom assessment and are often confused and frustrated by the difficulties that they experience as they try to reconcile the demands (Hargreaves, Earl, Moore, & Manning, 2001).

Who Is This Book For?

I have written this book for those teachers and school leaders who are struggling with and trying to come to grips with the conflict that they feel in relation to assessment. I hope that it will provide some alternate perspectives and beliefs about the role that assessment can play in the daily working of schools and classrooms, with real examples of how teachers are making assessment work to enhance student learning.

Teachers and school leaders can use this book as a focus for their discussions about what assessment means, especially as a part of learning and as a stimulus for deciding how they might change their practices. But changing practices will not be enough. An important element of these discussions and reflections should be the role of schooling and the role of educators in schools. Why? Because embedding some of the changes into routine practices without this discussion is unlikely to have much influence. Assessment as learning is premised on assumptions and beliefs that are simple in their articulation and very difficult in their application. Throughout the book, I have highlighted these assumptions by placing them in boxes. I invite you to consider your personal assumptions as you read mine and think about how your beliefs contribute to the way you engage in your work as a teacher.

I have also included examples from my own experience and the experience of colleagues, preservice candidates, and graduate students with whom I have worked throughout the book. These are all identified as "The Case of. . . ." I find them all compelling and exciting images of the challenges and the possibilities that exist for making assessment work for students. I hope you do, too. Here is the first one.

"The Case of Understanding Mathematics Learning and Assessment"

I have had the pleasure, over several years, of working with a wonderful young secondary mathematics teacher who came to me because of an interest in learning more about assessment. During our association, she has given me insights into the difficulties associated with changing deeply held beliefs that are based on a lifetime of personal experience. At one point, she came to me with a new understanding on her part. "I know how to teach calculus," she said. "I just don't know what to do when they don't get it." After her own time in school, always successful and delighting in the intellectual challenge that mathematics provided, she had had a major epiphany. Her experience was not the same as the experience of her students, and she did not know what they were encountering when calculus was not "obvious" to them, as it was to her. Helping them learn meant finding out what concepts, misconceptions, skills, and relationships make up "getting calculus" so that she could help them unpack their own learning.

After being part of several graduate courses about classroom assessment and attending a range of workshops and conferences dedicated to the topic, this same teacher read the draft manuscript for this book. Another epiphany: "I've heard lots of people talk about ideas like connecting assessment to learning, giving feedback, encouraging students to talk about their thinking, but you know what? I didn't get it. I kept saying to myself, 'I do that.' And I do, but not for the same reasons. At the end of the day, I still focused on what the information told me about how to give them a grade. Their learning was secondary."

Taken together, these realizations on her part not only are dramatic shifts in her thinking that are resulting in some serious changes to her practice and even her knowledge about the underpinnings of her subject area, but they also demonstrate how subtle and challenging making these changes can be. It seems so easy, even commonplace, to change the language and not the concepts, to believe that the work is done, when it has barely started.

What Is This Book About?

This book is about classroom assessment—the kind of assessment that happens every day in classrooms everywhere. Certainly, there are other kinds of assessment in education, and much has and will be written about them, but not in this book. Instead, the focus is on what teachers and students do, what they *can* do, how they think, and how they might think about routine classroom assessment as an inextricable part of learning. The ideas in this book arise out of my musings, observations, and conversations with students and teachers; from hours of reading material; and from discussions with people around the world who are struggling with the same issues. Consequently, this book is premised on a number of beliefs and assumptions about the nature and purpose of schooling and the role of teaching and assessment in the learning process. The major and most dramatic assumption is that assessment can and should be much more than a check on learning that comes at the end. It is an integral part of the learning process that, all too often, has been ignored. Historically, educational assessment has largely been assessment *of* learning, designed to accredit or judge the work of students. Sometimes, it has been assessment *for* learning, with feedback loops to ensure that students are given cues to review their learning and move forward. Assessment *as* learning goes even deeper, however, and draws on the role of personal monitoring and challenging of ideas that are embedded in the learning process, and the role of both students and teachers in fostering this process. *Assessment As Learning* is not superficial tampering. It is a fundamental shift in thinking about teaching and assessment, and about the relationship between them.

Throughout the book, my assumptions and perspectives will become clearer. When they do, I will attempt to provide a rationale and support for choosing this route as a compelling one for moving toward the kind of schooling that I believe will serve us all well. To that end, I have tried to shed some light on the assessment dilemmas that teachers feel, provide some insights into the complexity behind these tensions, and offer some suggestions for consideration in classrooms. I have not provided detailed directions for implementing classroom assessment strategies. Instead, I have tried to offer the following:

- An understanding of the reasons behind the confusion and discomfort that surround classroom assessment by detailing the way that the changing role of schooling and our increasing knowledge about the nature of learning have made classroom assessment much more complex

- Insight into the powerful influence that classroom assessment can have on students' learning

- Examples of mechanisms for effective use of assessment as learning in a variety of contexts, many of them drawn from actual examples provided by teachers whom I have come to know through my work

Organization of This Book

The book is organized into 11 chapters. Chapter 1 sets the stage for considering a new view of learning and assessment that argues for connecting them as part of the same process. Chapter 2 is a brief history of assessment, with attention to the influence of the current large-scale reform movement on classroom assessment. In Chapter 3, I make the case for considering assessment *of* learning, *for* learning, and *as* learning and make a concerted effort to rationalize shifting the existing balance among them in schools. Following the discussion of the purposes of assessment in relation to learning, Chapter 4 is about learning as the primary purpose for schools, and Chapter 5 details the links that exist between learning and assessment.

The next five chapters revisit what we know about learning and consider how assessment can contribute to deeper and better learning for students. Chapter 6 addresses diagnostic assessment—finding out what students believe to be true. The focus in Chapter 7 is motivation and the role that assessment can play in motivating students. In

Chapters 8 and 9, I get to the heart of the matter: How can assessment enhance and extend learning? Chapter 10 addresses the essential role of reflection and self-assessment in learning.

Finally, in Chapter 11, I have tried to identify some of the specific demands that looking at assessment as learning will make on teachers and to offer glimpses of what teachers should think about as they work to get to assessment that maximizes learning for all students.

At the end of each chapter, I have included some "Ideas for Follow-Up" that might be useful as groups of educators read and think about assessment as learning together. The questions are not comprehensive, but perhaps they can offer a starting point for conversation and sharing.

Writing this book has been a powerful learning experience for me. I have been forced to clarify my own thinking, challenge my assumptions, and put my ideas forward for constructive criticism from my colleagues and mentors, from my students and their students. I now find myself in the space between the production and the feedback. All comments are welcome. I hope this volume helps to stimulate conversation and challenge ideas—my own as well as others'.

Acknowledgments

First and foremost, thank you to all of the teachers, students, and colleagues who have challenged my thinking and pushed me to make classroom assessment my passion. In particular, thanks to Karen Allin, Rich Cornwall, Mary Lou McKinley, Rick Parsons, and Nancy Torrance, who provided assistance, insight, and wonderful examples of classroom assessment as learning, and to Louise Stoll, Karen Allin, Michele Schmidt, and Steven Katz for being, as always, my "critical friends."

Many teachers have known, in their hearts, about the role that classroom assessment plays in learning. To all of the researchers who continue to examine and describe the power of classroom assessment, you have given them the evidence that they need to continue with the struggle to make learning the raison d'etre of schools. From these teachers and the others who follow—thank you.

My own journey of awareness about the potential for classroom assessment as a vehicle for learning came from a lucky encounter (and subsequent long friendship) with Rick Stiggins, who had the courage to say, "I believe in teachers, I believe in classroom assessment, and I'll stake my career on it." We are all so grateful that he did and still does speak out with integrity, passion, and truth. Closer to home is my mentor and good friend, Bob Wilson, who pushes, cajoles, and never ceases to remind me that teachers are at the heart of learning in schools, and that they often do know best, even when they don't have the language to articulate their knowing. He inspires me to listen, and listen, and listen.

Once I was hooked on assessment, I have had the privilege to work with some wonderful and insightful colleagues and graduate students who constantly push me and teach me. To all of you in Scarborough, at OISE/UT, and around the world, thank you.

Finally, to family and friends who have listened to my ranting and watched me avoid writing in every possible way. You know what you have contributed—from a place at the table on Arran Lake to write, to answering midnight phone calls with a request for a virtual hug. I love you all.

About the Author

Lorna Earl, Ph.D., is Associate Professor in the Theory and Policy Studies Department at the Ontario Institute for Studies in Education at the University of Toronto and Head of the OISE/UT International Centre for Educational Change. Her experience as a Research Director in a large school district and as the first Director of Assessment for the Ontario provincial Education Quality and Accountability Office, when it was formed in 1995, have kept her immersed in the study of assessment in schools for almost 30 years. Her work in Canada, England, the United States, Australia, and New Zealand, and her interest in the international applications of assessment ideas, have given her experience in many contexts. This allows her to see similarities and differences that emerge as educators and governments struggle with the challenges that face schools in many locales.

CHAPTER 1

The Evolution of Assessment

Educational reform in the past decade has felt like a roller coaster ride for most teachers and schools. Schools reflect the changes that are occurring more broadly in society, and there seems to be no end to the changes (economic, cultural, political, and socioeconomic) that schools are expected to keep up with, or even lead. As Hargreaves (1994) reminds us, "Few people want to do much about the economy, but everyone—politicians, the media, and the public alike—wants to do something about education" (p. 17). The role of education is hotly debated in boardrooms, living rooms, and staff rooms.

Teachers and administrators are caught in the middle of what often appear to be conflicting and countervailing demands, struggling to maintain their balance. They are expected to navigate their passage through the unrest and uncertainty about how schools should be organized, what should be taught, how it should be taught, and how assessment should occur. At the same time, they are expected to continue to exert their professional influence by staying abreast of advances in understanding of human learning and of effective schools. The prospects are daunting, but the possibilities are compelling.

For a long time, extended education was available only to a small elite group. Schools were designed to provide the minimum education required for employment and engagement in the broader culture. For most students, this meant attending school long enough to learn the 3Rs and get a minimal understanding of the society in which they lived. Only a few students continued on to secondary school and beyond. Over time, as societies have changed, schools have evolved progressively from serving this elite group, to working with the larger numbers and wider aspirations of a middle class, to dealing with the responsibility for educating all young people.

For most of the 20th century, the conception of learning was a behaviorist one that focused on learning specific, discrete skills and facts in a hierarchical sequence. Schools were charged with their transmission to students. Over time, these theories have been challenged by a social constructivist view of learning that emphasizes learning as a cognitive process that is shaped by prior knowledge and cultural perspectives. Teachers are expected to attend both to the demands of a fixed school curriculum generated by cultural/societal demands and to the needs of individual children with varied understandings, backgrounds, and interests who make up a class. They are caught between an awareness that young people construct their own view of the world through ideas that have some meaning for them and the expectations of the social milieu in which they live (Katz, Earl, & Olsen, 2001).

Traditionally, assessment and tests or examinations were synonymous, and their role was clear and consistent with the purposes of schooling—testing of segmented competencies and knowledge from the school curriculum as a way of sorting students into groups and deciding about future schooling. Assessment was based on the "concordance" or "fidelity" of the students' responses to the material that was delivered. As we come to know more about how learning happens, assessment takes on a different sheen. In our work, we have found that teachers are uneasy about having a single purpose for assessment. They are increasingly aware that assessment has multiple purposes and that they need a toolbox full of assessment ideas to address them all.

"The Case of Standards-Based Assessment"

In our book, *Learning to Change,* Andy Hargreaves and I wrote about how middle school teachers were responding to mandated changes in curriculum and assessment. In this longitudinal study, we followed 29 teachers from four different school districts who were actively engaged in efforts to incorporate the changes into their practices. When it came to assessment, they were confused, frustrated, and anxious. They told us that assessment was the hardest part of their work and gave us vivid examples of the inconsistencies and contradictions that they were facing.

> *We are having trouble because the marks don't mesh with the standards-based report card. I don't know how to relate them.*

> *We're supposed to be teaching to the standards and helping kids learn how to learn. But then they have the large-scale tests. What does the curriculum have to do with common testing?*

What about the students who don't get it? There is so much in the curriculum, I can't stop and work with them but that's my job, isn't it?

The high school mathematics department would like to issue a standardized test to all the incoming students. It makes me think about what I've been doing all year. I send the kids to them with detailed reports based on the standards. I talk about integers and decimals and geometry. What are they going to do with those reports?

These teachers were struggling with the paradox of classroom assessment. It does have multiple purposes. As Wilson (1996) describes it, assessment must satisfy many goals, such as providing feedback to students, offering diagnostic information for the teacher to use, providing summary information for record keeping, proffering evidence for reports, and directing efforts at curriculum and instructional adaptations. There is no single activity called "classroom assessment," and inherent tensions exist among the different purposes that are not trivial. Contradictions in classroom assessment processes are unavoidable. The challenge that these teachers were facing was how to untangle the issues that are embedded in these tensions and formulate plans that honor the complexity of the assessment process, in ways that made sense to them.

Defining the Future

Navigating these troubled waters requires more than tinkering with practice. It means that teachers and administrators are having to rethink their beliefs about issues as lofty as "What are schools for?" "Whom do schools serve?" and "What is our professional role in creating the schools we need?"

Hedley Beare (2001), an Australian researcher, identified the following three categories of futures for education and for societies as a whole:

- *Possible futures*—things that could happen, although many of them are unlikely

- *Probable futures*—things that probably will happen, unless something is done to turn events around

- *Preferred futures*—things that you prefer to have happen and/or that you would like to happen

He also issued a challenge to educators everywhere when he stated that it is possible to take deliberate actions to maximize the chance of achieving preferred futures—for young people, for the teaching profession, for schools, and for societies. We each need to take the time to decide what it is that we believe education is for and what role assessment should play: not because someone tells us, or the rules dictate, but because we believe it is right and just. Once we have an image of the future we prefer, getting there is possible. It may be difficult; we may have to change, to learn, to live in dissonance, and to stand firm in our beliefs. But it is possible.

My preferred future is a world in which young people not only possess competence and confidence in a broad range of areas, but also the tools to adapt to new knowledge as it comes along, and the dispositions to function wisely and with civility in a fast-paced and unpredictable world. I also have an image of how assessment fits in this preferred future. I described it first in an earlier book about classroom assessment (Earl & Cousins, 1995) as follows:

> I can imagine a day, in the not too distant future, when assessment and evaluation are not viewed with foreboding and terror; not separated from teaching and learning; not used to punish or prohibit access to important learning; and not seen as private, mystical ceremonies. Instead, assessment and teaching/learning will be reciprocal, each contributing to the other in ways that enhance both. Assessment will reveal not only what students know and understand, but will also capture how those new learnings came about and will provide a range in variety and quality of work that show the depth, breadth and growth of each student's thinking. This wealth of information will, in its turn, be used to provoke further learning and focused instruction. (p. 57)

In the rest of this volume, I offer ideas, suggestions, and images to illustrate the potential of realizing this preferred future.

Ideas for Follow-Up

1. How comfortable are you with your current approach to classroom assessment? What questions do you have about what you are doing?

2. What is your preferred future for education and for assessment? What is the probable future, given how things are now?

CHAPTER 2

Rethinking Assessment

Although assessment is a relatively new word in education, the process of gathering information about student performance and using it in schools has had a long and contentious history. One way of understanding assessment better is to situate it in the social, economic, and political context of the times.

A Brief History of Assessment

Formal and informal assessment of learning has existed for centuries—from the early Chinese civil service exams for entry into high public office, to public presentations by students of Aristotle, to practical assessments for entrance to craft guilds. It wasn't until industrialization and universal schooling at the turn of the past century, however, that schools became significant social institutions and evaluation of student achievement, as we know it, became a significant dimension of schooling. For centuries, the young in a community followed traditional occupations for which they learned "on the job," and schooling was a luxury. With the industrial revolution, people moved from rural to urban communities, and large numbers of newcomers emigrated from many countries and cultures. This led to larger organizations and a need to absorb and educate many young people in urban centers with a different social structure and economic base. The notion of universal education was born.

For most of the 20th century, and even now, factories have dominated the economy, and schools organized around a factory model have been consistent with the world around them. Kindergarten-sized units of raw material are put onto the first bench of the "plant" and

Learning by direct sharing in the pursuits of grown-ups becomes increasingly difficult except in the case of the less advanced occupations. Much of what adults do is so remote in space and in meaning that playful imitation is less and less adequate to reproduce its spirit. Ability to share effectively in adult activities thus depends upon a prior training given with this end in view. Intentional agencies—schools—and explicit material—studies—are devised. The task of teaching certain things is delegated to a special group of persons.

—Dewey (1916)

sequentially moved through the "stations" (grades) on the assembly line. They spend a fixed amount of time at each one (a school year). If, at the end of the allotted time, they aren't "done," they are sorted into "streams" or "tracks" and moved to other parts of the building. This metaphor for schools has largely fit the times. Society has been content because it worked for most people. Many students left school for work at an early age, but this was not viewed as a problem. Those who left were not called "dropouts." There were legitimate places for the majority of young people to go that did not require much schooling—places like factories, mines, and places for farming and fishing. Assessment, in the form of classroom tests and final examinations, was the set of gates through which students had to pass to move to the next level of education. Education, beyond the basics, was a scarce resource, necessary only for a few.

Not everyone agreed that schools should be organizations to serve economic imperatives. Dewey, as early as 1916, wrote eloquently about the need for education to serve all students, and that education was necessary in order for society to continue to grow in democratic, social, and moral ways. However, the major model for schooling mimicked the industrial model of work, and teachers were the quality control agents who decided which of their students continued on to higher levels of schooling.

The rise of the middle class and capitalism in the middle of the century threw the social order into flux, and many groups began to demand equity in society. Schools were becoming the key to social mobility, and there was considerable pressure to ensure that decisions about access to advanced schooling were made based on merit, rather than social status. It was time for an efficient mechanism in schools to identify and categorize students so that they were placed in the appropriate slots—something that was based on predictions about their likely success in a range of future endeavors. Assessment of achievement became the basis for awarding of privileges, with tests and exams as the process used to sort the students in a way that satisfied the expectations held by the mainstream society and that would be accepted as fair. This kind of sorting became an important function of schools (Stiggins, 2001).

Although teachers were often involved in the testing process, there was considerable pressure for mechanisms that were not biased by the teachers' subjective judgment. There was also tremendous optimism about social science in general and mental testing in particular (Lemann, 1999). Don't forget, the Army Alpha had been enormously successful in selecting officer candidates for the military in World War I (Popham, 2002), and a whole range of mental measurements was being developed in its image.

In many countries, the focus moved to seemingly scientific and objective mechanisms for measuring student achievement. In some, examinations became the arbiter of admission to differential secondary education and to universities. In England, they established the 11+ examinations that consigned young people to their lifelong social fates at age 11. If they did well, they went to grammar schools. Otherwise, they stayed in the local comprehensive school. Entrance to university in England changed from a system of "friends at court" to success on A-level examinations. In Canada, provincial exit exams defined access to universities. The Baccalaureate in France did the same. In the United States, the SATs were developed for the same reasons. As Nicholas Lemann (1999) describes it, Henry Chauncey, the first president of the Educational Testing Service (ETS), had a plan:

> To depose the existing, undemocratic American elite and replace it with a new one made up of brainy, elaborately trained, public-spirited people drawn from every section and every background. (p. 5)

The mechanism for this transformation was the administration of a series of multiple-choice tests to everyone and, on the basis of the scores, deciding what each person's role in society should be. The SATs were born.

In all of these different contexts, external tests or examinations were the means by which the "gatekeepers" exercised power and gave the illusion, at least, of objective measurement. The important decisions about access to higher education were determined outside schools and classrooms using so-called scientifically developed instruments.

It is no surprise that the control embodied in the examinations filtered down to affect those who were anxious to provide their students with access. Assessment in schools quickly took on the summative role, designed not only to report the achievement of individuals to parents, other teachers, and the students themselves, but also to make decisions about student placements and life choices. Students were given different programs, sorted into different "tracks," and set on the voyage toward their various destinations. Assessment in schools became the local gatekeeper, emulating the external exam models and reinforcing the need to sort and select. Schools and teachers contributed to this process through a system of ongoing reporting, rewards and penalties, and program decisions.

Once again, however, other perspectives and voices were clamoring in the background. In 1971, Bloom, Hastings, and Madaus wrote a landmark book titled *Formative and Summative Evaluation of Student Learning* that described a view of education in which the primary purpose of schooling was the development of the individual. In their view, assessment and evaluation were a part of learning, and classroom teachers played a prominent role in using evaluation to improve and extend student learning. Although their work influenced a generation of teachers and administrators, their voices often have been overwhelmed by the power of testing as a mechanism for social control and social mobility.

Over time, in the United States in particular, external standardized testing took on a dominant role in this process of identifying and selecting students for favor or censure. Standardized tests offer an image of "scientific credibility" and have the advantage of being easily mass-produced, administered, and scored (Stiggins, 2001). Because of this concrete, apparently scientific mechanism for deriving scores that appear to have the same meaning for all students, standardized tests have dominated the landscape for more than 50 years. In the 1980s, a number of researchers and educators began to challenge the stranglehold of multiple-choice tests on education. There was evidence that multiple-choice tests could not assess a student's ability to produce answers, that mass-produced tests may not test what local schools are actually teaching, and that the tests push teachers into narrowing the curriculum until the test becomes the instruction (Barton, 1999). A great deal of debate occurred about the quality of tests and the implications of test use (Broadfoot, 1996; Haney, Madaus, & Lyons, 1993; Popham, 2002). Challenges and counterchallenges continue to keep many lawyers, bureaucrats, test makers, and educators employed and busy defending, devising, challenging, and changing standardized tests.

For many states and districts, the solution to the concerns was to demand or create more authentic assessments. They began using portfolio assessments or performance assessments meant to reflect more closely what is expected of students in the real world. New assessment systems were born. Some died early. Others have lived on. Some have been reversed, and others have been replaced.

Thousands of people have been involved in trying to get large-scale assessment right. Mountains of books and articles have been written about the various approaches to large-scale assessment and whether or not they work. The debates will undoubtedly continue. I do not intend to try to capture the content of the arguments about large-scale assessment, because that would be another book. I do want to note, however, that throughout the sometimes heated and rancorous debates, often focusing on the technical quality and merit of the tests, there has been remarkably little public discussion about the purpose of these assessments and how they contribute to student learning. In fact, although the rhetoric about educational reform always cites improvement as the goal, all too often, improvement is defined in terms of increased test scores, with little attention to what the scores represent in terms of learning. Because large-scale assessment has become the vehicle of choice for accountability purposes and the lever for holding schools accountable for results (Firestone, Mayrowetz, & Fairman, 1998), other purposes have fallen away. The stakes are too high. Superintendents, principals, teachers, and policymakers watch closely to see what has happened to the test scores. But who is watching student learning?

Looking for Change in All the Wrong Places

The persistent determination to use large-scale assessment as the primary lever for school reform may be fundamentally misdirected. Most of the rhetoric about school reform is about improving the quality of what schools do and, by inference, the quality of student learning. Standardized tests are intended to provide information for accountability, evaluation, or comparative purposes; focus public and media attention on educational concerns; and change educational practice and instruction (Haertel, 1999). Unfortunately, existing standardized tests and even large-scale performance assessments are remarkably insensitive to the detection of the things students have learned (McDonnell, 1994; Popham, 2002). They are designed to spread students out on a continuum, but they do not provide sufficient information to direct the work of schools or tell the people who work in them what to do next. Evidence is also emerging that large-scale assessment really doesn't change *how* teachers teach (Firestone, Winter, & Fitz, 2000), although some teachers and administrators have enhanced their scores by using the test as the curriculum or by tampering with test scores. The major influences of these massive assessment programs seem to be in making concerns about education visible to the public, supporting the political desire for accountability, and focusing attention on raising test scores. They are used to grade schools, scold schools, and judge whether schools are achieving their goals (Barton, 1999). Learning is not a central issue.

As many authors have described, educational change is much more complex than most reform agendas have allowed for, and many reforms have had very little impact on practice (Elmore, 1996; Fullan, 2000; Hargreaves et al., 2001). More than a decade ago, Larry Cuban (1988) at Stanford drew attention to a fundamental puzzle in school reform. He pointed out that through a whole century of rhetoric about school reform, the basics of schooling have remained remarkably similar. His explanation for this paradox is that reformers have concentrated largely on "first-order" changes—*changes that try to make what already exists more efficient and effective.* Very few reforms focused on "second-order" changes—*changes designed to alter the fundamental ways in which schools operate.* The few second-order changes that did emerge (e.g., open space, team teaching, flexible scheduling) were quickly diverted by teachers and administrators, who saw minimal gain and much loss in embracing the changes and either adapted them to fit what existed or ignored them (Cuban, 1988). Nevertheless, second-order changes are probably necessary if schools are going to prepare young people for a future in which they are required to be competent, confident, and creative learners as a starting point for dealing with the complexity of their lives.

Rethinking Assessment for Real Change

This book is about changing assessment in ways that will challenge the status quo. The ideas that are included clearly suggest second-order changes that will influence how teachers view their work and act on a daily basis in their classrooms, not just a few superficial changes in delivery or resources. This kind of change is hard. Cuban (1988) warned us that trying to implement second-order changes in schools can lead to a sense of impotence and pessimism. He also reminded us that fundamental changes can occur when teachers themselves believe that the changes are worth making and when there is a parallel change in the social and political structures that exist outside schools.

The history of assessment described above shows a long line of first-order changes designed to inject quality control into education using a testing system designed to measure student performance and hold schools accountable. We have been consumed with more frequent and rigorous testing as the obvious mechanism for improving schools. Even well-meaning reformers offer testing as a politically feasible solution to the problems in schools. Unfortunately, criticizing educators does not improve schools, and higher test scores do not equal higher standards or better learning. Although policymakers often find ways to straddle the fence, educators are independent actors who can wield their own influence in their classrooms and schools. The time may be right for rethinking assessment in schools.

In a recent editorial in the journal *Assessment in Education,* Patricia Broadfoot (2001) bemoaned the fact that

> Current developments in society are set within a context that is characterised by a confused muddle of institutions and practices that are the enduring product of previous eras. Such institutions and practices were, more often than not, conceived in response to very different social and economic priorities of the past. Not surprisingly, their continuing contemporary influence can provide a significant drag on our collective capacity to address present day challenges. We cling to the familiar like a much-loved old garment, even when it is long past its best and ought to have been discarded long ago. (p. 109)

Assessment, as she points out later, is one of these muddled processes in transition from the past. Government policies are routinely placing conflicting demands on schools. This is not an indictment of government. Rather, it is a genuine reflection of a society divided about what schools are for. Much of the debate (both overt and hidden) in education focuses on the purpose of schooling. Some legislation is premised on schools as instruments of social control that need to be controlled themselves. Large-scale assessment, sanctions, and incentives for schools are a visible example. Other legislative directions identify schools as the mechanism for maximizing opportunities for all, with rhetoric about fairness and equity. At the same time that there is an increasing focus on accountability, there is also a societal push toward enhancing learning for all students.

Schools and districts are caught in an era with the contradictory purposes of "education for all" and "education as gatekeeper" with control of the nature of goals and rewards. Teachers and administrators are the instruments of these contradictory demands and are both recipients and perpetrators of these competing messages.

Despite the amount of research evidence that testifies to the shortcomings of many assessment techniques as a means of measuring educational achievement, existing assessment practices are so deeply rooted in our collective intellectual and political consciousness that they have been almost impossible to challenge. They may even become more entrenched as policymakers realize the power of large-scale assessment to monitor, compare, and leverage educational systems.

In this confused and emotionally charged assessment environment, the stakes are high to "get it right." Educators find themselves in a difficult position. They are part of the transition, laden down with the burdens of the past, while contemplating the possibilities of the future. They know how it has always been and have a great deal invested in maintaining stability, but at the same time, many of them acknowledge that it just doesn't feel right. What better way to bring some clarity to a murky subject than to return to first principles: What is our purpose? What are we trying to accomplish? What is assessment for?

Purpose Is Everything

As I and others have written about elsewhere, classroom assessment has a multitude of purposes, many of them contradictory. In a book about reinventing education for young adolescents (Hargreaves, Earl, & Ryan, 1996), we discussed the multiple and competing purposes of assessment as the motivation of students, the diagnosis of difficulties, certification of achievement, and accountability to the public. In our discussion, we draw attention to the paradoxes and contradictions inherent in trying to fulfill all of these purposes together. For example, traditional classroom assessment and reporting processes permit comparisons among students, fulfill accountability demands, and certify students for entry into other educational programs or institutions. But they do not provide any specific information about what the student has achieved. Diagnostic assessment cannot occur when a test event is high-stakes. Why would a student take the risk of making errors or showing misunderstanding to a teacher if the result is likely to work to the student's disadvantage?

Paul Black (1998) identified three broad purposes of assessment in schools: support learning; report achievement of individuals for certification, progress, and transfer; and satisfy the demands for public accountability. He goes on to point out that tensions among these purposes involve choices about (a) the best agencies to conduct assessments and (b) the optimum instruments and appropriate interpretations to serve each purpose.

Rick Stiggins (2001), in a discussion of standardized testing, points out that we have been relentless in our attempts to make standardized tests powerful instructional tools that are relevant in the classroom. Unfortunately, such tests tend to provide little information of value for day-to-day instruction. They do a good job of assessing broad classifications of content and spreading students out on the basis of the scores (considered against a reference point of other students or specific, preset standards) so that they can be sorted into groups. They do not provide timely or sufficient information to inform classroom practice.

In all of these discussions, the theme is the same. It is not possible to use one assessment process for the many purposes that we want it to fulfill. Different purposes require vastly different approaches, and mixing the purposes is likely to ensure that none of them will be well served. It is becoming more and more obvious that we must first decide about the purpose and then design the assessment program to fit (Gipps, 1994).

Like learning and teaching, assessment is not a singular entity. It is complex and dynamic, and it deserves to be differentiated and understood in all of its intricacy. Educators need to think about the various purposes for assessment and make choices about the purposes

> Using one assessment for a multitude of purposes is like using a hammer for everything from brain-surgery to pile driving.
>
> —Walt Haney (1991)

that they believe are important and how to realize these purposes every day in their classrooms. The good news in this story is that many other educators and researchers have been thinking, writing, and talking about these ideas for some time. Strong voices have been emerging with alternative visions for assessment in schools—visions that make purpose paramount and shift the focus from large-scale assessments for accountability to classroom assessment for teaching and learning. Many others agree with Linda Darling-Hammond (1994), who envisions an era in which the goal of schooling is to educate all children well, rather than selecting a "talented tenth" to be prepared for knowledge work. This new era will be one in which it is no longer sufficient for schools to sort their students and cull out the ones who don't fit the school's recipe for learning. Instead, learning will be the fundamental purpose of schooling (Earl & Cousins, 1995).

Since the mid-1980s, there has been a steady stream of advocates for assessment being educationally useful (Black, 1998; Gipps, 1994; Popham, 1995; Shepard, 1989; Stiggins, 1991; Sutton, 1995; Wiggins, 1993; Wiggins & McTighe, 1999; Wolf, Bixby, Glenn, & Gardner, 1991). They, and others, have focused on the importance and value of the assessment that teachers do every day in classrooms as a critical element in helping students learn. A great deal has been written already about these alternative images of classroom assessment, and teachers flock to professional development sessions to learn about new ways to perform assessment. Still, the practices that are being advocated are more the exception than the rule and are not encouraged or supported in many educational settings.

But the seeds have been sown for a genuine revolution, and ideas are there to be nurtured and to blossom. This assessment revolution is not happening in the halls of power, although governments can assist in its development and hasten its influence, if they so choose. Instead, assessment is situated in schools and particularly in classrooms, as students and teachers work together. The shift that these various authors envision depends on teachers and others rethinking how and why assessment and teaching happen.

Lorrie Shepard (2000) worried aloud, in her presidential address to the American Educational Research Association, that external accountability testing can lead to deskilling and deprofessionalizing of teachers and will teach students and teachers that effort in school should be in response to externally mandated rewards and punishments, rather than the excitement of ideas. I agree. However, I also worry that moves to empower teachers to take back assessment will result in reinforcement of the traditions that Broadfoot (2001) mentioned—traditions of teachers judging students using questionable methods, without the changes in assessment purpose or approach that will make it an integral part of learning. Just moving assessment back to teachers' control, on its own, is not a positive change. Returning to some fictional golden age will not move the agenda forward. Even when they were relatively autonomous, teachers retained control mainly of their own "secret gardens." More recently, they have been victims of change. Teachers should and can be agents of change, not victims. But the road is long and likely difficult.

The revolution is much larger than just assessment. It is a revolution about learning. And the purpose is very clear—high-level learning for all students. Approaching this vision of schools as learning institutions requires a dramatic change in the assumptions underlying education, and it requires a different view of schools, schooling, teachers, teaching, and, particularly, assessment. In this conception, *schools* have the responsibility for preparing *all* students for tomorrow's world; *teachers* have the wherewithal to guide all students to high levels of learning; and, *assessment,* first and foremost, is part of student learning. This seemingly straightforward shift requires dramatic changes in the way teaching and learning happen in schools.

After researching almost 7,000 classrooms across the United States, from 1900 to 1980, Cuban (1984) reported that most of the teachers taught the entire class as a group, with classroom activities built around students listening, writing, and watching. He suggested that this approach was consistent with societal expectations:

> The overriding purposes of the school . . . are to inculcate in children the prevailing social norms, values and behaviors that will prepare them for participation in the larger culture. . . . Those teaching practices that seek obedience, uniformity, productivity, and other traits required for minimum participation in bureaucratic and industrial organizations, are viewed as both necessary and worthwhile. . . . As the students grow older, homework, tests and grades focus on classroom

competitiveness and productivity. . . . Certain teaching practices are functional: whole-group instruction where waving hands vie for teachers attention; a question-answer format that rewards those better at factual recall; classroom furniture arranged to produce a uniform appearance; textbooks, a primary source of knowledge, yield reams of homework to which credit is given or withheld and becomes the basis for tests and quizzes. Dominant teaching practices, then, endure because they produce student behaviors consistent with the requirements of the larger society especially in the high school. (pp. 240–241)

So, changing classroom assessment is the beginning of a revolution—a revolution in classroom practices of all kinds. A tall order, but not an impossible one. Educational change is a process of creeping incrementalism, with tiny changes, day after day, in many different and unpredictable ways and places. We have already taken many of these first steps and made many of the tiny changes. We are embarking on an evolutionary path toward the revolution. Over time, teachers, parents, and students can re-form the nature of assessment in schools from a culture of judging and categorizing to one that fosters learning for all.

Taking Up the Challenge

In the current climate, educators are uniquely positioned to make fundamental changes in the purposes and processes of assessment in their classrooms, but it will not be an easy road. Powerful forces are operating in several different directions. The push of large-scale reform is for more centralized control, with national or state curricula and concomitant testing systems. At the same time, the veneer over teachers' moral purpose is very thin. Most of them entered the profession to make a difference in students' lives, and they are routinely concerned about how to serve their students well. When students are at stake, many teachers are willing to consider new approaches. The public is still undecided and probably uninformed as well. They need images of another way, of alternatives to what has always been.

Although the challenges are immense, this is not a time for inertia. As one of my favorite cartoon characters, Pogo, once said: "We seem to be surrounded by insurmountable opportunities." Teachers and administrators have the potential to use assessment as an exciting and powerful means for enhancing learning. Getting classroom assessment right is not a simplistic, either-or situation. It is a complex mix of challenging personal beliefs, rethinking instruction, and learning new ways to assess for different purposes. It requires educators who are excited about learning, imaginative, and willing to formulate strategies of "resistance" that allow them to use assessment in productive ways in their classrooms and honor the complexity of learning and assessment. None of the assessment purposes described above is right or wrong. They are situational. They work in different ways under different conditions.

Oddly enough, the large-scale reform agendas of the past decade provide the possibility of movement toward a different kind of classroom assessment, assessment that is more consistent with alternative images than is obvious at first glance.

Classroom Assessment and Large-Scale Reform

Education is in the foreground of many legislative agendas, and many governments have embarked on large-scale reform agendas designed to change entire systems. As Michael Fullan (2000) describes it, "Large-scale reform has returned with a vengeance" (p. 19). Over the past decade, large-scale reform has been surprisingly similar around the world. Geoff Whitty and his colleagues (Whitty, Power, & Halpin, 1998) studied legislative changes to education in Australia, England, Wales, New Zealand, Sweden, and the United States. Each country had its unique history and context, but the various governments had introduced policies that sought to reformulate the relationship between government, schools, and parents. All involved increased responsibility for individual schools, a reduction of power for district school boards or local education authorities, more power and responsibility to parents, changes to and centralization of curriculum, the introduction of standards or expectations for student learning, and centralized assessment schemes.

When governments mandate reform agendas, they are generally focused on first-order changes that are intended to put pressure on schools through external quality control, with scores from large-scale assessment as the ultimate measure of success. All too often, educators deplore and resist the changes or engage in superficial compliance to satisfy their masters. In my mind, this process is a diversion that takes us away from the work at hand. However, the current wave of large-scale reform contains much of value that can be cultivated and colonized by educators to transform the first-order changes into second-order changes, particularly in relation to learning, teaching, and assessment; second-order changes designed to change the very fabric of what schools are for.

Table 2.1   Characteristics of Large-Scale Reform

- Vision and goals
- Standards
- Curriculum frameworks and other teaching resources
- Focus on teaching and learning
- Accountability and incentives based on performance
- Coherent and integrated policies
- Sufficient funding and workable governance structures

SOURCE: Leithwood et al. (1999).

In a recent review of characteristics of large-scale reform, Leithwood, Jantzi, and Mascall (1999) identified the elements that seem to be present in most large-scale reform efforts. Their headings are displayed in Table 2.1.

The authors go on to say that, even with all these dimensions, change is not likely to happen in schools unless teachers are motivated to change, have the capacity to make the changes, and work in a context where support is readily available. In this section, I've taken the characteristics that they have identified and offered suggestions for how they can become the basis for exciting and serious change in schools, founded on the simple assumptions that permeate this text.

Vision and Goals

Most reform initiatives purport to be about enhancing student learning. The rhetoric about high standards for all and no child left behind provides a perfect starting point for educators to make learning the fundamental purpose of schools and to focus all of their efforts in that direction. What could be more worthy of attention in schools than quality learning for every student?

Standards

Virtually every state, province, and country has or is engaged in setting standards or expectations for student learning. Standards may be the reference point for large-scale assessments, but they are also the best descriptions available of what we expect of students in schools. Standards can make the work of schools visible to the public that they serve and give students clear learning targets. The process of looking at actual student work, discussing expected levels of achievement, and setting standards can lead to a constructive dialogue about what should be taught in schools and at what level. In particular, the active involvement of teachers and the public in writing standards has developed alliances among educators and the public in the struggle to define directions for education for children. Even more compelling is the fact that learning is easier when both the teacher and the student have a clear image of where they are headed (Black and Wiliam, 1998). Standards offer the basis for describing the expectations and making them concrete and accessible to everyone.

Curriculum Frameworks and Resources

Curriculum frameworks, when they do not become straitjackets for teachers, provide the backdrop for consistency and rigor in what gets taught. One of the most salient complaints about education has been the lack of consistency in what gets taught and how well it is taught from one district to another, one school to another, and one classroom to another. The current wave of reform has brought the essentials of curriculum into center stage. Virtually all of the reform-driven curriculum frameworks have a major focus on early literacy and numeracy. This renewed focus is quite different from the 3Rs of our past. In the 21st century, it is essential that all children (and eventually all adults) have solid facility with language and numbers, as well as many other more sophisticated skills. Children need concepts of literacy and numeracy so that they can move from *learning how* to read, write, and work with numbers to *using* reading, writing, and mathematics as tools to learn in other areas and to communicate their ideas to others.

This is not to suggest that literacy and numeracy are the only building blocks for learning. They are essential for future learning, but they are not all that young children need to learn, nor should they displace other important learning. They can use the symbol systems of language and numbers to develop competence and expertise in other areas by engaging in the learning work of developing and internalizing knowledge, organizing knowledge in a broad range of areas of study, and connecting ideas together in ways that make sense. This requires facility with the conventions, knowledge, concepts, and ideas embedded in the particular discipline, as well as comfort with a whole range of ways of thinking about and analyzing them.

When governments and teachers' associations produce curriculum documents, they provide teachers not with a roadmap to follow slavishly, but with a framework to inform their practice and challenge their conceptions of what ought to be included. When the work of producing curriculum is a collaborative effort that includes expert teachers, teachers are able to spend their valuable time refining and adjusting the material for use in their setting.

Focus on Teaching and Learning

Success in large-scale reform is related to the extent to which the reforms focus on teaching and learning. Teachers may resent the implications that they do not focus on teaching and learning already. Unfortunately, many things happen in schools that divert attention from learning. Even when it is a central purpose, there is always more that can be done. When teachers and students make learning the ultimate goal, their actions are not only consistent with the reforms but also deeply connected to the moral purpose of schooling. There may appear to be many hurdles, but nothing needs to stand in the way of making learning paramount.

Accountability and Incentives Based on Performance

Although accountability in policy terms is often defined by standardized test scores and target setting, accountability for teachers and students can be shown directly, every day, in the work that they do and the learning that occurs. Incentives in this case are not just extrinsic rewards. They emerge from the recognition of successful action and the knowledge that it came from personal commitment and hard work. The rewards are in the satisfaction of learning that is well done.

Coherent and Integrated Policies

When governments manage to align their policies in relation to things like curriculum and special education so that there is clear direction for schools, educators have less to unravel in order to integrate the policies into schools and classrooms and can concentrate on learning and teaching.

Sufficient Funding and Workable Governance Structures

These final components of large-scale reform efforts are certainly important dimensions for making implementation of reforms easier. They can also be assets for engaging in assessment reform in schools. At the same time, they may not be essential if teachers and administrators have the will and the determination to embark on the kinds of second-order changes that are described in this book.

Often, the opportunities embedded in large-scale reform are difficult to see, even when the reforms are well intentioned. Considering reforms dispassionately can be particularly hard when teachers feel denigrated, devalued, and under scrutiny. It seems that every intended outcome of a policy comes with its shadow of unintended outcomes, and the eclipse caused by the shadow is sometimes more dramatic than the original image. This being the case, teachers and administrators have it in their power to act rather than react and to move the educational change agenda forward in ways that they believe can really benefit students.

Ideas for Follow-Up

1. What was the purpose of classroom assessment when you were a student?

2. How is *large-scale assessment* being used for educational change in your district?

3. How is *classroom assessment* being used for educational change in your district?

CHAPTER 3

Assessment *of* Learning, *for* Learning, and *as* Learning

In Chapter 1, I described a "preferred future" for assessment. My vision is one that makes assessment an integral part of learning—guiding the process and stimulating further learning. The word *assessment* is derived from the Latin *assidere*, meaning "to sit beside or with" (Wiggins, 1993). Although this notion of a teacher sitting with her students to really understand what is happening as they pursue the challenges of learning is far removed from the role that assessment and evaluation have typically played in schools, many teachers have always done it. In this chapter, I look more closely at the various purposes for assessment that occurs routinely in classrooms. Classroom assessment is a complex undertaking that means something different to different audiences and in different situations. And so it should. Assessment has many purposes that sometimes support one another and sometimes compete or conflict with one another. As Wilson (1996) noted, teachers engage in a broad range of assessment roles, and keeping them straight is a challenging task (see Table 3.1).

Clearly, these roles overlap, and watching teachers try to manage the assessment activities and juggle them to satisfy the various goals shows how complex the process of classroom assessment really is. Also, tensions are embedded in these various roles and goals that cause concern for teachers. I hope that these tensions become more visible and understandable after I describe three different approaches to classroom assessment that have guided my thinking as I have contemplated the role of classroom assessment in my preferred future. The three approaches are Assessment *of* Learning, Assessment *for* Learning, and Assessment *as* Learning. Although I intend to highlight the contribution of Assessment *for* Learning and Assessment *as* Learning as part of a preferred future, Assessment *of* Learning is also

Table 3.1   Assessment Roles and Goals

Role	Goal
Teacher as mentor	Provide feedback and support to each student.
Teacher as guide	Gather diagnostic information to lead the group through the work at hand.
Teacher as accountant	Maintain records of student progress and achievement.
Teacher as reporter	Report to parents, students, and the school administration about student progress and achievement.
Teacher as program director	Make adjustments and revisions to instructional practices.

SOURCE: Adapted from *Assessment Roles and Goals* (Wilson, 1996).

valuable and has its place. In my mind, it is important to understand them all, recognize the inevitable contradictions among them, know which one you are using and why, and use them all wisely and well.

Assessment *of* Learning

The predominant kind of assessment in schools is Assessment *of* Learning. Its purpose is summative, intended to certify learning and report to parents and students about students' progress in school, usually by signaling students' relative position compared to other students. Assessment *of* Learning in classrooms is typically done at the end of something (e.g., a unit, a course, a grade, a Key Stage, a program) and takes the form of tests or exams that include questions drawn from the material studied during that time. In Assessment *of* Learning, the results are expressed symbolically, generally as marks or letter grades, and summarized as averages of a number of marks across several content areas to report to parents.

This is the kind of assessment that still dominates most classroom assessment activities, especially in secondary schools, with teachers firmly in charge of both creating and marking the tests. Teachers use the tests to assess the quantity and accuracy of student work, and the bulk of teacher effort in assessment is taken up in marking and grading. A strong emphasis is placed on comparing students, and feedback to students comes in the form of marks or grades, with little direction or advice for improvement. These kinds of testing events indicate which students are doing well and which ones are doing poorly. Typically, they don't give much indication of mastery of particular ideas or concepts because the test content is generally too limited and the scoring is too simplistic to represent the broad range of skills and knowledge that has been covered. But this lack of specificity hasn't presented a problem because the teachers' perceived purpose of the assessment is to produce a rank order of the students and assign a symbol to designate the students' position within the group, whatever group it might be. Teachers maintain voluminous records of student achievement that are used only for justifying the grades that are assigned.

Although much of this book focuses on the next two approaches to assessment, there are and will always be milestones and junctures where "summative" assessment is called for and Assessment *of* Learning is essential. Doing it right is a challenge in itself.

Assessment *of* Learning and grading have a long history in education. They have been widely accepted by parents and the public. If they have served us so well, why would we worry about a process that works? Without moving too far away from my primary purpose, I'd like to highlight a few of the issues that are currently contentious about what we have always done. Although the public has been largely supportive of grading in schools, skepticism is increasing about its fairness and even its accuracy. Educational researchers and theorists have been critical of traditional grading practices for quite some time (Marzano, 2000). In terms of measurement theory, grades are highly suspect. Why? Because teachers consider many factors other than academic achievement when they assign grades; teachers weight assessments differently, and they misinterpret single scores on assessments to represent performance on a wide range of skills and abilities (Marzano, 2000). As education becomes an essential ingredient for a successful future, more attention will be paid to how grades are calculated and how well they actually reflect what they are taken to mean. The book is not yet closed on Assessment *of* Learning, and educators have a great deal to learn to ensure that it and the grades that result from it are defensible and worthwhile.

> To measure or to learn; that is the question.
>
> —Broadfoot (1996)

Assessment *for* Learning

Assessment *for* Learning offers an alternative perspective to traditional assessment in schools. Simply put, Assessment *for* Learning shifts the emphasis from summative to formative assessment, from making judgments to creating descriptions that can be used in the service of the next stage of learning.

When they are doing Assessment *for* Learning, teachers collect a wide range of data so that they can modify the learning work for their students. They craft assessment tasks that open a window on what students know and can do already and use the insights that come from the process to design the next steps in instruction. To do this, teachers use observation, worksheets, questioning in class, student-teacher conferences, or whatever mechanism is likely to give them information that will be useful for their planning and teaching. Marking is not designed to make comparative judgments among the students but to highlight each student's strengths and weaknesses and provide them with feedback that will further their learning.

> Assumption: Classroom assessment can enhance learning.

Clearly, teachers are the central characters in Assessment *for* Learning as well, but their role is quite different from that in the prior approach. In Assessment *for* Learning, they use their personal knowledge of the students and their understanding of the context of the assessment and the curriculum targets to identify particular learning needs. Assessment *for* Learning happens in the middle of learning, often more than once, rather than at the end. It is interactive, with teachers providing assistance as part of the assessment. It helps teachers provide the feedback to scaffold next steps. And it depends on teachers' diagnostic skills to make it work.

> When the cook tastes the soup, that's formative; when the guests taste the soup, that's summative.
>
> —Robert Stake

Recordkeeping in this approach may include a grade book, but the records on which teachers rely are things like checklists of student progress against expectations, artifacts, portfolios of student work over time, and worksheets to trace the progression of students along the learning continuum.

> In reality, it is through classroom assessment that attitudes, skills, knowledge and thinking are fostered, nurtured and accelerated – or stifled.
>
> —Hynes (1991)

Assessment *as* Learning

Assessment *for* Learning can go a long way in enhancing student learning. By introducing the notion of Assessment *as* Learning,

I intend to reinforce and extend the role of formative assessment for learning by emphasizing the role of the student, not only as a contributor to the assessment and learning process, but also as the critical connector between them. The student is the link. Students, as active, engaged, and critical assessors, can make sense of information, relate it to prior knowledge, and master the skills involved. This is the regulatory process in metacognition. It occurs when students personally monitor what they are learning and use the feedback from this monitoring to make adjustments, adaptations, and even major changes in what they understand. Assessment *as* Learning is the ultimate goal, where students are their own best assessors.

At some point, students will need to be self-motivating and able to bring their talents and knowledge to bear on the decisions and problems that make up their lives. They can't just wait for the

> Assumption: Self-assessment is at the heart of the matter.

teacher (or politicians, or salespeople, or religious leaders) to tell them whether or not the answer is "right." Effective assessment empowers students to ask reflective questions and consider a range of strategies for learning and acting. Over time, students move forward in their learning when they can use personal knowledge to construct meaning, have skills of self-monitoring to realize that they don't understand something, and have ways of deciding what to do next.

Recordkeeping in Assessment *as* Learning is a personal affair. Students and teachers decide (often together) about the important evidence of learning and how it should be organized and kept. Students routinely reflect on their work and make judgments about how they can capitalize on what they have done already. Comparison with others is almost irrelevant. Instead, the critical reference points are the student's own prior work and the aspirations and targets for continued learning.

Getting the Balance Right

These three approaches all contribute to student learning but in vastly different ways. Table 3.2 gives a summary of the salient features of each approach.

As I mentioned earlier, all three assessment approaches have their place. The trick is to get the balance right. At the current juncture, almost all classroom assessment in a traditional environment is summative Assessment *of* Learning, focused on measuring learning after the fact and used for categorizing students and reporting these judgments to others. A few teachers use Assessment *for* Learning by building in diagnostic processes—formative assessment and feedback

Table 3.2   Features of Assessment *of*, *for*, and *as* Learning

Approach	Purpose	Reference Points	Key Assessor
Assessment *of* Learning	Judgments about placement, promotion, credentials, etc.	Other students	Teacher
Assessment *for* Learning	Information for teachers' instructional decisions	External standards or expectations	Teacher
Assessment *as* Learning	Self-monitoring and self-correction or adjustment	Personal goals and external standards	Student

at stages in the program—and giving students second chances to improve their marks (and, it is hoped, their learning). Systematic Assessment *as* Learning is almost nonexistent.

Obviously, there are times when information about students' achievement of key outcomes and the degree to which they compare with others is important and the approach should be Assessment *of* Learning. The issue is whether schools should be utilizing Assessment *of* Learning over and over again to such an extent that it leaves no place for other approaches to assessment. Figure 3.1 shows this traditional relationship of the approaches to one another.

Figure 3.2 shows a reconfiguration of the pyramid to suggest a different kind of balance—one that emphasizes increased attention to Assessment *for* and *as* Learning. In this scenario, Assessment *of* Learning has a role to play when decisions must be made that require summative judgments, or when teachers and students want to see the cumulative effect of their work, but this role is relatively small. The major focus is on classroom assessment that contributes to student learning, by the teacher (for learning) and by the student (as learning).

Given the history of schools as sorting institutions, the notion that assessment and learning are intimately and inextricably intertwined is revolutionary. On the surface of it, the ideas are appealing, but the fit with schools as we know them is uncomfortable and awkward. I suspect this is the dilemma that teachers have talked about when they say, "Assessment is the hardest part." They have always been caught between monitoring learning and categorizing students on the basis of their assessments, and teaching students, and they have struggled with these contradictory responsibilities. One teacher whom I interviewed recently expressed it this way:

Figure 3.1   Traditional Assessment Pyramid

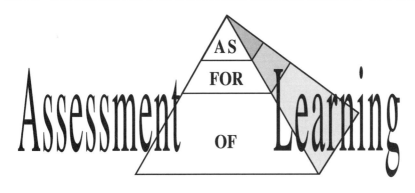

Figure 3.2   Reconfigured Assessment Pyramid

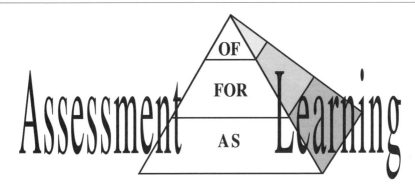

> I really struggle with assessment. I'm supposed to be teaching for mastery of learning skills. What does that have to do with common testing?

This tension, which has always existed, is exactly the reason for reconfiguring the balance. Teachers and administrators can implement this reconfiguration without creating a major upheaval in what the community, especially parents, expect of schools. Parents always have their own children's interests at heart. When they can see how Assessment *for* and *as* Learning can contribute to enhanced learning and success for their child, it may draw them into the fray as willing allies in the focus on learning.

In this reconfigured assessment environment, assessment would make up a large part of the school day, not in the form of separate tests, but as a seamless part of the learning process. And there would be tests when the decisions to be made require identification of a few individuals or groups, or when a summative description is important for students and others as a milestone or rite of passage. In the real world, these incidents are far fewer than the experience of schools would lead us to believe.

Ideas for Follow-Up

1.   Interview teachers in your school to identify the balance of purposes for assessment. What does the assessment pyramid look like?

2.   Analyze samples of assessment tasks being used in your school. Are they designed to be Assessment *of, for,* or *as* Learning?

CHAPTER 4

A Focus on Learning

The underlying idea behind this book is that learning is the imperative. Learning has always provided the advantage for human survival through difficult, even seemingly impossible times. Human beings are able to learn, unlearn, share their learning, and pass on learning to those who follow. Learning is at the core of our being, as individuals and collectively. It is the key to equipping future generations to respond and to survive in a frenetically and unpredictably changing world. And perhaps most important, *we have not even approached the limits of what can be learned.*

The challenge for educators is to apply our emerging understanding about learning to help students become the citizens for a "preferred future" where all students, not just a

> Assumption: Learning is the imperative in schools.

few, will learn. They will learn not only the foundation skills of language and mathematics, but also a whole range of "new basics," such as accessing, interpreting, and applying information; performing critical thinking and analysis; solving novel problems; making informed judgments; working independently and in groups; and discerning the appropriate course of action in ambiguous situations.

Learning is intellectual. Learning is social. Learning is emotional. It is ordered, and it is erratic. It happens by design and by chance. We all do it, and we take it for granted, even though we do not have a clear understanding of what it means or how to make the most of it.

There are a multiplicity of conceptions of the nature of learning, from something that *happens to* the learner, with knowledge as the "stuff" to fill students' waiting minds, to a view suggesting that learning is a completely unique experience of constructing reality for each

Figure 4.1   What Makes Humans Human?

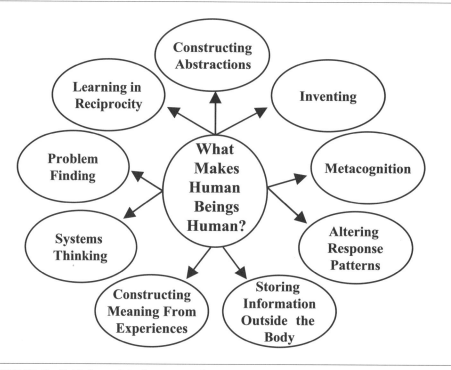

SOURCE: Stoll, Fink, and Earl (2002) (adapted from Costa, 1996).

individual. Clearly, learning is a complex and mysterious process that continues to challenge our understanding. In the past 50 years, however, we have learned a great deal that can and is being applied in classrooms. Figure 4.1, adapted from work by Costa (1996), shows the powerful and unique learning qualities that human beings have at their disposal for harnessing information and making sense of the world.

These human qualities that Costa (1996) outlined are the foundation of our ability to learn.

- *Metacognition.* Human beings can reflect on their own thinking processes. Experts describe such thinking as an internal conversation—monitoring their own understanding, predicting their performance, deciding what else they need to know, organizing and reorganizing ideas, checking for consistency between different pieces of information, and drawing analogies that help them advance their understanding.

- *Constructing abstraction.* Humans have the capacity to use language, images, and numbers as symbols to transform events into categories and patterns. These symbolic systems make it possible for people to think in abstractions and to order and reorder the world in thought.

- *Storing information outside the body.* Humans store, organize, and retrieve information in and from locations other than their bodies. From cave drawings, to books, to videodisks, external storage and retrieval systems provide access to information far beyond the limits of memory.

- *Systems thinking.* Humans are able to see patterns, congruencies, and inconsistencies while still focusing on the whole. This capacity allows them to consider many perspectives and to imagine how changing one element can have an impact on the total system.

- *Problem finding.* Not only are humans able to search for problems to solve, but they also appear to enjoy it. Humans question and sense ambiguities and anomalies in the world around them. Once there is some doubt, they look for better ways of understanding the nature of things.

- *Reciprocal learning.* Human beings are social creatures with a compulsive craving to engage with each other. They learn best in groups as they listen to one another, strive for agreement, and rethink their beliefs and understanding.

- *Inventing.* Human beings are creative and often motivated intrinsically, rather than extrinsically, to work on tasks because of the challenge. They constantly strive for greater fluency, elaboration, novelty, parsimony, simplicity, craftsmanship, perfection, harmony, beauty, and balance.

- *Deriving meaning from experience.* One of the most significant attributes of human beings is that they can reflect on and learn from their experiences. They can stand back, monitor activities, and modify actions or beliefs.

- *Altering response patterns.* Although a certain amount of human activity may be hard-wired, people are able to make significant conscious and deliberate choices about their behavior. They are always capable of learning and altering their responses based on new ideas or understanding.

Costa's (1996) framework accentuates the view that learning is not a static trait. It is a dynamic process that can be learned and developed as we go through the iterative process of fitting information into patterns or schema of similarities, differences, likeness, and regularities. The human mind operates by constructing something like a mental map, an internal representation allowing the individual to retrieve information efficiently and use it by making connections to other ideas. As learning progresses, learners move beyond the basic rules associated with any field until it becomes automatic, when they are comfortable in a domain, and when they begin to build their own understanding by acting, assessing what happens, reflecting, designing new strategies, and acting again. This is the "stuff" of classrooms and schools.

Although large-scale reform efforts often give the illusion that learning can be directed from outside, it is important to remember that things like centralized curriculum, testing programs, targetsetting, and inspections are all means to an end. And the end, I believe, is learning—better learning and more learning for all students.

In a recent book, *It's About Learning (And It's About Time)* (Stoll et al., 2002), several colleagues and I have described the changing nature of our knowledge about learning and how this knowledge can be channeled into new learning at all levels in education—students, teachers, leaders, schools, and educational systems. As you read this section, imagine some possible implications for assessment.

Learning for Understanding

Learning is not a passive process. Young minds are not empty of ideas and ready to receive our wisdom any more than adult minds are sponges absorbing new ideas from the air. From the earliest days, the minds of infants are active and toiling to make sense of the world around them. Over time, this sense-making activity is made up of conscious attention, organizing and reorganizing ideas, assimilating or accommodating new ideas, and constantly reshuffling and reorganizing in efforts to connect ideas into coherent patterns. Learning begins with some level of *consciousness* when someone focuses attention on it or because something about it commands attention. Once something enters consciousness, the human mind goes to work to organize it and connect it to what the mind already knows. This involves processing the information, searching for and retrieving information from memory or experience, checking the match between the new information and prior knowledge, monitoring comprehension, reorganizing ideas, and coming to decisions about what the new information means and where it fits. All of this activity happens at lightning speed; generally, the learner is completely unaware of the process. Somehow, the wealth of information existing outside a person becomes part of an individual's internal "knowing."

When the new information is largely consistent with prior ideas and beliefs, it usually combines easily with existing knowledge and reinforces the existing views. If the new information is inconsistent or in conflict with existing ideas, the learner may be required to transform his or her beliefs. When this happens, the learner experiences dissonance and disorder, and needs sustained attention and energy to keep going. This is not just a cognitive process; it is emotional, because every piece of information gets evaluated for its bearing on the self and the potential effect on the learner's environment. Even though the dissonance causes discomfort, it is essential for conceptual change and, therefore, serious learning. Learning results from these episodes of dissonance (Linn & Songer, 1991; Olsen & Bruner, 1996).

In his book *Smart Schools: From Training Memories to Educating Minds,* David Perkins (1992) makes the bold statement that we already know enough about how learning works, how teachers teach, and how to cope with diversity to do a much better job of educating. His claim comes in response to one of the most dramatic discoveries in learning research—that being able to recall and even apply concepts doesn't necessarily mean that the ideas have been understood. Most students, including the best students in the best schools, don't really understand (Gardner, 1991). All too often, children learn how to plug numbers into a formula or memorize descriptions of complex phenomena, but when they encounter the concepts in a new situation, they do not know how to use them. Material is kept in memory and drawn out (often erroneously) when it might fit. Unfortunately, students often know far more than they understand about subjects they have studied and suffer from many misconceptions or misunderstandings (Perkins & Unger, 2000).

> New insights don't happen by osmosis. They come from facing ideas that challenge the familiar ways of viewing issues.
>
> —Earl and Katz (2002)

Learning for understanding suggests a much deeper grasp of underlying ideas and concepts, not just recitation of algorithms or rules. Understanding is knowledge in action. Students who understand can take knowledge, concepts, skills, and facts and apply them in new situations where they are appropriate. Brandsford and colleagues (Brandsford, Brown, & Cocking, 1999) provide an example using Einstein's theory of relativity that should resonate for many of you. What would constitute evidence that someone understood $E = MC^2$? Reciting the equation only shows that it has been remembered; it does not show that it has been understood. Understanding involves knowledge about energy, mass, velocity of light, and mathematical notions such as "squaring." But this isn't enough. One would have to be able to use these concepts according to rules of physics, support the theory with evidence, identify the problems the theory solves and the theories it replaces, and so on. Deep understanding is having a grasp of the structure of a discipline, seeing how things are related, using the ideas in novel situations, and evaluating, even challenging, the knowledge claims embedded in the discipline.

Prior knowledge of a topic or idea provides the foundation for linking new ideas and building complex mental models, but as the Einstein example shows, knowledge in itself doesn't guarantee understanding. People need a rich base of knowledge about the subjects under consideration and a great deal of experience to become comfortable with the ideas and create the mental models that organize them.

Studies that examine differences between experts and novices have provided enormous insights into how knowledge and understanding work together (Brandsford et al., 1999). Certainly, novices possess less knowledge than experts, and less skill. But it is not merely the amount of knowledge or the number of skills that distinguishes experts from their less experienced peers. Experts also have well-honed regulatory systems that come into play when they become aware that something (facts or skills) is missing or doesn't fit. They display planning, control, and reflection in their actions. They are aware of the knowledge and skills that they possess, or are lacking, and use a range of strategies to actively implement them or acquire them (Ertmer & Newby, 1996). Novices may lack important knowledge or may have memorized a wealth of disconnected facts, without any organizing structure or concept to provide understanding or transfer to new situations. Because they do not yet have these organizers, they need rules to help them see the order of things and develop knowledge and schemata for future reference. Over time, as they become more proficient, some parts of the process no longer require conscious attention; they become automatic. When this happens, they can start to move outside rigorous adherence to the rules and begin to adapt and to make the learning their own, reflecting a unique constellation of talents and ideas. When something doesn't appear to be working, however, even experts go back to the rules as a strategy for self-monitoring and correction. Imagine a professional tennis player executing a serve. When it's working, it's an ace. When it's not, even a professional goes back to the practice court and to first principles, often with a video camera as an aid.

> The research . . . shows clearly that "usable knowledge" is not the same as a mere list of disconnected facts. Experts' knowledge is connected and organized around important concepts (e.g., Newton's second law of motion); it is "conditionalized" to specify the contexts in which it is applicable; it supports understanding and transfer (to other contexts) rather than only the ability to remember.
>
> —Brandsford et al. (1999)

Experts organize and classify their knowledge around important concepts and draw on these configurations of "usable knowledge" in their thinking because the ideas have become automatic parts of their thinking. With this kind of automaticity, experts can use the concepts in an unstructured world where there are complex interactions of multiple factors. They use metacognition and reflection to control and perfect their learning. Perhaps most important, they take personal responsibility for the outcomes of their learning, fine-tune their understanding by checking it against other information, and use self-monitoring to signal the need for a return to the rules or a search for new information.

As if it isn't complicated enough to think about making connections that stimulate "deep understanding," it is also important to remember that each individual is unique. As with all other human characteristics, learning is diverse and different for each learner. It is a function of heredity, experiences, perspectives, backgrounds, talents, interests, capacities, needs, and the unpredictable flow of any particular life. Learners have different emotional states, rates and styles of learning, stages of development, abilities, talents, feelings of efficacy, and needs. It is exactly this diversity that provides innumerable opportunities for expanding learning—first, by acknowledging differences in physiological, personal, linguistic, cultural, and social backgrounds, and second, by focusing on the common features that make all of us human. But the differences must be taken into account as well, to provide all learners with the necessary challenges and opportunities for learning and self-development.

Learning Is Hard Work

Living in dissonance and challenging "taken to be true" notions is hard work. People tend to strive for relative stability between their internal conceptions and new information and may even avoid conditions that disrupt the way they see the world. The challenge is to move beyond dissonance into productive learning. But what is it that compels people to live in the dissonance, experience the discomfort of not understanding something, and strive to integrate new knowledge, even when it requires serious adjustments to their prior beliefs? What motivates learning? Understanding how motivation works provides the key to keeping learning at the forefront and building patterns of learning that are automatic and last a lifetime.

Clearly, motivation to learn is more complicated than we thought. If learning is not primarily dependent on external rewards, what else influences it? And how does it work? According to motivational researchers, students are motivated by both success and competence. And they are influenced by their beliefs about what contributes to success. Students who believe that academic achievement is determined by fixed ability are more likely to work toward performance goals (i.e., grades) to please the teacher and appear competent. For these students, grades are the currency in school, and the exchange value of the grades is more important than the learning. Unfortunately, that means that they tend to pick easy tasks and are less likely to persist once they encounter difficulty (Stipek, 1996, cited in Shepard, 2000). Students who attribute academic success to their own efforts are more likely to adopt learning goals, which means they are motivated by an increasing sense of mastery and by the desire to become competent. When people succeed or fail, they explain their success or failure to themselves in various ways: effort, ability, task factors, or luck. Only the first of these attributions is likely to promote adaptive motivational tendencies. The student can decide to try harder and be successful. The other explanations—ability, task difficulty, or luck—are all out of the student's control. When students do not believe that they have control over their achievements, they are much less motivated to work in school.

Although motivation is an individual attribute, there are also dramatic cultural differences in the way teachers, parents, and students view the relative importance of ability and effort in their success. The relative emphasis that is given to ability and effort can have direct implications for the way people think about learning. Stevenson and Stigler (1992), in their book *The Learning Gap,* described a series of studies comparing American with Asian schools:

> In American society, learning tends to be regarded as an all-or-none process. A student who is "bright" is expected to just "get it," whereas duller students are assumed to lack the requisite ability for learning certain material. Under the "ability" model, motivation to try hard depends . . . a great deal on the individual child's assessment of whether s(he) has the ability to succeed. By contrast, the effort model, such as the Chinese and Japanese tend to hold, portrays learning as gradual and incremental, something that almost by definition must be acquired over a long period of time. (p. 102)

This difference in attitude, they believe, leads to a weakness in North American educational systems because of the pessimistic image that it offers most of our students. Stevenson and Stigler (1992) summarized their findings by saying,

> Ability models subvert learning through the effects they have on the goals that parents and teachers set for children and on

children's motivation to work hard to achieve these goals. Effort models offer a more hopeful alternative by providing a simple but effective formula for ensuring gradual change and improvement: "work hard and persist." (p. 106)

If motivation to learn is something that can be influenced, educators need to take a long, hard look at what they believe inspires students to learn.

The extent to which individuals see themselves as competent and capable has a dramatic effect on their willingness to attempt new learning (see Figure 4.2). People consciously or unconsciously ask questions such as, How uncomfortable will it make me? For how long?

When people consistently fail, they lose their motivation to learn and go to great lengths to avoid the pain of failure, the possibility of public humiliation, and additional confirmation of their incompetence. In essence, human beings deal with threat by down-shifting, turning off, and resisting engagement.

> Learning is a constructive process that occurs best when what is being learned is relevant and meaningful to the learner and when the learner is actively engaged in creating his or her own knowledge and understanding by connecting what is being learned with prior knowledge and experience.
>
> —Lambert and McCombs (1998)

Motivation also flags when someone succeeds too easily. There is no reason to continue to expend energy. Csikszentmihalyi (1990) explains that if a person has few skills and faces little challenge, he or she is apathetic, whereas if challenge is low but the skill level is higher, he or she is likely to experience boredom. When both levels of challenge and skill are high, he or she is in "flow." When people believe they are able to succeed, they are willing to try new and challenging tasks, even when such tasks are difficult. Therefore, continuous learning appears to depend on a combination of effort and obvious success. When students are in flow, as Csikszentmihalyi (1990) describes it, they are completely absorbed in the task at hand and will work hard and unflaggingly toward a goal, no matter how hard the new learning might be. The motivation for learning comes from achieving mastery of a skill or body of knowledge, and the initial passion can be the seed for higher levels of attainment.

On the other hand, if the work is boring and undemanding, or if the risk of failure and embarrassment is too high, young people quickly fill the time with activities they find more compelling, often to the chagrin of the adults around them.

Biggs and Moore (1993) talk about four broad categories of motivation, all of which can influence learning. *Extrinsic* motivation comes

Figure 4.2   Motivation as a Function of Challenge and Skill

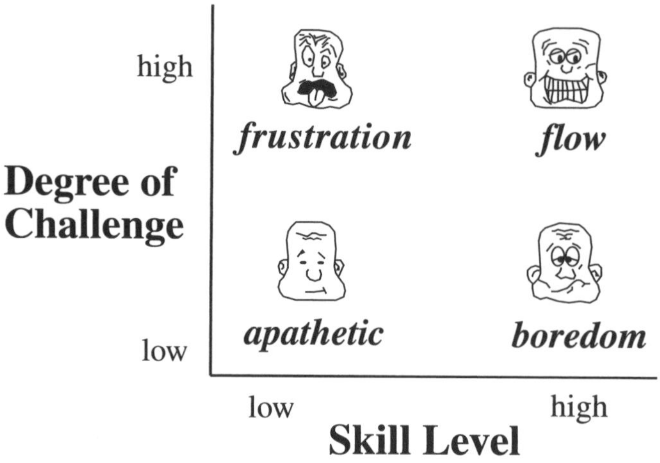

from outside and is central to surface learning. With extrinsic motivation, the task is carried out because it provides positive or negative reinforcing consequences. *Social* motivation is related to the influence of the person who formed the motive (i.e., parent, peer, or teacher) and the nature of the process (modeling, conformity, or cooperation) that he or she uses to engage the learner. *Achievement* motivation is what drives learning for the purpose of passing a test or getting a job. It is surface motivation, exemplified in actions such as rote learning, which may, nevertheless, produce academic success. *Intrinsic* motivation is internal and comes from a need to engage in learning for its own sake, with personal commitment.

For a long time, reinforcement and rewards have been considered important motivators. When initial interest in a task is low, rewards can increase the likelihood of academic engagement and performance of tasks. However, there is an interesting paradox about the nature and power of rewards when the behavior is intrinsically interesting. Extrinsic rewards have the potential to undermine performance, especially when the behaviors are ones that people are likely to do in the absence of the reward because they are inherently interested. There is a danger that when people who are highly intrinsically motivated are faced with a heavy accountability system of extrinsic rewards, they lose some of the intrinsic motivation and replace it with reinforcement from the reward. It is then very hard to return the behavior to the category of "important to do without a reward," and the behavior is likely to be less prevalent, not more.

As you can see, learning is not the exclusive purview of the intellect. It is also deeply emotional. As Daniel Goleman (1995) describes in his book *Emotional Intelligence*, thinking and rationality are the engine of our choices, but feelings and emotional intelligence help to streamline decisions by eliminating some options and highlighting others. It is the complementarity of feeling and thought that provides the balance to harmonize head and heart.

Learning, because it involves something new and unknown, inevitably triggers a range of emotions. New learning often includes a risk of failure and the possibility of discomfort and disorientation as the learner struggles to make sense of new ideas. As Goleman describes it, the body experiences an emotional hijacking, where surges in the limbic system capture the rest of the brain. This can result in a feeling of helplessness and a "down-shifting" to self-protective behaviors. It can also trigger flow, where the individual is totally and unself-consciously absorbed and engaged in the pleasure of the learning and doing (Csikszentmihalyi, 1990). Needless to say, people learn more and sustain their interest when they have experienced and are motivated by experiences of flow in their learning than when their learning is forced and the emotional response is fear and anxiety. This state of engagement is based on relaxed alertness, a combination of perceived safety and challenging learning experiences.

Learning Happens in Context

Learning doesn't take place in a vacuum, and learners are never tabula rasa (blank slates). They are not containers to be filled; rather, their minds are whirling, spiraling, dancing—connecting and challenging everything that they encounter in their social and physical environment. This process begins in tiny infants, and as they grow, they create coherent and (for them) reasonable patterns of the world around them. These beliefs about what the world is like come very early from interaction with the family and the community. Early experiential knowledge forms the fabric of children's lives and is often very resistant to change. It is the "stuff" that life has taught them. Learners test the veracity of their beliefs and their ideas (and those of their community and culture) by comparing them to the beliefs and ideas

> Learning occurs best in an environment that contains positive interpersonal relationships and interactions, comfort and order, and in which the learner feels appreciated, acknowledged, respected, and validated.
>
> —Lambert and McCombs (1998)

held by the people and the culture around them. This testing process often involves books, media, teachers, parents, and experts. Social interactions, formal and informal, are important contributors to learning and to the beliefs that people hold.

Vygotsky (1978) enhanced our understanding of learning as a social process. He argued that the capacity to learn from others is fundamental to human intelligence. With help from someone more knowledgeable or skilled, the learner is able to achieve more than he or she could achieve alone. Cooperation lies at the heart of success.

Assumption: Learning in school is driven by what teachers and students do in classrooms.

Learning in schools, in particular, takes place in a social context. The nature of this social milieu has a profound effect on how, why, and what learning occurs. Classroom and school settings can be more or less learning friendly. One Australian study found that classrooms that are personalized encourage active participation, and the use of investigative skills produces more meaning-oriented approaches to learning in the students (Dart, Burnett, & Boulton-Lewis, 1999). People may also learn in one context but fail to transfer their learning to different contexts. When a subject is taught in many different contexts, however, and includes examples demonstrating broad applicability of what is taught, people are more likely to be able to abstract what is relevant and construct their own knowledge to apply flexibly as the situation arises. Perhaps most important, the learning context can influence learners' motivation and identities. Teachers' values and beliefs influence the type of structure they create in the classroom and their responses to students. Children are astute observers of teachers and can identify differential treatment by them (Weinstein, 1998), frequently lowering the motivation of students who see themselves as less able. Through detailed case studies of individual children throughout their primary schooling, Pollard and Filer (1999) demonstrate how they are continuously shaping, maintaining, and actively evolving their pupil identities as they move from one classroom context to the next. What this means is that each child's or young person's sense of self as a pupil can be enhanced or threatened by changes over time in their relationships, structural position in the classroom, and relative success or failure. It can also be affected by their teachers' expectations, learning and teaching strategies, classroom organization, and, as you will soon see, assessment and evaluation practices.

Ideas for Follow-Up

1.   Use Figure 4.1 as an organizer for a mind map activity in which you identify things that you do (or could do) in your classroom assessment activities to capitalize on the human qualities identified by Costa.

2.   Think of something you remember learning that is now automatic for you (e.g., a sport, driving a car). What was it like when you were learning it? What helped you get good at it?

CHAPTER 5

Assessment and Learning

As I mentioned in Chapter 3, Assessment *of* Learning is still the predominant approach to assessment in most schools, and the modes of choice are tests, essays, and projects. Even when teachers use informal assessments such as questioning in class and observing students, they typically do so to make or confirm judgments about individual students, and they rarely retain the information for very long or find a way of preserving it for future consideration.

In this book, I am proposing a major and fundamental shift in the way we think about assessment. Moving to a more equal place for Assessment *for* Learning and Assessment *as* Learning in the operation of schools and classrooms is a massive undertaking, but it is possible. Although Chapter 11 is dedicated to "getting there," the first step in this process is one of understanding and considering alternative views to the ones that have dominated our culture for so long.

In this chapter, I introduce the ideas, theory, and research that have led me and others to believe that assessment can and should be a key part of learning. Why do we think that classroom assessment is so important? How can classroom assessment be linked to learning? If classroom assessment can be that powerful, how does it work?

> Never doubt that a small group of thoughtful, committed citizens can change the world; indeed, it's the only thing that ever has.
>
> —Margaret Mead

How Does Assessment Contribute to Learning?

Classroom assessment will always have an impact of some kind on students and their learning. It is the basis for decisions that teachers make about things like what to teach and to whom, what to communicate to parents, and promotion to the next grade. It is the basis for decisions that students make as well—about such things as their sense of personal accomplishment, their feelings of self-worth, and their willingness to engage in the academic work of schools. It defines consolidation of learning and affects the development of enduring learning strategies and skills. Ultimately, it influences the value that students attach to education. If assessment has this kind of impact, it deserves careful attention so that it supports learning rather than hampering it.

> Assessment that is explicitly designed to promote learning is the single most powerful tool we have for raising standards and empowering life long learning.
>
> —Assessment Reform Group (1999)

Just doing classroom assessment doesn't necessarily contribute to learning, however. Remember, most classroom assessment is summative Assessment *of* Learning. Even more child-centered approaches using performance assessments, portfolios, or records of achievement are only a small step toward using assessment that really encourages students to progress.

Researchers studying classroom assessment have found that formative assessment can contribute to learning. In 1988, the *Review of Educational Research* published a comprehensive review of literature about the impact of classroom assessment practices on students done by Terry Crooks, from New Zealand. He made a strong, research-based case that classroom assessment has both short- and long-term effects on learning. In the short term, classroom assessment can

- Focus attention on important aspects of the subject
- Give students opportunities to practice skills and consolidate learning
- Guide further instructional or learning activities.

In the medium and long term, assessment holds the possibility of

- Influencing students' motivation as learners and their perceptions of their capabilities
- Communicating and reinforcing teaching goals, including performance criteria and desired standards of performance
- Influencing students' choice of and development of learning strategies, skills, and study patterns
- Influencing students' subsequent choice of courses, activities, and careers (Crooks, 1988).

In the United States, people such as Walt Haney and George Madaus (1989), Lorrie Shepard (1989), Grant Wiggins (1989), and Rick Stiggins (1991) were proposing that we needed better assessments and that classroom assessment held the key to learning for students.

A decade later, Paul Black and Dylan Wiliam (1998), in England, synthesized evidence from more than 250 studies linking assessment and learning. The Assessment Reform Group (1999), also in England, described their finding as follows:

> The outcome was a clear and incontrovertible message: that initiatives designed to enhance effectiveness of the way assessment is used in the classroom to promote learning can raise pupil attainment. (p. 4)

This review reinforced the potential of classroom assessment. The authors indicated that classroom assessment that promotes learning

- Is embedded as an essential part of teachers' views of teaching or learning
- Involves sharing learning goals with students
- Aims to help students to know and to recognize the standards they are aiming for
- Involves students in self-assessment
- Provides feedback which leads to students recognizing their next steps and how to take them
- Is underpinned by confidence that every student can improve
- Involves both teachers and pupils reflecting on assessment data. (Assessment Reform Group, 1999, p. 7)

Black and Wiliam (1998) also identified several inhibiting factors:

- Teachers' tendency to assess quantity of work and presentation, rather than quality of learning
- Greater attention given to marking and grading, much of it tending to lower the self-esteem of students, rather than to providing advice for improvement
- A strong emphasis on comparing students with each other, which demoralizes the less successful students
- Teachers' feedback to students serving social and managerial purposes rather than helping them to learn more effectively
- Teachers not knowing enough about their students' learning needs

Using assessment practices to add to learning is clearly a complex undertaking. It means paying attention to student engagement and motivation. It means making connections, referring to progressions of learning and to learning goals, and planning relationships and linkages between instruction and assessment. It means thinking about students individually as well as collectively. It means reinforcing important ideas, identifying gaps or misconceptions, and building on students' beliefs to steer them toward clear understanding.

This Is Not Just About Assessment

It is obvious that assessment is not everything. But it should also be clear that teaching without assessment as an integral part of the process is also not enough. Rethinking assessment is one small part of boosting the quality of teaching and learning in schools. Classrooms where assessment is viewed as an integral part of learning are very different from other classrooms. Teachers who are working with a new view of assessment as part of learning are finding that it isn't possible to change assessment and leave everything else the same. When assessment changes, so does teaching, so does classroom organization, and so does interaction with students and parents.

The biggest change that I can foresee in changing the balance of the links between assessment and instruction is a fundamental power shift. Assessment as learning requires the involvement of both students and parents. It is not a private activity for teachers, and certainly not a process that governments can control. It is a personal, iterative, and evolving conversation in which teachers are assessing and describing performance in ways that are useful to others, who will make their own decisions about what to do next.

> Assumption: Assessment and learning are intimately intertwined and often indistinguishable from one another.

In the following chapters, I have used examples from both colleagues and graduate students with whom I have worked that highlight occasions when assessment was designed to enhance students' learning. Although I have organized the material into separate chapters, using the examples to highlight particular ideas, each of them offers a range of insights into the role of assessment. They all represent integrated, whole, and thoughtfully prepared approaches to assessment that have learning as the goal. Taken together, they give a range of examples of what good assessment looks like.

Ideas for Follow-Up

1. What have you read in this chapter that reinforces beliefs that you hold already? What has challenged your beliefs?

2. What are the barriers in schools to using assessment as learning?

CHAPTER 6

Using Assessment to Identify What Students Believe to Be True

As I described in Chapter 4, learning is an interactive process by which learners try to make sense of new information and integrate it into what they already know. Students are always thinking, and they are either challenging or reinforcing their thinking on a moment-by-moment basis. Before teachers can plan for targeted teaching and classroom activities, they need to have a sense of what it is that students are thinking. What is it that they believe to be true? This process involves much more than, "Do they have the right or wrong answer?" It means making students' thinking visible and understanding the images and patterns that they have constructed in order to make sense of the world from their perspective.

The choice of assessment task is a critical feature if it is going to help the teacher see the students' thinking. It has to provide the opportunity for the students to deploy the knowledge and skills that the teacher is trying to investigate, from a variety of points of view. Teachers need detailed images so that they can foresee the possible responses of the students, a feat of imaginative prediction that demands considerable expertise (Black, 1998).

"The Case of the Pool Table"

At the beginning of the school year, a middle school mathematics teacher uses a series of games that he has devised to give him insights into his students' knowledge and depth of understanding of concepts in the mathematics curriculum. One of these games uses a modified pool table to help him ascertain the students' conceptions of algebraic relationships, either

Figure 6.1   The Pool Table Task

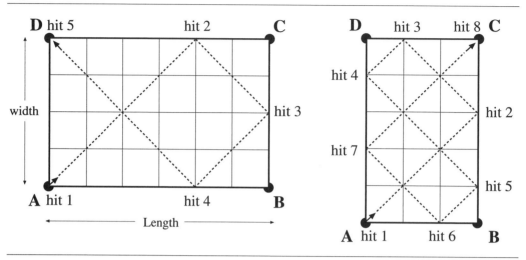

formally or intuitively. Students in a Grade 7/8 mathematics class were given a graphic of a four-pocket pool table (see Figure 6.1).[1]

The students were told that the ball always leaves Pocket A at a 45° angle, rebounds off a wall at an equal angle to that at which the wall was struck, and continues until it ends up in a pocket. Students counted the number of squares through which the ball passed, as well as the number of hits the ball made, the first and last hit being the starting and finishing pockets. They experimented with tables of various dimensions and recorded their observations on a chart (see Table 6.1).

As the students gathered data (with many more data combinations than I have included in the table), they began to make predictions about the number of hits, the number of squares, and the destination of the ball, based on the patterns that they observed. Some moved to general statements of relationships, such as, "You can tell the number of hits by adding the width and the length together and dividing by their greatest common factor," or "The number of squares that the ball goes through is always the lowest common multiple of the width and

Table 6.1   Recordkeeping of Hits (Pool Table Task)

Length	Width	Number of Hits	Number of Squares
6	4	5	12
3	5	8	15
5	4		
3	2		
8	4		

the length." Other students continued to count to reach the answers without seeing the relationships that existed.

During this task, the teacher wandered around the room observing and noting the thinking that was occurring for individual students. He stopped and asked questions, not about the answers that they were recording but about the process that they were using. He prompted students to think about the patterns and to take a chance at making predictions. All the while, he was making notes on a scratch pad that contained the names of the students and blank fields for writing his observations. From this information, he decided how to proceed in teaching the next series of lessons and how to group the students for the various instructional elements to come. For some, the work progressed quickly to an introduction of formal notation of an algebraic equation to symbolize the general patterns that they had identified. For others, the teacher used a number of patterning exercises to help them see the patterns that arose and formulate them in concrete ways. He was conscious of the importance of moving from concrete experience and direct consciousness of the phenomenon to the more abstract representation. The pool table task gave him a window into the students' thinking and a starting place for planning instruction, resources, grouping, timing, and pacing. When he moves on to another concept, all of these are likely to change. Once again, he needed to see what the students see, what they think, and what they understand before he could decide what he was going to do.

Start With What Students Believe to Be True

Students come to school with preconceptions about the way the world works. If their initial understanding is not engaged, they may fail to grasp new concepts and information or may memorize material for the immediate purposes (e.g., the test) but revert to their preconceptions outside the classroom. Often, these preconceptions include stereotypes and simplifications. Nevertheless, they have a profound effect on the integration of new concepts and information. Unless teachers really figure out what students believe is true and confront their notions about the world, they will continue to hold onto many misconceptions, some of which will make it impossible for them ever to truly understand more complex phenomena that build on this prior knowledge.

Assessment is the window into students' preconceptions, a way of finding out not just what they know, but what they believe to be true. Teachers need an accurate grasp of what students (individually and collectively) believe to be true in order to use this knowledge as a starting point for teaching, all the while monitoring their changing conceptions and altering teaching to fit. Errors are the window into students' learning. Understanding students' incomplete understandings, false beliefs, misconceptions, and naïve interpretations of concepts gives teachers some clues for creating conditions for learning. These preconceptions must be addressed before any new learning can take place, particularly if they are inconsistent with the new knowledge and the learner must accommodate to the new information by changing beliefs. Unless the teacher can figure out what students believe and what would convince them that their ideas are flawed or simplistic, students will continue to hold on to their preconceptions.

Teachers need constant information about what students know and the strategies being used to process and comprehend new concepts. By embedding diagnostic assessment in instructional activities, teachers can preserve the integrity of assessment tasks and protect instructional time that would otherwise be diverted (Shepard, 1989). They can also get closer to the images that students hold.

"The Case of the Bog"

In a local school district, all students in Grade 8 participated in a writing assessment based on a real decision by the city to build a new school on fragile land. Table 6.2 shows the task for the students.

The district used the rubric in Table 6.3 to assess the students' performance. This typical scoring strategy satisfied the district's accountability needs and also provided district curriculum consultants and teachers with insights about the dimensions of written language that needed attention in elementary schools.

One teacher, who happened also to be a talented graduate student, took the process further. She believes that teachers need to unpack the process of writing in order to help their students move forward. For her, the information in this rubric was useful, but it wasn't enough to allow her to understand what students needed next. She used the Cognitive Domain of the Taxonomy of Educational Objectives (Gronlund, 2000) and Core Thinking Skills (Marzano et al., 1988) to devise a mechanism for considering the students' responses in relation to their learning (and teaching) needs. Table 6.4 is the combined organizer that she created.

By using this framework for the analysis, she could gain additional insights into how the students are thinking and what teachers can do to help them improve. Imagine a group of teachers receiving student papers from the assessment and collectively reviewing those papers as a way of making detailed diagnostic notes about each student as a

Table 6.2   The Bog Task

Background Information	Recently, the City of XXX and the District School Board have been debating a proposal for the construction of a new elementary school, Sherwood Mills Public School. The proposed school site is adjacent to the XXX Bog, which has been the habitat of many wetland creatures for the past century. The controversy centers on the need for the new school and the preservation of the wetlands. You will be asked to do the following:
Description of the Task	• Collect data about both the conditions of the XXX Bog and the need for a community school in that area. • Identify the main problems. • Form an opinion as to whether or not the school board should go ahead with the construction of the Sherwood Mills School. • Substantiate your opinion by creating diagrams, graphs, or maps to support your point of view. Include personal experiences to enrich your argument. • Make recommendations about the building proposal. Validate your answer. • Draft an article that includes your opinion, your supporting reasons, and your recommendations regarding the proposed building. • Refine your draft, and make sure to include a powerful concluding statement of your point of view.

starting point for planning the next term and ensuring that students received the assistance that they needed. I have included just one student paper (with a pseudonym, of course) to illustrate what they can learn. Jonathon's report is displayed in Table 6.5.

In a joint planning session, a group of teachers analyzed Jonathon's responses to the questions and his final report using the District Writing Scales and the more detailed consideration of his thinking (see Table 6.6).

Table 6.7 gives their observations of gaps based on the framework described above.

On the basis of their analysis, the teachers made a number of suggestions for Jonathon's teacher. These are displayed in Table 6.8.

(Text continues on page 66)

Table 6.3 District Writing Rubric

Grade 8 Performance Assessment . . . the Bog

Trait/Level	1	2	3	4
Voice	• Not successful in capturing attention • Text lacks sincerity • Little or no evidence of tone	• Not very successful in capturing and maintaining attention • Text not very convincing and sincere • Minimal tone	• Fairly successful in capturing attention • Text somewhat convincing and sincere • Tone is fairly effective, i.e., creates mood	• Successful in capturing and maintaining attention • Text convincing and sincere • Tone effective, i.e., creates mood
Organization	• Minimal logical plan and sequence interferes with comprehension • No clear intro and/or conclusion • Transitions are omitted • Paragraphs: no evidence	• Overall logical plan and sequence present but weak • Intro and/or conclusion weak • Transitions are not always used • Paragraphs are sparse	• Adequate overall logical plan and sequence • Intro and conclusion are adequate and related • Transitions are used where needed • Paragraphs may not appear throughout entire text	• Very good overall logical plan and sequence • Intro and conclusion are strong and effective • Transitions are used appropriately and skillfully • Paragraphs at appropriate times
Ideas & Content	• Unclear main idea/purpose • Text wanders • Simplistic • Inaccuracies in info	• Main idea/purpose recognizable • Focus somewhat flawed • Predictable	• Main idea/purpose reasonably clear • Text shows focus, some lapses • Fairly interesting	• Very clear main idea/purpose • Text focused • Interesting, original, insightful

(Continued)

Table 6.3 (Continued)

Grade 8 Performance Assessment . . . the Bog

Trait/Level	1	2	3	4
(Ideas & Content, continued)	• Poorly blended from source	• Supporting details repetitive, unrelated • Not well blended from source	• Supporting details fairly accurate • Fairly well blended from source	• Supporting details accurate • Well blended from source
Conventions	• Weak command of grade-appropriate conventions • Minimal command of advanced conventions	• Fair command of grade-appropriate conventions • Inconsistent command of advanced conventions	• Good command of grade-appropriate conventions • Fair command of advanced conventions	• Excellent command of grade-appropriate conventions • Good command of advanced conventions
Effective Use of Language	• Many lapses in fluency • No variation in sentence length/structure • Word choice is limited • Figurative language rarely used	• Some lapses in fluency • Little variation in sentence length/structure • Word choice somewhat limited • Figurative language used occasionally	• Fairly fluent, smooth, and natural • Some sentences vary in length/structure • Word choice is generally appropriate • Figurative language used fairly successfully	• Fluent, smooth, and natural • Sentences vary in length/structure • Word choice is appropriate • Figurative language used successfully

Table 6.4   Links Between the Bog Task and the Cognitive Domain of the Taxonomy of Educational Objectives (Gronlund, 2000) and the Core Thinking Skills (Marzano et al., 1988)

Question on the Bog Task	Cognitive Domain Categories (Gronlund, 2000) Required for This Question	Core Thinking Skills (Marzano et al., 1988) Required for This Question
1. Collect data about both the conditions of the XXX Bog and the need for a community school in that area.	Knowledge: Remembering previously learned material • Recall of information pertinent to environmental issues (including appropriate vocabulary) • Able to identify, define, describe facts pertinent to environmental issues Comprehension: Grasps the meaning of material • Identification of the main problem • Shows comprehension of facts and principles by summarizing, sequencing, generalizing, inferring, explaining, and extending facts presented in reading materials and discussions	Information gathering: Obtaining information through observation and formulating questions by clarifying issues and meaning through inquiry • Remembering: activities and strategies used to retrieve pertinent information • Activating prior knowledge regarding environmental and/or wetland issues Organizing skills: Used to arrange information so that it can be understood or presented effectively • Comparing and identifying similarities and differences, and classifying this information so that it makes sense and student can make personal links with information
2. Identify the main problem	Comprehension: Grasps the meaning of material • Shows comprehension of facts and principles by paraphrasing, predicting, and inferring • Can estimate future consequences implied in the reading material, data, websites, etc.	Analyzing skills: Clarifying existing information by examining parts and relationships • Identifying the key components regarding the issue of building on an environmentally sensitive piece of land vs. building a community school

(Continued)

Table 6.4 *(Continued)*

Question on the Bog Task	Cognitive Domain Categories (Gronlund, 2000) Required for This Question	Core Thinking Skills (Marzano et al., 1988) Required for This Question
		• Identify main ideas Focusing skills: Defining problems in order to clarify puzzling situations • What is the statement of the problem? • Who has the problem? What makes it a problem? • Give examples
3. and 4. Form an opinion about whether or not XXX District School Board should go ahead with the construction of Sherwood Mills School. Substantiate your opinion through the use of diagrams, graphs, or maps to support your point of view. Include personal experiences to enrich your argument.	Application: Use learned material in new and concrete situations • Applies concepts and principles to new situations • Makes predictions about cause and effect Analysis: Break down material into its component parts so that its organizational structure becomes apparent • Recognizes logical fallacies in reasoning • Distinguishes between facts and fiction • Evaluates the relevance of available information and/or data Synthesis: Put parts together to create a new whole • Draws conclusions through gathering information from varied and reliable sources	Analyzing skills: Clarifying existing information by examining parts and relationships • Identify relationships and patterns from discussions, key articles, primary and secondary sources Generating and integrating skills: Use of prior knowledge to add information beyond primary and secondary sources • Experiential and/or personal links • Makes inferences due to inductive (making generalizations and logical statements based on observation or analysis of various cases) or deductive reasoning (ability to extend an existing principle or idea in a logical manner)

(Continued)

Table 6.4 *(Continued)*

Question on the Bog Task	Cognitive Domain Categories (Gronlund, 2000) Required for This Question	Core Thinking Skills (Marzano et al., 1988) Required for This Question
	• Integrates learning from different constructs into a plan for solving a problem	• Anticipation of an outcome (predicting) based upon prior knowledge, discussions in class, reading materials, etc. • Adding details, explanations, examples, or other relevant information to support and/or improve understanding (elaboration) . . . indicates that student is able to relate the new information to prior experiences and/or knowledge
5. Think of any recommendations that you would make about this building proposal. Validate your answer.	Synthesis: Put parts together to create a new whole, with an emphasis on the creation of new patterns or structures • Draws conclusions through gathering information from varied and reliable sources • Integrates learning from different constructs into a plan for solving a problem • Categorizes, compiles, reconstructs, relates, reorganizes, revises, rewrites, or summarizes information pertinent to the topic and/or opinion Evaluation: Judge the value of materials for a given purpose, with the	Analyzing skills: Clarifying existing information by examining parts and relationships Integrating skills: Ability to put together the relevant pieces of a solution • New information and prior knowledge connected to make meaningful connections Evaluation skills: Being able to assess the reasonableness and quality of ideas • Verification of ideas; ability to confirm or prove the truth of an idea based upon reliable primary sources of information

(Continued)

Table 6.4 *(Continued)*

Question on the Bog Task	*Cognitive Domain Categories (Gronlund, 2000) Required for This Question*	*Core Thinking Skills (Marzano et al., 1988) Required for This Question*
	judgments determined by a set of criteria (either predetermined or gathered independently) • Appraises, compares, concludes, contrasts, describes, discriminates, interprets, or justifies pertinent information to form an opinion with validating evidence	
6. Draft an article that includes your opinion, your supporting reasons, and your recommendations regarding the proposed building of Sherwood Mills School.	Synthesis: Put parts together to create a new whole, with an emphasis on the creation of new patterns or structures • Draws conclusions through gathering information from varied and reliable sources • Integrates learning from different constructs into a plan for solving a problem • Categorizes, compiles, reconstructs, relates, reorganizes, revises, rewrites, or summarizes information pertinent to the topic and/or opinion Evaluation: Judge the value of materials for a given purpose, with the judgments determined by a set of criteria (either	Integrating skills: Ability to put together the relevant pieces of a solution Evaluation skills: Being able to assess the reasonableness and quality of ideas • Establishing criteria … being able to set standards for judging the value or logic of ideas • Checking the accuracy of facts through several reliable sources Integrating skills: Ability to put together the relevant pieces of a solution • Restructuring; bringing in new information that might challenge old beliefs, concepts . . . student actively modifies, extends, recognizes that previously held beliefs might be flawed or valid

(Continued)

Table 6.4 *(Continued)*

Question on the Bog Task	Cognitive Domain Categories (Gronlund, 2000) Required for This Question	Core Thinking Skills (Marzano et al., 1988) Required for This Question
	predetermined or gathered independently)	
	• Appraises, compares, concludes, contrasts, describes, discriminates, interprets, or justifies pertinent information to form an opinion with validating evidence	
7. Refine your draft and be sure to include a powerful concluding statement pertaining to your point of view.	Synthesis: Put parts together to create a new whole, with an emphasis on the creation of new patterns or structures • Draws conclusions through gathering information from varied and reliable sources • Integrates learning from different constructs into a plan for solving a problem • Categorizes, compiles, reconstructs, relates, reorganizes, revises, rewrites, or summarizes information pertinent to the topic and/or opinion	Integrating skills: Ability to put together the relevant pieces of a solution • Ability to summarize information

SOURCE: Created by Mary Lou McKinley, doctoral student, OISE/UT, as part of her thesis, "Using the Analysis of a Performance-Based Writing Task to Address the Gaps in Student Learning and to Suggest Teaching Strategies for Teachers of Young Adolescents."

Table 6.5   Jonathon's Report

Final Draft Of Article   *April 9th 1999*

The city of _____, and the _____
District School Board, have been debating
the proposal of a new elementary school.
The elementary school's site is to be on
the _____ wetlands site, which is
home to very rare, flora and fauna, and
has been for the past century. This decision
will be based on the need for the new ___
school, and the preservation of the _____
___ wetlands.

I am strongly against the proposal
to build this new school where the
wetlands stand. The bog should be preserve
d for natural history. It holds quiet a bit
of geological history. It Carbondates to a
melting glacier some 12,000 years ago.
Also, it is home for a lot of very rare
flora and fauna, which cannot be found
in any other peace in Ontario and
___

The _____ wetlands existed from
the time of mammoth's and mastadons,
with being the only _____ location
for over 21 native plants and other species,
it is like an outdoor museum and it
is educational for present and future
generations. Also it is a "priceless legacy".
The _____ wetlands is a high
quality habitat and one of only two
provincially signifigant wetlands in
the city of _____.

The wetlands are signifigant due to the
rarity in it's region. Proof of it's signifiga-
nce is that it is the only place in
_____ which has gooseberry bushes,
Tamaracks and mud peat. It is also
home to the Northern Harrier and the
Short-eared Owl.

(Continued)

Table 6.5 (*Continued*)

The bog is 12,000 years old, Paul Mayort, a botany at _____ College, says to have "the mud to prove it". James Bradley, an Enviroment minister, proposed that it could be a "three way participation" which would result to preserving the wetlands and the buffer zone. Gary Gallon, who is an assitant of James Bradley, says the cost of bringing property into public hands, would be alot less than the original cost of $54 million dollars.

Dr. McAndrew's, who is a proffesor of botany and geology, and the Curator of botany for the Royal Ontario Museum, says that a lot of questions can be answered by the study of the wetlands. Beth Bremner and Herb Ruch say that the wetlands are "unbelievably unique", they also said that "they benefit to science, schools and public is truly obvious".

The CVCA want the rare flora and fauna to be re-examined and re-evaluated. The citizen's Commitee recommend a "mediator". Local politicians should wist the bog before making a final decision. There should be a re-evaluation based on information from a botanist. It could go to the OMB for final agreement seeing as it is taking over 10 years to make a decision. Vocal support from the community could make a difference, Arranging a land Swap could work out as well.

The _____ wetlands should be preserved for educational Reasons. It is very interesting to have all the rare flora and fauna to learn about, and we need some kind of natural resource in our city, rather than buildings and what not.

Table 6.6   Jonathon's Scores and the Rationale Using the District Writing Scale

XXX District Writing Scales and Student's Score	*Rationale for Score*	*Examples From Student's Paper*
Voice 2+	• Fairly successful in capturing attention • Attempt made to persuade, but text is very routine & not convincing • Minimal level of tone is evident . . . only slightly effective in evoking reader response (e.g., increase in knowledge, understanding, insight, opinion/ attitude change)	"I am strongly against the proposal for a new school where the wetlands stand. The bog should be preserved for natural history. It holds quiet a bit of geological history . . . home for rare flora and fauna . . ."
Organization 2+	• Paragraphs do appear throughout text but occasionally run together or begin in the wrong places • Transitions not evident • Some evidence of structure (rambles at times) • Intro & conclusion recognizable but weak & not entirely related • Intro is simply a reorganization of the original question	"The city of XXX, and the XXX District School Board, have been debating the proposal of a new elementary school. . . . decision will be based on the need for a new school, and the preservation of the XXX wetlands." (intro) "The XXX wetlands should be preserved for educational reasons. It is very interesting to have all the flora and fauna . . . rather than buildings and what not."
Ideas and Content 2	• Some facts presented but argument not focused • Writer generally stays on topic but does not develop a clear theme	"I am strongly against the proposal to build this new school . . . Paul Maycoct, a botany at XXX College, says to have 'the mud to prove

(Continued)

Table 6.6 (*Continued*)

XXX District Writing Scales and Student's Score	Rationale for Score	Examples From Student's Paper
	• Paper states opinion but does not expand or give reasons to support the opinion nor develop the opinion with further explanation (personal experiences and/or readings) • Facts presented in isolation . . . not always related to stated opinion • Does not contain reference to opposite point of view • Paper includes numerous pieces of information from assigned reading materials but not well blended from sources • Attempt made to relate some of the information, but relationship not clearly established because ideas are incomplete and underdeveloped (amount of explanation is limited)	it.' James Bradley, an Environment minister, proposed that it could be a 'three way participation' which would result in preserving the wetland and the buffer zone . . ." "Beth Bremmer and Herb Ruch say that the wetland are 'unbelievably unique,' they also said that 'they benefit to science, schools and publish is truly obvious.'"
Conventions 3-	• Fairly good command of grade-appropriate spelling, punctuation, and grammar conventions (a bit of difficulty with homonyms) • Some inconsistency of more advanced conventions—	"The elementary school's site . . . holds quiet a bit of geological history."

(*Continued*)

Table 6.6 (*Continued*)

XXX District Writing Scales and Student's Score	Rationale for Score	Examples From Student's Paper
	e.g., correct use of the possessive; using a wide variety of subordinate clauses; etc. • Minimal-to-moderate revision/correction of conventions required	
Effective Use of Language *2*	• Text is fairly smooth but sometimes tends to show lapses in fluency • Vocabulary & choice of words directly from reading materials but sometimes used awkwardly and/or inappropriately when transferred to own work	"The CVCV want the rare flora and fauna to be re-examined and re-evaluation. The citizen's committee recommend a 'mediator.' Local politicians should visit the bog before making a final decision. There should be a re-evaluation based on information from a botanist. It could go to the OMB for final agreement seeing as it is taking over 10 years to make a decision. Vocal support from the community could make a difference. Arranging a land swap could work out as well . . ."

Table 6.7   Gaps Identified Based on Detailed Analysis of "The Bog" Task for Jonathon Smith

---

Gaps in Student Learning . . . Derived From the Criterion-Referenced Scale

Organization

- Some evidence of structure (rambles at times)
- Intro & conclusion recognizable but weak & not entirely related
- Intro is simply a reorganization of the original question

Ideas and Content

- Some facts presented but argument not focused
- Writer generally stays on topic but does not develop a clear theme
- Paper states opinion but does not expand or give reasons to support the opinion nor develop the opinion with further explanation (personal experiences and/or readings)
- Facts presented in isolation . . . not always related to stated opinion
- Does not contain reference to opposite point of view
- Paper includes numerous pieces of information from assigned reading materials but not well blended from sources
- Attempt made to relate some of the information, but relationship not clearly established because ideas are incomplete and underdeveloped (amount of explanation is limited)

Effective Use of Language

- Text is fairly smooth but sometimes tends to show lapses in fluency
- Vocabulary & choice of words directly from reading materials but sometimes used awkwardly and/or inappropriately when transferred to own work

Gaps in Student Learning . . . Links to the Bog Task

- Difficulties in collecting information with regards to the issues of preserving a unique environmental area and the need for building a school in a high growth area
- Question as to whether there are gaps in student's understanding of wetlands, environmental issues, etc. (prior knowledge)
- Appeared to have difficulties in identifying main problem
- Stated an opinion . . . supported this opinion with random statement from the readings provided . . . no links to personal experiences
- Opinion not substantiated
- No recommendations given . . . references to reading materials but no specific recommendations given as to why building on the wetlands should not be supported

---

(Continued)

Table 6.7 (*Continued*)

Gaps in Student Learning . . . Links to Cognitive Domain & Core Thinking Skills (Gronlund, 2000; Marzano et al., 1988)

- Difficulties in recalling, explaining, extending facts pertaining to environmental issues . . . no experiential or personal links (knowledge, comprehension, Gronlund, 2000; information gathering, organizing skills, Marzano et al., 1988)
- Difficulties in grasping the meaning of the materials presented and blending the sources as supporting evidence in order to identify the main problem (comprehension, Gronlund, 2000; analyzing skills, focusing skills, Marzano et al., 1988)
- Stated a definite opinion but appeared to have difficulties in supporting opinion from available sources . . . facts presented in isolation and not well blended from sources (analyzing skills, generating and integrating skills, Marzano et al., 1988; analysis, Gronlund, 2000)
- Difficulties in identifying relationships and patterns from discussions and key articles (application, Gronlund, 2000; generating and integrating skills, Marzano et al., 1988)
- Difficulties in putting together relevant information (prior knowledge and new information) to make meaningful connections (evaluation and synthesis, Gronlund, 2000; analyzing skills, evaluation skills, integrating skills, Marzano et al., 1988)

Table 6.8   Suggestions for Next Steps in Instruction With Jonathon

- Activation of prior knowledge using a graphic organizer (Know, Want to Know, Learned) to establish what the student knows or believes to be true
- Instruction on how to connect prior knowledge to new information . . . right-angled thinking
- Identification of critical terms and phrases used in a variety of different situations with emphasis on those terms that are pertinent to the topic being discussed—for example, a "naturally preserved, historical site"— through explicit teaching during discussion of reading materials
- Instruction about how to use pertinent facts to support a stated opinion. Teaching that facts

  – Are specific to the informational content
  – Convey information about issues pertaining to people, places
  – Relate to the argument

- Instruction in how to use cause/effect sequences to consolidate students' understanding about how fragile an ecosystem can be and the impact of changing the natural habitat

Once again, in this example, assessment, curriculum targets, planning, and instruction are seamless. The process is dynamic, and the teachers move from one to the next effortlessly, with a focus on identifying what they know already, what they need to know, and what his teacher can do to support Jonathon's learning.

Ideas for Follow-Up

Analyze assessment tasks that you use already to identify the prerequisite learnings embedded in the tasks. Look at student papers to identify the places where they have misconceptions or lack the prerequisite knowledge to do the task. What instructional strategies could you use to scaffold their learning?

Note

1. This task was first described in Katz (1999).

CHAPTER 7

Using Assessment to Motivate Learning

Motivation has always been a central factor in learning, as I described in Chapter 4. Simply put, motivation affects the amount of time and energy students are willing to devote to any task. Much of what we currently know about motivation to learn, however, is contrary to the folk wisdom of the past. Our view of motivation has been heavily influenced by the behaviorist psychology of the 1960s and 1970s. This theory describes how schedules of rewards and punishments lead to behavior being either reinforced or extinguished. In schools, this theory has been translated into practices of encouraging academically productive behavior with rewards and eliminating academically nonproductive behavior through punishment. This theory is deeply embedded in the way classrooms operate and has become almost an unquestioned "truth." Assessment has been the mechanism for doling out rewards and punishments in the form of grades (Stiggins, 2001). Marks have been cast as the ultimate motivator, but researchers have found that the relationship between marks and motivation is neither simple nor predictable. Marks have been found to be motivating for some students and demotivating for others (Stiggins, 1997). Students who generally do well often will be motivated by the likelihood of success and praise that accompanies doing well again. Students who typically do not do well may choose to avoid the likelihood of a failure experience by devaluing the assessment process and even devaluing school. What could be worse than failing a test? My guess would be working hard to pass

> The assessments that drive student learning and academic self-worth are those used in classrooms.
>
> —Stiggins (1990)

and still failing the test. If the student doesn't exert any effort, he or she can at least save face.

Assessment That Motivates

Motivation is essential for the hard work of learning. Even when students find the content interesting and the activity enjoyable, learning requires sustained concentration and effort. The cognitive demand of any new learning is a cost that has to be offset. Assessment can be a motivator, not through rewards or punishment, but by stimulating the intrinsic interest of students and providing them with the direction and confidence that they need to take the risk. When they don't have the tools or the capacities to reach the goals, the students have fallen through thin ice; without the strength to kick themselves out, they simply hang on with their fingertips, waiting to be rescued. Increasing capacity and fostering learning need to build both confidence and competence through early victories and a sense that the vision is doable in increments (Wiggins, 1998). Assessment can contribute to this process and enhance motivation by being relevant, appealing to students' imagination, and providing the scaffolding that they need to genuinely succeed.

Relevant Assessment

When assessment capitalizes on students' interests, enthusiasm, and talents and provides images of the world that lies ahead of them, it is much more likely to engage and inspire them so that the learning is itself the motivator. By making connections between curriculum, instruction, assessment, and students' daily lives—whether through looking at today's parallels for King Lear's behavior or comparing Mozart's life with that of a current popular composer—teachers can engage students and draw them into the learning that assessment encompasses. Assessment does not stand apart; rather, it is interwoven with teaching and learning to make connections for students, reinforcing what they know and challenging their thinking.

Imaginative Assessment

Children have vivid imaginations that allow them to see many possibilities in their minds that aren't available to them in real life. Assessment that is open-ended and allows for a range of solutions and approaches can capitalize on this natural interest and passion to engage students in reasoning critically, solving complex problems, and applying their knowledge in making novel connections between disparate things or seeing things in ways that might be missed otherwise. As less and less of what we thought was known remains stable and unchallenged, imagination may well be a critical faculty for students as they confront the world as it really is—a whole series of messy, seemingly insoluble problems to unravel, explore, and try to solve.

Assessment That Scaffolds Learning

Students are very aware that they are likely to face challenges and the unknown in their futures. They need to be confident that they can handle whatever they encounter. And they learn best when they are in a context that provides moderate challenge. When the task is too difficult, students may feel threatened and become self-protective. When the task is too simple, students may coast into inattention and boredom (Jensen, 1998). A task is appropriately challenging when students are expected to risk and move into the unknown, but they know how to get started and have support for reaching the new level of learning. This is what Vygotsky (1930/1978) called the "zone of proximal development"—that zone of competence that learners can navigate with support and that they are able to negotiate successfully with reasonable effort. In this zone, students get stuck but have the skills to consider various options and get themselves unstuck.

Assessment can be the vehicle that keeps new learning from being so obscure, difficult, or complicated that most students lose interest or find it impenetrable. Motivation is enhanced when errors and mistakes are treated as a normal part of learning, with timely feedback and a chance to rethink and redo the work, and when assessment is designed to provide students with access to their progress and allows them to stay engaged with the task. When assessment is designed to give students and teachers insight into what they are able to do independently as well as with guidance, students are empowered to seek help and the teacher is able to provide assistance at the point of learning, not at the end of instruction. When teachers intervene during learning, they can provide opportunities to see, imitate, and try out complex skills under their guidance. This kind of assessment has to occur in the middle of teaching and learning. It can (and should be) idiosyncratic and targeted. Why? Because it creates the perfect opportunity for teachers to teach exactly what students need to know and to provide focused feedback to move their learning forward. Sometimes, it even fosters flow—the kind of engagement in a task that is so focused and so absorbing that everything else disappears (Csikszentmihalyi, 1990).

"The Case of *Othello*"

To the chagrin of most English teachers, Shakespeare's plays are often viewed by students as ancient and boring, without any relevance for their lives. Making Shakespeare come alive for students is a perennial challenge. In this vignette, a teacher of gifted adolescents uses assessment as a mechanism to draw the students into *Othello* while also challenging their analytic skills and using the assessment to gauge both individual and collective skills of comprehension and analysis of characters during the reading of the play. The task is described in Table 7.1, the assignment handout for the students.

This task was explicitly designed to engage the students in thoughtful attention to various characters, with some personal investment in getting to know them well. The teacher preselected characters and scenes to ensure that all characters were discussed as they developed throughout the play. On a more practical note, he was also able to schedule the students' presentations and individual preconferences. The assignment was not a trivial undertaking and required considerable advance instruction and practice so that the students were ready to tackle it. They had already studied plays and how they are structured, the sociopolitical structures and cultural values of the Elizabethan and Jacobean periods, and how literary terminology and literary devices work to create vivid images and lead the audience. The teacher had also provided many organizers for making oral presentations and supporting their comments.

Although the complete *Othello* unit addressed more than character revelation, this assessment process, designed to motivate and promote learning, gave the teacher access to the thinking and understanding of his students individually and collectively. The conferences, coupled with the teacher's ongoing observation and questioning in class, offered tremendous scope for altering the pace, reviewing or reteaching concepts, solving problems collectively, or doing whatever seemed appropriate given the group's perception of need.

The rubric that the teacher and students used following the initial conference is included in Table 7.2. Although rubrics come up later in Chapter 9, please note that this one has detailed descriptors of the "look fors" in this assignment as a foundation for discussion and clarification. There is no suggestion that the teacher intends to use the rubric for marking or grading the assignment. It is a tool for discussion and an aid for the student to refine the presentation for the "public" exhibition in front of the class.

In an ongoing conversation with this teacher, we have started to explore the adjectives that differentiate his Levels, with the intent of making these targets more concrete for the students.

Table 7.1   Student Handout for *Othello* Character Revelation Assignment

---

Individual Character Revelation in Othello

Character Revelation

Throughout the play, various characters win your sympathy, stir your ire, excite your frustration, or inspire your contentment. Indeed, many characters have the power to evoke a myriad of responses from the audience throughout the production. The capacity for this lies in the playwright's ability to create characters that may grow from static creations to emotionally and intellectually charged human beings whose desires, motives, and actions can be readily understood and believed by the audience. Authentic characters must evolve within the context of conflicts, relationships, emerging action, and plot development. Each of these elements provides an avenue through which the playwright reveals the true nature of the character, and the audience comes to understand, contemplate, and even judge the merits of characters within the context of the play.

Each student has been assigned one character from a particular scene in the play.

The Task

You must each do a character analysis, with particular attention to your respective scene, to determine how the character has developed or is further revealed to the audience. You will apply prior context of the character's revelation up to that scene, but the focus of the inquiry and analysis should remain within the scene itself. More specifically, the focus within the scene should be directed toward three areas that help reveal characters: dramatic function, relationships, and language.

- *Dramatic Function.* In this area of inquiry, you are interested in how a character's role is used to move the action or conflict forward or aid in the development of the plot. You need to ask questions about the character's role and determine how the role is manifested in the scene. Some possible questions are, What is your character's relationship to the central events in the play? How does the character function to support central events, themes, or conflicts? What is your character's relationship to other characters in the play? Might he or she act as a foil to another character? How does the nature of your character shape or motivate the necessary actions and responses that such a role demands?
- *Relationships.* This area of inquiry requires a consideration of the character through observation of behavior and attitudes borne out of human relationships. Characters are often best understood relative to others. This allows the audience to make value judgments regarding a character's interaction with others in various situations.

(Continued)

Table 7.1 (*Continued*)

Individual Character Revelation in Othello

Some possible questions are, How would you define the prevailing attitude of your character? What underlying emotions motivate the actions of your character? What attitudes or perspectives are displayed in your scene? Are these consistent with your previous understanding of his or her nature? How has your character changed from the opening scene, and do you foresee more changes? What other characters seem to affect your character most? Why?

- *Language.* The power that a playwright uses to create authentic characters and moments on stage exists in the ability to manipulate language. The poetry of Shakespeare (remember, Shakespeare called himself a "poet," not a "playwright") helps to reveal his characters, especially considering the array of literary devices that he employs. He uses metaphors and similes. He uses rhyme. He uses tone and diction as well. Some questions to consider: What literary devices does Shakespeare use to expose your character's nature? How does the choice of diction relate to your character's status, attitude, education, passion, intelligence, humor, and so on? Does this change at all? If so, why? How might the character's tone be understood as a reflection of his or her nature? Why?

Ultimately, you will present your ideas orally to the rest of the class when we, as a group, reach that particular scene during our in-class reading. One week before the class presentation, you will meet with me in a conference and deliver your character revelations. The conference should last about 15 minutes, and you should be prepared to offer between 5 and 10 minutes of material for us to discuss. After the conference, both you and I will use the attached rubric to assess the character revelation. We will meet the subsequent day to discuss our perspectives, and you can use this feedback to prepare for the class presentation.

Assessment to Reverse Socialization

Teachers need to keep in mind another motivational issue. External assessments and routine reporting requirements can have a demotivating effect on students. Students enter school already socialized by the long-standing history of schools as places where they are judged and marked, often with important consequences (from parental reactions, to entry to further and higher education). These factors tend to focus pupil attention on meeting demands rather than on any intangible personal benefits of the learning. For some, the certainty of praise and success in this enterprise has become a drug; they continually

(*Text continues on page 76*)

Table 7.2 Character Revelation Rubric

Level	Dramatic Function	Character's Relationships	Character's Language
5	• Character's response to events, conflict, or action within the scene clearly identified, *insightfully*, thoroughly, and *confidently* explained using *superior* range and depth of relevant textual support • Motives for character's behavior within the scene clearly identified, *insightfully*, thoroughly, and *confidently* explained using superior range and depth of relevant textual support • Character's contribution to conflict and/or plot development clearly identified, *insightfully*, thoroughly, and *confidently* explained using *superior* range and depth of relevant textual support	• Character's attitudes toward other characters clearly identified, *insightfully*, thoroughly, and *confidently* explained using *superior* range and depth of relevant textual support • Character's historic and developing relationships clearly identified, *insightfully*, thoroughly, and *confidently* explained using *superior* range and depth of relevant textual support • Demonstrates a thorough and *insightful* understanding of motives behind character's actions, and responses to other characters, using *superior* range and depth of relevant textual support	• Clearly identifies, *insightfully*, thoroughly, and *confidently* explains how a character's diction reveals his or her status and perspective, using three *effective* examples from the text • Clearly identifies, *insightfully*, thoroughly, and *confidently* explains how literary devices serve to reflect the character's attitude or point of view, using three *effective* examples from the text • Clearly identifies, *insightfully*, thoroughly, and *confidently* explains the consistency or shift in character's tone that reveals the character's stage(s) of development, *effectively* using language from the beginning, middle, and end of the scene
4	• Character's response to events, conflict, or action within the scene *clearly* identified and	• Character's attitude toward other characters *clearly* identified and *thoroughly* explained	• Clearly identifies and *thoroughly* explains how a character's diction reveals his or her status and

(Continued)

Table 7.2 *(Continued)*

Level	Dramatic Function	Character's Relationships	Character's Language
	thoroughly explained using *relevant* textual support • Motives for character's behavior within the scene *clearly* identified and *thoroughly* explained using *relevant* textual support • Character's contribution to conflict and/or plot development *clearly* identified and *thoroughly* explained using *relevant* textual support	using *relevant* textual support • Character's historic and developing relationships *clearly* identified and *thoroughly* explained using *relevant* textual support • Demonstrates a *thorough* understanding of motives behind character's actions, and responses to other characters, using *relevant* textual support	perspective, using *three relevant* examples from the text • Clearly identifies, *thoroughly* explains how literary devices serve to reflect the character's attitude or point of view, using *three* relevant examples from the text • Clearly identifies and *thoroughly* explains the consistency or shift in character's tone that reveals the character's stage(s) of development, using *relevant* language from the beginning, middle, and end of the scene
3	• Character's response to events, conflict, or action within the scene *identified* and *explained* with *some* reference to characters or events in the text • Motives for character's behavior within the scene *identified* and *explained* with *some* reference to characters or events in the text	• Character's attitude toward other characters *identified* and explained using some textual support • Character's historic and developing relationships with other characters *identified* and *explained* with *some* reference to characters and events in the text • Demonstrates an *adequate*	• *Identifies* and *explains* how a character's diction reveals his or her status and perspective, using at *least two* examples from the text • *Identifies* and *explains* how literary devices serve to reflect the character's attitude or point of view, using at *least two* examples from the text

(Continued)

Table 7.2 *(Continued)*

Level	Dramatic Function	Character's Relationships	Character's Language
	• Character's contribution to conflict and/or plot development *identified* and *explained* with *some* reference to characters and events in the text	understanding of motives behind character's actions, and responses to other characters, using *some* reference to characters and events in the text	• *Identifies* and *explains* the consistency or shift in character's tone that reveals the character's stage(s) of development, using language from two *different parts* of the scene
2	• Character's response to events, conflict, or action within the scene only *partly identified or explained* • Motives for character's behavior within the scene *only partly identified or explained* • Character's contribution to conflict and/or plot development only *partly identified or explained*	• *Partially* demonstrates the character's attitude toward other characters in the text • Character's historic or developing relationships with other characters only *partly identified or explained* • Demonstrates *partial* understanding of motives behind character's actions and/or responses to other characters	• *Partially* identifies or explains how a character's diction reveals his or her status and perspective, with *some* reference to language in the text • *Partially* identifies or explains how literary devices serve to reflect the character's attitude or point of view, with *some* reference to language in the text • *Partially* identifies or explains the consistency or shift in character's tone that reveals the character's stage(s) of development, with *some* reference to language in the text

(Continued)

Table 7.2 *(Continued)*

Level	Dramatic Function	Character's Relationships	Character's Language
1	• Character's response to events, conflict, or action within the *scene not identified or unable to be explained* • Motives for character's behavior within the scene *not identified or unable to be explained* • Character's contribution to conflict and/or plot development *not identified or unable to be explained*	• *Cannot* coherently demonstrate the character's attitude toward other characters in the text • Character's historic or developing relationships with other *characters not identified or unable to be explained* • Demonstrates *little to no* understanding of motives behind character's actions or responses to other characters	• *Cannot* identify or explain how a character's diction reveals his or her status and perspective • *Cannot* identify or explain how literary devices serve to reflect the character's attitude or point of view • *Cannot* identify or explain the consistency or shift in character's tone that reveals the character's stage(s) of development

need more. For many other students, year upon year of "not good enough" has eroded their intellectual self-confidence and resulted in a kind of mind-numbing malaise.

Teachers can use assessment to foster motivation to learn, not just to pass the test. But breaking old habits will not be easy. Instead, it will be a long process of little steps, with setbacks and failures along the way. Nevertheless, I believe it is worth taking up the challenge. When assessment is integrated into the learning process, students and teachers can work together with a shared expectation of finding out what makes sense. This can unleash students' natural curiosity and encourage them to engage in the work in order to acquire knowledge or skills. I have to repeat, however, that the process will take time. Changes this dramatic cannot be accomplished abruptly. Any meaningful reordering of important phases of instruction takes time, but teachers, students, and parents can develop the dispositions and habits of mind of taking learning seriously, recognizing the value or assessment for learning, and seeing assessment as a positive experience. Like all socializing activities, these kinds of dispositions develop gradually, in this case, through exposure to a different kind of assessment experience.

Traditional Assessment *of* Learning is not likely to disappear, nor should it. The trick is to balance its effects by ensuring that students have alternative views about themselves and their learning, and that these views are valued and shared as well. Over the long run, the cumulative effect of Assessment *for* Learning and Assessment *as* Learning should encourage students to develop motivation to learn as an enduring disposition.

Ideas for Follow-Up

1. Examine a sample of your assessment strategies. How relevant are they? How much do they capture the imagination? What information do they provide to the student that can scaffold learning?

2. How might these assessment strategies be modified to make them better motivators for student learning?

3. What changes might you make in your classroom assessment as a result of your discussions about using assessment as motivation?

CHAPTER 8

Using Assessment to Make Connections

In Chapter 4, I talked about how learning is different for novices and experts and the stages in between. Biggs and Collis (1982) studied students as they responded to questions in a variety of subjects in classrooms. They characterized the responses of the students in five categories:

- *Prestructural level.* The student had little idea about how to approach a new idea, so he or she produced an irrelevant response or no response to questions posed.

- *Unistructural level.* The student selected one piece of information and focused on it, with no attention to other details.

- *Multistructural level.* The student focused on more than one piece of information but made no attempt to link one piece to another.

- *Relational level.* The student tied several pieces of information together under headings or categories.

- *Extended abstract level.* The student took the categorized information and carried it into new areas or ideas.

This conception of learning draws attention to the value of depth of learning, rather than coverage. It highlights that teaching is enabling others to learn by finding ways of helping each student see the connections among the bits of information and relate new ideas to his or her previous understanding. The focus shifts from presenting the same information to all students at the same time to helping individual students see their own learning in relation to personal markers, as well as to external ones. For many people, learning feels like a random activity. It just seems to happen (or it doesn't). Unless a person knows how to order his or her thoughts, attention goes to whatever is in the immediate environment, and the learner will often wallow in confusion and uncertainty, without any mechanisms for bringing order to things. But learning can be controlled and enhanced by focusing attempts to make sense of information in order to relate it to prior knowledge and master the skills involved.

In the early stages of learning something new, students (regardless of their age) need supporting structures and rules to give them a framework for seeing patterns. As their learning becomes more complex and they internalize these organizers, they are able to work with and sometimes even construct new ones that reflect combinations of, sophisticated connections to, and subtle changes to the originals. These organizers allow students to monitor what is being learned and use the

> People learn best when they make connections between what they already know and what they are learning, when they can draw on their experiences and make greater meaning of them, when they see how ideas relate to one another, and when they can use what they are learning in concrete ways.
>
> —Darling-Hammond (1992)

feedback from this monitoring to make adjustments, adaptations, and even major changes in what is understood. These organizers also help students come to understand that learning is not a random accumulation of bits of information. Rather, it is a dynamic process of making sense of ideas by manipulating, altering, and transforming them in their heads. The most important learning becomes the students' own learning and its progress over time. Unfortunately, many see little connection between the bits of information that accrue at school and the world that they experience after school lets out for the day. Teachers are the only bridge that can connect them. These connections are much more likely when students can see what they are aiming for, have organizational structures to help them see the connections, and can make personal connections between their expectations and their own view of the world.

Curricula as Visible Targets for Learning

As Black and Wiliam (1998) found, learning is easier when both the teacher and the student have a clear image of where they are headed. This is not to say that they need a long list of the bits of information that they need to store inside their brains. Rather, teachers need a big picture of the whole course or learning agenda to frame the learning tasks. They also need more detailed breakdowns that identify the inter-relationships and connections embedded in the concepts, skills, and knowledge that make up the successful learning so that they can create appropriate activities along the way.

> Students can reach any targets that they can see and that stand still for them.
>
> —Stiggins (1993)

Students also need to see the big picture to make it worth their while to travel this road. All too often, we ask students to get on the "learning train" with no idea of what the destination will be or why they should go there. When they know the purpose and direction of their learning and can see the connection of the learning intention of any particular task to the larger agenda, they are likely to be more motivated and task-oriented. Even more important, they can plan their own learning and see their own progress.

Mapping the relationships may seem straightforward, but this process is much more than a scope-and-sequence chart. The goal is to make the next step in learning visible to the students so that they can use their minds to unravel ideas and see patterns.

As I mentioned in Chapter 2, content standards are a legacy of large-scale reform. These standards provide a starting point for teachers to articulate the learning targets for their classes. Fortunately, the standards that have been developed, especially by subject organizations, include challenging subject matter and describe what it means to know and learn in each of these disciplines. I have included a segment from the National Council of Teachers of Mathematics (NCTM) standards in Table 8.1 as an example to show the richness and detail that the standards can provide.

> Learning is seeing patterns in the world around us. Teaching is creating the conditions in which students can see the known patterns of our collective understanding. Nobel prize winners see patterns where they have not been seen before.
>
> —John Polanyi, Nobel Laureate–Chemistry

As you can see, these standards offer a worthy starting place for creating the day-to-day work of teachers and students. They can serve many purposes, from stimulating the beginning of a conversation about what should be taught in schools and at what level; to guiding the program planning for teachers; to describing detailed benchmarks, with examples of what is expected of students.

Table 8.1 NCTM Measurement Standard: "Applying Appropriate Techniques, Tools, and Formulas to Determine Measurements"

Grade	Standard
Pre-K-2	• Measure with multiple copies of units of the same size, such as paper clips laid end to end • Use repetition of a single unit to measure something larger than the unit, for instance, measuring the length of a room with a single meter stick • Use tools to measure • Develop common referents for measures to make comparisons and estimates
3–5	• Develop strategies for estimating the perimeters, areas, and volumes of irregular shapes • Select and apply appropriate standard units and tools to measure length, area, volume, weight, time, temperature, and the size of angles • Select and use benchmarks to estimate measurements • Develop, understand, and use formulas to find the area of rectangles and related triangles and parallelograms • Develop strategies to determine the surface areas and volumes of rectangular solids
6–8	• Use common benchmarks to select appropriate methods for estimating measurements • Select and apply techniques and tools to accurately find length, area, volume, and angle measures to appropriate levels of precision • Develop and use formulas to determine the circumference of circles and the area of triangles, parallelograms, trapezoids, and circles, and develop strategies to find the area of more complex shapes • Develop strategies to determine the surface area and volume of selected prisms, pyramids, and cylinders • Solve problems involving scale factors, using ratio and proportion • Solve simple problems involving rates and derived measurements for such attributes as velocity and density
9–12	• Analyze precision, accuracy, and approximate error in measurement situations • Understand and use formulas for the area, surface area, and volume of geometric figures, including cones, spheres, and cylinders • Apply informal concepts of successive approximation, upper and lower bounds, and limit in measurement situations • Use unit analysis to check measurement computations

SOURCE: Reprinted with permission from *Principles and Standards for School Mathematics*, copyright 2000 by the National Council of Teachers of Mathematics. All rights reserved.

The power comes not from having standards or objectives, but from routinely using them to clarify what the learning is about and how it all connects. Curriculum expectations have always been used to judge students' performance, or as reference points for a process of deriving information from students in order to modify teaching. If assessment is going to link curriculum to student learning, then standards must become the "stuff" of discussion in classes. All too often, students have very little understanding of the purpose of classroom activities or of the assessment tasks. If they are going to take responsibility for their own learning, they need to know what the "grand scheme" is and how the piece with which they are working fits. A simple chart of curriculum objectives on the classroom wall can be useful for students as they are working; so can regular statements of the intent of the learning throughout a lesson or a unit. Students also need to be able to distinguish between what teachers want them to do, what they want them to learn, how teachers and the students themselves will know what they have achieved, and what comes next.

Although curriculum standards provide an image of what students are expected to learn, they do not give a sense of how the students should go about the learning process. Often, students are expected to think about something without having learned how to think or having practiced thinking. Thinking, however, is a multifaceted, complex neural activity that requires a range of prior skill development. Art Costa and Bena Kallick (2000) have produced a series of books focused on what they call "habits of mind." The basic premise is that young people (and adults, for that matter) can come to deeper understanding and do much better on critical and creative thinking tasks when they are taught and internalize these habits of mind. Simply, habits of mind are "broad, enduring and essential life-span learnings" (p. xiii). These include persistence; listening with understanding and empathy; questioning and posing problems; applying past knowledge to new situations;

> Habits give control over the environment, power to utilize it for human purposes. Active habits involve thought, invention, and initiative in applying capacities to new aims. They are opposed to routine, which marks an arrest of growth. Since growth is the characteristic of life, education is all one with growing; it has no end beyond itself. The criterion of the value of school education is the extent in which it creates a desire for continued growth.
>
> —Dewey (1916)

gathering data through all of the senses; and creating, imagining, and innovating. Habits of mind obviously do not replace standard curriculum or teaching. They complement and extend it by explicitly pushing the limits on students' thinking and equipping them with tools to go the distance in both school and life. Orchestrating the conditions for students to make connections and use their developing habits of mind requires careful planning on the part of teachers, individually and together.

Plan Learning, Plan Assessment, and Expect the Unexpected

Learning is not a linear process. Assessment doesn't come at the end. Teaching is not the filling in the sandwich between curriculum and assessment. Taken together, curriculum, teaching, learning, and assessment interact in an iterative and sometimes cyclical process. They feed into one another and sometimes dart back and forth in seemingly unpredictable patterns. This does not mean that they are independent of or disconnected from one another. On the contrary, the interconnections are key. Curriculum, teaching, and assessment all need to be consistent for effective learning. If teachers are going to see the connections and recognize trends, they will need to map the curriculum topic by topic and identify the threads of skills and learning that make up the program—horizontally, to see what is intended for this class, and vertically, to follow the progressions that will occur across classes, subjects, and years (Sutton, 1995). All of this means that the curriculum is not the first element of planning that teachers should consider. Learning intentions and assessment are connected so closely to curriculum that it is impossible to plan them in isolation from one another.

This is not to suggest that planning should set the day in stone. The wonderful thing about planning is that once you've done it, you can make all kinds of changes and adjustments and not lose the plot. Or, if you do, it's on purpose. Careful planning is the skeleton for the school day. You can't see it, but its absence would be a disaster. Plans should provide the blueprint and the organizers that teachers and students can use to constantly identify the intentions, make the connections explicit, reinforce the relationships, and identify the misconceptions that can get in the way. Whether or not activities are appropriate and fulfill learning intentions should be in constant question. Ongoing assessment is the key to making on-the-spot corrections or modifications, or even abandoning the whole thing for another direction.

"The Case of the Literacy Hour"

During the past 4 years, I have been involved in the external evaluation of the National Literacy and Numeracy Strategies in England (Earl et al., 2000). One of the characteristics of the literacy strategy is the organization of material and the focus on teaching within a Literacy Hour, with clear curriculum targets. At the same time, there are high-profile national numerical targets for schools. The Secretary of State for Education has publicly stated that he would resign his post if the targets of 80% achieving level 4 in literacy and 75% reaching level 4 in mathematics by 2002 were not reached. Each school has set annual percentage targets that are reported and monitored regularly to see how it is doing. A public and numeric process like this runs the risk of focusing attention on students as "widgets." "If I can just get Sonia over the bar, we'll be OK." The Directorate of the Strategies, however, has put considerable effort into making the connections between the National Curriculum and target setting for schools. Teachers are encouraged to think about curriculum targets and what they mean for individual students.

I have been lucky enough to observe some talented teachers who have internalized and are using the target-setting exercise as more than a quantitative series of ticks on a record sheet. They are using the curriculum targets to clarify the learning goals and establish the criteria of quality for individual tasks. From then on, modifying them for individual children or groups of children is relatively straightforward.

In a small, rural primary school, the Year 3 (Grade 2) teacher started the lesson with a whole-group activity—shared reading of a Big Book. This book, about a youngster and his experience with growing vegetables that took over the garden, had been introduced to the class the day before, so they spent a few minutes reviewing the title, the author, the picture on the cover, and what they had read the day before, and they made predictions about what might happen next in the story. Then, several of the children each read a portion of the book aloud, as did the teacher. During the shared reading, the teacher routinely drew attention to how the author used descriptive words to help the reader see the images in the story, even without looking at the pictures. On the blackboard behind her head was the curriculum target for the day: *Objective: Identify and use expressive, figurative, and descriptive language, especially adjectives, to create effects in poetry and prose.*

A class lesson followed in which the teacher read the objective aloud to the children and discussed what it meant, reviewing with them the terms *adjective, expressive, figurative,* and *descriptive.* She then explained to the class that adjectives could be used to create interesting effects in writing—to cause a feeling or an emotion in the reader or to try to make an image or a picture of the object in the mind of the reader. During this part of the lesson, she showed the children some simple sentences she had already written on the board and asked them to try to think of interesting adjectives to help a reader get a feeling or create a mental picture about the object in the sentence. Children enthusiastically raised their hands to offer suggestions. The teacher took a half-dozen suggestions in turn, each discussed by teacher and child with a combination of questioning—"Why did you choose the word *massive?*" "And does that adjective, *massive,* tell us something about the zucchini?" "Think carefully. Is that word, *massive,* an adjective?"—and careful explanations of what made a good response. Several examples were worked in this way. The children seemed eager to offer suggestions and attempt explanations, and the teacher praised the efforts of all who volunteered—"Excellent," or "That was a great try, but *nice* doesn't really describe the zucchini. We want a word to describe the zucchini that would help the reader see what the author had in mind. How would *nice* do that?"

When a child gave an evocative response, she modeled writing for the children by writing the new sentence on the board as the child repeated it. At one point, she misspelled a word deliberately to be greeted by a show of hands eager to help her out. She found this was something that gave the children great delight and helped to keep some of them focused during this part of the lesson.

After this sentence-level teaching session was finished, the teacher told the class that the group activities for today would continue working with figurative language by using adjectives, or *words that describe an object or tell you something about the object that makes it easier for the reader to picture it.* She was going to work with one group to construct sentences about plants using adjectives. The other groups were each going to their tables to work on the assignments she had placed there for them. Propped on each table was the specific target for the day: *using expressive, figurative, and descriptive language, especially adjectives, to create effects in prose.*

When the teacher was working in the guided writing exercise with the small group, she was observing, asking questions, and making on-the-spot adjustments to fill in the gaps in each child's learning. I listened for a while as she worked with them. Instruction and assessment were seamless. She was regularly reiterating the goals ("We're using descriptive adjectives to help readers make a picture in their mind, to make others see the plants the way we want them to be seen"); providing examples ("How about a nubbly pumpkin?"); and asking focused questions ("What did the sunflower look like? How did it feel?"). The children were having a ball thinking of words to make ordinary plants into exciting images, such as "wispy dandelions" and "terrified tomatoes," and explaining why the adjectives that they were suggesting were exactly the right ones for the impression that they were trying to make. All the while, the teacher was listening and probing to get a sense of their understanding and using her analysis to focus and extend their learning.

The rest of the class was equally busy. In one group, the students were completing a "cloze" passage that required them to insert reasonable adjectives from a list the teacher had set out on a laminated sheet. In another, the task was more open-ended. The students were writing short sentences using adjectives and nouns from lists set out for them. A fourth group was revising a short passage by crossing out the existing adjectives and replacing them with more expressive or imaginative adjectives. Afterwards, she explained that the tasks had been created for different groups based on her assessment of the practice that would help them now.

Although the teacher was completely occupied with one group, the rest of the students were producing paper artifacts that she could quickly scan and also read more carefully later. She spent a few minutes with each group asking pointed questions and checking the level of understanding. In the next phase of the Literacy Hour, she moved into a brief plenary session in which she pulled together the ideas and used the children's work from all of the groups to illustrate the power of adjectives. As a finale, the children identified the image that they found the most interesting, and some of them described it to the class in words and explained why they thought it was interesting. You might say that this example sounds more like instruction than assessment. And you would be partially right. The teacher began with key objectives that were readily visible and gave the children a clear sense of the learning expectations. The assessment happened throughout the lesson and the group work in ways that contributed to learning. The intimate connection between instruction and assessment was evident in the questions that the teacher asked and in the students whom she chose to answer them. It showed in the choices of assignments for the groups' independent work, and it guided the decisions that the teacher made about how to conduct the plenary session. This is "scaffolding" in action: students and the teacher engaged in challenging conversation and questioning to elicit and embed understanding.

Differentiation

Differentiation is making sure that the right students get the right learning tasks at the right time. Once you have a sense of what each student holds as "given" or "known" and what he or she needs in order to learn, differentiation is no longer an option. It is an obvious response. But it can be a formidable task. To many of you, it probably feels like a recipe for failure. How can you possibly individualize teaching for all of those students, especially in secondary schools, where you see more than 100 students a day?

Differentiation doesn't mean a different program for each student in the class, and it doesn't mean ability grouping to reduce the differences. It means recognizing and accepting that each student is a unique individual. It means using what you know about learning and about each student to improve your teaching so that students all work in ways that have an optimal effect on their learning. And assessment provides the necessary information to do it.

Ruth Sutton (1995) says it best:

> The key to effective differentiation is the accuracy and relevance of the information that we use to decide appropriate learning tasks for pupils, and our willingness to challenge these decisions from time to time by allowing students to surprise us. (p. 26)

All too often, we confuse children's lack of experience with lack of ability. We view diversity as limiting and slow down instruction rather than accelerating it. Instead of delaying learning, we should be finding a different approach to learning to meet the special needs and unique qualities of each student. Assessment, instead of being the means for categorizing students and avoiding working to help them learn, becomes the mechanism for deciding what to do to push the learning forward.

When teachers are asked about the factors that affect learning, they mention things like those listed in Table 8.2. Most of these will be familiar. They are qualities that differentiate all students, not just a few of them labeled as "special needs."

Finding out about students as learners and as people is the key to differentiation. When teachers are equipped with detailed knowledge about their students and have a clear idea about what the students need to learn, differentiation can happen all of the time. If the lesson is in science, but reading the instructions is hampering some students, the teacher can read the instructions for some of them or write instructions that are succinct and short so that those who are daunted by a lot of reading feel comfortable. If the mathematics task in the next unit requires that the students have a solid grasp of basic shapes, the teacher can use manipulatives, at the beginning of the class for a few days before, to review the material, ascertain the nature of each student's understanding, and provide support. Activities like the Pool Table task provide every student with access to the ideas and give

Table 8.2   Factors That Affect Students' Learning

- Reading ability, confidence, and speed
- Writing ability, confidence, and speed
- Concentration span
- Spatial awareness
- Hand-eye coordination
- Ability to listen to instructions and absorb information aurally
- Ability to absorb information visually, from pictures or diagrams
- Skill in manipulating numbers
- Functioning of the senses, particularly sight and hearing
- Learning styles (i.e., the approach to learning with which the learner feels most comfortable, and the ability to learn in different ways when the circumstances change)
- Previous experience, knowledge, and skills
- Support and encouragement from parents
- Self-esteem
- High or low expectations from themselves, peers, their families, and their teachers
- The belief among teachers and schools that they can make a difference

SOURCE: Sutton (1995).

teachers a chance to work with some students as they do it. Individual attention can be focused on what they need to do now to move on in their learning. What insights can teachers help them achieve? What is the next obvious piece in this puzzle?

Ideas for Follow-Up

1. Pick a student in your class. Make a detailed list of what you know about this student's learning, about the conditions in which the student learns best, about the patterns with which he or she is familiar, about his or her learning habits and prior knowledge and learning style, and so on.

2. Now think about a unit you are currently teaching. What patterns are you trying to make visible for students? What are the learning targets? What are the essential qualities of successful mastery?

3. How can you match what you know about the student with the curricular expectations?

CHAPTER 9

Using Assessment to Extend Learning

B y now it should be obvious that assessment is an integral part of learning. It provides a window into how and what students are thinking and signals the kind of feedback that is necessary to support learning. As I discussed in Chapter 6, diagnostic assessment provides feedback to teachers about student learning so that they can use it to coordinate teaching and tailor support for students. From the research that has been done so far, assessment is such a valuable part of learning because it can make learning visible to both teachers and students.

Feedback for Learning

It isn't enough for teachers to see the next steps and use them in their planning. Students need to see them as well. Feedback for learning is the process that provides the conceptual link between what students believe to be true and the collective wisdom of the culture as it is captured in the knowledge carried by teachers and in the texts, resources, and so on that are available to them as reference points. As Grant Wiggins (1993) puts it, "Feedback is information that provides the performer with direct, useable insights into current performance, based on tangible differences between current performance and hoped for performance" (p. 182).

Feedback can lead to increased effort or engagement, alternative strategies to understand the material, and the restructuring of understanding. A major role for teachers in the learning process is to provide the kind of feedback to students that encourages their learning and provides signposts and directions along the way, bringing them closer to independence.

Feedback for learning can take many forms. It can be formal or informal. It can be individual or collective. Feedback can also be evaluative or descriptive, as Caroline Gipps and her colleagues (Gipps et al., 2000) have described it (see Table 9.1).

> Feedback can be the vital link between the teachers' assessment of a child and the action following that assessment, which then has a formative effect on the child's learning.
>
> —Hargreaves et al. (2000)

All too often, teachers provide evaluative feedback in the form of grades and short (usually nonspecific) comments, often praise or censure. This kind of feedback tells students whether they are okay or not and affects their sense of themselves and their position in relation to learning, but it offers little direction for moving their learning forward. Thinking back to the earlier comments about motivation, evaluative feedback leaves students feeling either good or bad about themselves, without any sense of what is inspiring their feeling except the external symbol of their success or lack of it. Some of them have a momentary feeling of self-esteem, especially in relation to a social comparison with their peers. Others are left to lick their wounds. After a while, learning, and even school itself, is pushed into a less important role in their lives, as they use the negative feedback to discount school and adjust their expectations in other directions.

Descriptive feedback, on the other hand, makes explicit connections between students' thinking and other possibilities that they should consider. It is linked to the learning that is expected. It addresses faulty interpretations and lack of understanding. It provides students with visible and manageable "next steps" based on an assessment of the work at hand and an image of what "good work looks like" so that they can begin to take on the responsibility of self-assessing and self-correcting. Feedback is not an independent activity. Rather, it is part of the teaching process—the part that comes after the initial instruction takes place, when information is provided based on the way that the individual has processed and interpreted the original material.

When students are aware of the reason for the task, see the task as possible, and know what they are striving for, they are almost always motivated to go for it. Good feedback keeps this activity in balance. It allows them to set reasonable goals, track their performance, and set the next goal in the ongoing process of learning.

In a wonderful book called *Unlocking Formative Assessment,* Shirley Clarke (2001), from the Institute for Education at the University of London, describes her program of research directed at understanding

Table 9.1   Evaluative and Descriptive Feedback Strategies

Evaluative feedback	• Giving rewards and punishments
	• Expressing approval and disapproval
Descriptive feedback	• Telling children they are right or wrong
	• Describing why an answer is correct
	• Telling children what they have achieved and have not achieved
	• Specifying or implying a better way of doing something
	• Getting children to suggest ways they can improve

SOURCE: Gipps et al. (2000).

feedback and how it works. Although she is working in primary classes and concentrating on literacy, the principles that she describes hold the promise of being generalizable to many settings and age groups. In her research, she has found that feedback is most useful when it focuses on the learning intentions of the task. She advocates displaying the specific learning intentions for the lesson or unit prominently in the classroom and regularly returning to them throughout the lesson, as the central focus of the work. While the students are working on a task, it is easy for the teacher to be distracted by other occurrences or behaviors. The message to the students, however, is that student behavior, being neat, and so on are more important than the lesson at hand, and they get distracted as well. Instead, the teacher's major focus should be feedback to individuals and groups that helps them to see the ideas and make the connections in their thinking.

Clarke (2001) also tackles the sticky issue of how to give feedback on written work to guide students' learning. She suggests focusing feedback on a few things that are directly connected to the learning intentions for the task. She uses simple strategies, such as using a highlighter pen to identify examples of the learning intentions in the child's work, selecting a few of these highlighted elements to show where some improvement could be made, drawing an arrow from the selected items to a white space on the page, and writing what she calls a "closing the gap" prompt—prompts for making changes to their work that are geared to the particular student and what the teacher already knows about that student. Table 9.2 is an example from her book.

It is interesting to me that teachers often use reminder prompts when students would benefit from more structure and could be pushed in their learning with scaffolding prompts. Often, when students see example prompts, they immediately produce their own

Table 9.2   An Example of Possible Closing-the-Gap Prompts

Learning Intention: To effectively introduce a character at the start of a story.

Activity: Choose someone you know but the class doesn't to describe in a written paragraph.

We are Learning to: Write about people's characters for our stories.

How Will We Know We've Done It? (created with the class): We will have written something about their appearance, their likes and dislikes, their personality, their attitudes, and other things that help others know more about them.

Let's assume that a child has written about someone he knows from a summer camp. After highlighting several phrases that successfully give information about this person, the teacher asterisks the phrase "This person is a good friend." The arrow to the closing-the-gap prompt could take any of the following forms:

A Reminder Prompt: Say more about how you feel about this person.
A reminder prompt is most suitable for a student who probably has a good command of figurative language but has not used it here, for whatever reason.

A Scaffolding Prompt: Can you describe how this person is a good friend? (question) Or, Describe something that happened that showed you what a good friend this person is. (directive) Or, He showed me he was a good friend when . . . (finish the sentence).
Scaffolding prompts work well with students who need more structure or some direction but are likely to carry on from here.

An Example Prompt: Choose one of these sentences to tell me more about your friend. "He is a good friend because he never says unkind things about me." Or, "My friend helps me do things."
When students are struggling or don't appear to understand the concept, example prompts can provide them with actual models of the learning intention.

SOURCE: Adapted from Clarke (2001).

improvement and go beyond the teacher's expectations. Students are very motivated by these closing-the-gap strategies, and teachers are astounded by how quickly and thoughtfully they respond. A number of exciting spin-offs have come from this approach to feedback in marking. Once students get the hang of it, it lends itself to self- and paired student marking. Students start to think about what the teacher would highlight, develop arguments and reasons for their choices, offer one another suggestions for improvement, and revisit their own work with a critical eye.

As with all feedback, the quality of students' work depends on the quality of the closing-the-gap comments. Just giving feedback is not necessarily useful and may not even be motivating. By itself, feedback has no power to initiate action. Instead, it is a signpost or a guide for consideration by the student, which is all the more reason for providing the kind of high-quality feedback that makes the links between the current state of knowledge and the target. When feedback is vague or faulty, students make inappropriate modifications or don't see any reason to learn more or make adjustments to their thinking.

Although teachers are the most obvious purveyors of feedback, they are not the only ones. Peers and parents are just as important. Why? Because learning is social. Early experiential knowledge forms the fabric of children's lives and is often resistant to change. It is the "stuff" that life has taught them. People are constantly testing the veracity of their beliefs and ideas (and those of their community and culture) by comparing them to the beliefs and ideas held by the people around them. This testing process often involves books, media, and other resources, but the key contributors to the internal dialogue for students are teachers, parents, and peers.

So, what does good feedback look like? Good feedback provides evidence that confirms or refutes an idea. It gives students a chance to reflect on their learning and their learning needs. It gives recognition and appropriate praise for achievement and growth. It is targeted to the specific learning needs of each student or group of students. It gives clear directions for improvement and allows students the time to think about and respond to the suggestions. Finally, it focuses on quality and learning.

Although it is difficult to describe the iterative nature of feedback, I think it is important to reinforce that it is an ongoing process. When the process of feedback is running smoothly, it is a reciprocal flow of influence (Senge, 1990). Teachers use assessment to provide feedback to students about their conceptions and misconceptions; students use their feedback from teachers to adjust their understandings, rethink their ideas, and put their new conceptions forward, leading to another round of feedback and another extension of the learning. This process doesn't happen after the fact, or even once a term. It is part of a continuous conversation between teachers and students and among students.

When feedback is descriptive and iterative, it has a very different effect on the students' perceptions of themselves as learners and their overall self-esteem. When students see the effects of their efforts and know what comes next, they are more likely to remain motivated and to see how their progress is linked to their work.

Rubrics and Exemplars as Tools

I laughed recently when a teacher in a professional development session asked me if I was there to "rubricize" him. It sounded like an inoculation was all that he needed to gain access to this magical world of rubrics. There is no doubt that rubrics have become the "flavor of the year" in education; you have already seen several rubrics in earlier chapters. In this chapter, I expand on the use of rubrics and give some suggestions about how to make them effective. Unfortunately, many people still cling to the notion that the purpose of rubrics is to slot students into a category. By now, it should be clear that the kind of assessment that I am advocating is more concerned with helping students learn than it is with finding a slot in which to put them.

> A rubric is a particular format for criteria—it is a written down version of the criteria, with all score points described and defined. The best rubrics are worded in a way that covers the essence of what teachers look for when they judge quality and they reflect the best thinking in the field about what constitutes good performance.
>
> —Arter and McTighe (2001)

Rubrics can be useful tools for teachers, students, and parents. They are more than just evaluation tools to use at the end of instruction; they help clarify instructional goals and serve as teaching targets (Arter & McTighe, 2001). All too often, educators see rubrics as replacements for grading categories. Instead of recognizing that the power of rubrics is as mechanisms for making performance criteria visible, they transform the descriptions into the number designations. A student is quickly labeled as a "2" or a "3." The end result is counterproductive. A useful tool for learning becomes another sorting mechanism, and the value that it might have added to learning and teaching disappears.

Sometimes a rubric, even a good one, is not enough. Royce Sadler (1989) wrote a landmark paper describing why students need to have visible images of what excellence looks like. This knowledge of excellence develops progressively through a series of cognitive tacking maneuvers. Criteria and descriptions offer reference points along the way, but there is no substitute for "seeing" excellence. There is no one model of excellence for any area. Many of them exist, and students need to see (or hear, or imagine) what these various images of excellence are like.

When students are striving toward a difficult goal, especially one that is complex and requires the integration of new learning and a number of different skills, they benefit from seeing how it looks when it's done and from the process that an expert went through to get there. Having an image of where they are going, how long it takes to get there, and what the stages look like both motivates and provides targets that students can visualize and strive for along the way.

Think about athletes as they perfect and extend their performances. Personal video cameras have become essential tools for them as they watch the way that recognized experts do it, videotape their own performance, and make adjustments to fine-tune their own style so that it is more effective. The footage of experts in action provides targets for changes, but the individual athletes consider what they see in relation to their own body type and what they already do well to enhance their performance, rather than just emulating the expert.

"The Case of the Brass Band"

A music teacher in a small, rural secondary school, himself an accomplished trumpet player who played swing music with a brass band, offered an extracurricular program in the school for students who wanted to learn to play brass instruments. He made an announcement to the school that the "band" would meet after school on Tuesdays. Anyone in the school could come. The only requirement was that the students attend every session and practice in between. His promise to them: "We'll perform for the school at the spring concert. And you'll be great."

He was surprised and delighted that more than 20 people showed up at the first after-school class, including one teacher who "used to play the trombone" and the junior custodian, who played drums with a rock band and thought he might be able to add something to the group. The music teacher gave the motley crew an initial pep talk:

> We're all in this together. A band can only work as a whole group. So, each of us has to learn alone and learn together so that we can make the music work. Here's how we're going to

do it. Today, I want you to listen to some big band music, and we'll talk about what you like or don't like about each piece. I'll introduce you to the instruments and let you hear how each of them sounds and see how they work. I have copies of the tapes you're going to hear so you can take them home and listen to them again. When we meet next week, we'll decide who is going to play which instruments and what pieces we want to start with. You can take an instrument with you this week as well, if you think you know the instrument that you want. Or you can come in after school and try out any ones that you want.

This initial statement set the tone for the rest of the big band program. Everyone eventually selected an instrument, and the group agreed about the selections that it wanted to learn. From there, the real work began. The routines of the weekly class were straightforward. In early sessions, they involved the following:

• Listening to the segment of the piece that they were working on, using the recording

• Practicing the segment as a group

• Practicing individually (those members of the band identified by the teacher as doing something well)

• Giving feedback to these individuals based on a simple PMI (plus, minus, interesting)

• Listening to a recording of the particular instrument alone

• Analyzing the recordings in relation to the individual performances, with discussion about what is essential for a good performance, especially within a group, and what is unique to the particular performer

After each session, the teacher identified several students to meet with him during the week. Before they came for their private session, the students practiced a segment that they were finding particularly challenging and taped their playing while they were practicing. They brought three of these taped performances to the private session, and the teacher worked with them to help them "hear" their playing and to make adjustments. Once the session was over, the students received several tapes by experts on the instrument, performing the same piece, often very differently from one another. Their homework task was to analyze and describe what the different artists did that was similar and what was different, and to try to introduce some of these elements into their own playing.

As time went on, each student performed solo for the complete group, not as the perfect performance, but as a phase in the process of learning and creating the final production. The explicit expectation was that the group would provide helpful and challenging feedback to the individual about the performance as a solo, and as part of the band, so that the composition would work as a whole. The teacher used his considerable talent along the way to write (and rewrite) new arrangements for different individuals and different instruments. He even found a place for a big band drummer that built on the talents of the rock band drummer.

The final production was an enormous success, but that was the least important element in this lesson about learning. The students in this group learned that

- There is no single right answer;

- You get better when you practice, if you know what to practice and how to make it better;

- What sounds like confusing noise in the beginning can be taken apart and understood, and when it's put back together, you can hear the differences;

- When you can hear (or see) where you are headed, it's easier to get there;

- When you work together, you can create something that is bigger than any single person can on his or her own.

Ideas, Connections, and Extensions (ICE)

Young and Wilson (2000, p. 2) describe an approach to assessment that they call the ICE approach, which teachers can use "on the run" in classrooms. It is a portable technique for assessing growth that is generalizable across students, subjects, ages, and levels of schooling. I think that it offers a valuable organizer for teachers as they consider structuring instruction and feedback in their classes. ICE is described in Table 9.3.

These authors have found that the ICE approach makes sense and is manageable for teachers as they juggle all of the activities that make up their busy days. In fact, it serves as an organizer to keep them on track and focused on learning and individual students.

Table 9.3   ICE Approach to Assessment of Growth

ICE means	Description	Evidence
Ideas	*Ideas* are the building blocks of learning: the steps in a process, the necessary vocabulary, and the introductory skills that form the basis of learning. Sometimes, they are the bits of information in notes and textbooks; sometimes, they are steps in a process; sometimes, they are guidelines for action.	Students convey • The fundamentals • The basic facts • Vocabulary/definitions • Details • Elemental concepts
Connections	*Connections* are the relationships and patterns that exist between and among ideas and with previous knowledge and ideas. Novices follow prescriptions and manuals. Experts see patterns and can take shortcuts because they understand the underlying connections to other ideas.	Students communicate • The relationship or connections among the basic concepts • A relationship or connection between the new ideas and what they already know
Extensions	*Extensions* are the final stage in growth of learning and occur when individuals no longer need to refer to the rules for operations and no longer make conscious connections among the bits or even to their own experience. They have internalized the learning so much that it helps to define them as people. Rules have been abandoned for "maxims," or portable truths that have meaning even if they are not expressed.	Students show that relationships are internalized by • Using new knowledge in novel and creative ways to extend ideas or concepts, often well beyond the original learning context • Answering the hypothetical questions, "What does this mean? How does this shape my view of the world?"

SOURCE: Adapted from Young and Wilson (2000).

Ideas for Follow-Up

1.   Make an ICE chart for a unit that you are teaching. Identify the ideas, connections, and extensions that make up the unit. Create assessment tasks that allow you to ascertain students' facility with the ideas, connections, and extensions.

2.   Work as a team to consider student work and decide what kinds of feedback prompts you would use. Remember to identify the concept or skill that is the focus of the exercise before you begin.

CHAPTER 10

Using Assessment for Reflection and Self-Monitoring

A s I pointed out earlier, learning is an active process of constructing thoughts and making sense of the world around us. Ideas are the raw material for this process, and existing knowledge and beliefs can enable or impede new learning. Learning is also dependent on self-monitoring and awareness. We all decide when and how to use various skills; we check what we believe to be true against socially and culturally determined norms, and we continually decide how reasonable the resulting formulation feels. Effective learners develop cognitive routines for organizing, synthesizing, and reorganizing ideas. They also engage in self-monitoring and provide themselves with feedback that leads to the emergence of new ideas, combinations, or patterns.

> Assumption: Everyone can be an expert at something, sometime.

"The Case of Jojo"

When she was about 5 years old, my niece Joanna (Jojo to the family) came up to me and announced that "All cats are girls, and all dogs are boys." When I asked her why she believed cats were girls and dogs were boys, she responded, "Your cat *Molly* is a girl, and she's little and smooth. Girls are little and smooth, too. Cats are girls. The dog next door is a boy, and he's big and rough, just like boys are big and rough. Dogs are boys." Clearly, she had identified a problem, surveyed her environment, gathered data, and formulated a hypothesis. When she tested it, it held. Pretty sophisticated logic.

I pulled a book about dogs from my bookshelf and showed her a picture of a chihuahua.

"What's this?" I asked.

"Dog," she replied.

"Girl or boy?"

"It's a boy, dogs are boys."

"But it's little and smooth," I pointed out.

"Sometimes, they can be little and smooth," said Jojo.

I turned to a picture of an Irish Setter, surrounded by puppies. She was perturbed.

"What's this?"

"Dog," she replied, with some hesitation.

"Boy or girl?"

After a long pause, she said, "Maybe it's the dad." But she didn't look convinced, and she quickly asked, "Can dogs be girls, Aunt Lorna?"

This anecdote is a simple but vivid demonstration of the process of reflection and self-monitoring that we all use when we are trying to make sense of the world around us. Jojo had a conception of what she wanted to know (the gender of cats and dogs). She had come to a conclusion based on her initial investigation. With the intervention of a teacher (me), who gave her the wherewithal to compare her conceptions with other examples in the real world, she was able to see the gap between her understanding and other evidence. Once she had the new knowledge, she moved quickly to adjust her view and consider alternative perspectives.

Students as Their Own Best Assessors

We want students to become self-starting and self-motivated lifelong learners. If they are to become critical thinkers and problem solvers who can bring their talents and their knowledge to bear on their decisions and actions, they have to develop skills of self-assessment and self-adjustment. They can't just wait for someone to tell them the right answer. At this stage, all of the ideas that have emerged in other chapters come back into play as important factors in the work of learning. They include the following:

• Engaging students in the real work of learning is motivation at its best.

• Clear goals and visible examples of what "good work looks like," when it's done and while it's in process, set the stage.

- Student involvement in determining the goals, learning methods, and decisions about success increases their self-awareness and helps them see errors, consider alternatives, and make adjustments.

- Diagnostic assessment provides teachers with guides to share with their students.

- Descriptive feedback makes the next step manageable while providing maximum independence.

- Sharing the decision making and giving students practice in monitoring their own work gives them confidence and competence in making important judgments about their learning and their decisions.

- Bringing parents and peers into the process adds allies and co-conspirators to the learning process.

Developing Self-Evaluation Habits of Mind

A number of writers have referred to the "habits of mind" that creative, critical, and self-regulated thinkers use and that students (and many adults, for that matter) need to develop. These habits are ways of thinking that will enable students to learn on their own, whatever they want or need to know at any point in their lives (Marzano, Pickering, & McTighe, 1993).

> We must constantly remind ourselves that the ultimate purpose of evaluation is to enable students to evaluate themselves. Educators may have been practicing this skill to the exclusion of the learners. We need to shift part of this responsibility to students. Fostering students' ability to direct and redirect themselves must be a major goal—or what is education for?
>
> —Costa (1989)

When people succeed or fail, they can explain their success or failure to themselves in various ways: effort, ability, task factors, or luck. Only the first of these attributions is likely to promote adaptive motivational tendencies. The student can decide to try harder and be successful. The other explanations—ability, task difficulty, or luck—are all out of the student's control. When students do not believe that they have control over their achievements, they are not motivated to work in school.

In particular, several authors have identified an "inquiry habit of mind" as an essential component of profitable learning for individuals and groups (Earl & Lee, 1998; Katz, Sutherland, & Earl, in press; Newmann, 1996; Wiggins, 1993). If students are going to develop these "habits of mind" and become inquiry-minded, they need to experience continuous, genuine success. They need to feel as if they are in an environment where it is safe to take chances and where feedback and support are readily available and challenging. This does not mean the absence of failure. It means using their habits of mind to identify misconceptions and inaccuracies and to work with them toward a more complete and coherent understanding. Teachers have the responsibility of creating environments for students to become confident, competent self-assessors who monitor their own learning.

> I look at losing as research, not failure.
>
> —Billie-Jean King (tennis star)

Emotional Safety

Becoming independent and responsible learners who embrace assessment as a positive part of the process is not something that comes easily. In fact, it is downright scary for many adults, let alone young people. So don't be surprised if some (perhaps many) students do not wholeheartedly embrace the idea. The extent to which students are willing to engage in self-assessment is very much connected to their sense of self and their self-esteem. Persistence depends on expectations of success, even if they are not immediate. Students who have had a history of failure experiences or who fear failure will adopt techniques to protect themselves, even if it means avoiding opportunities for learning. Students who define themselves by their ability are often dependent on high grades as a visible symbol of their worth and find the challenge of moving away from their positions of confidence rather like a free fall into the unknown. It isn't enough to have a few safe moments or

> Emotional safety is necessary for intellectual risk taking.
>
> —Gipps et al. (2000)

episodes of learning. They need to be the norm. Through detailed case studies of individual children throughout their primary schooling, Pollard and Filer (1999) demonstrate how these students continuously shaped their identities and actively evolved as they moved from one classroom context to the next. What this means is that each student's sense of self as a pupil can be enhanced or threatened by changes in their relationships over time, structural position in the classroom, and relative success or failure. It was particularly affected by their teachers' expectations, learning and teaching strategies, classroom organization, and criteria for evaluation. This work shows how important the teacher is to students' sense of self and their views of themselves in school.

Lots of Examples of "What Good Work Looks Like"

Although curriculum guides and standards provide a skeleton image of the expectations for students, nothing is as powerful as multiple images of "what it looks like when experts do it." Not only do students begin to see and hear and feel the expectations for the work at hand, they become acutely aware of the variations that can occur and the legitimacy of those variations. Even in courses like mathematics, there are examples of the elegance and precision that come when experts understand the underlying principles and can apply formulas as shorthand mechanisms for solving problems. In the pool table examples, the students who moved from counting to pattern identification to algebraic notation as a symbolic representation of the relationships "saw" the way the patterns worked. They acquired "expertise" that they could transfer to new situations. The students who did not see the patterns needed more examples and practice with concrete activities to move to the next step. Although the students may never reach or even aspire to the heights of the experts in an area, seeing what the subject allows can have a value of its own. Students of art or music or literature are inspired by the work of masters in the field; students of geography or science or computer programming can be as well.

Once students have a sense of where they are aiming, teachers can offer many intermediate examples of the stages along the way and how experts struggle as well to meet their own expectations. I recently saw a senior English writing textbook that included images of the handwritten pages that author Margaret Atwood had written in the beginning stages of a new novel. One of the pages was messy, often illegible, with lots of words crossed out and marginal notes all over it. In a later chapter, the same page was displayed, now in a computer file, still with many ideas jumbled and half completed, and with lots of notes to herself in brackets. Near the end of the book, the same selection was shown as it appeared in the final manuscript—a very different piece from when it began. Students were using these artifacts to analyze how Atwood was thinking and why she was making the changes that she made, and they were practicing the kind of analysis that they could bring to their own thinking and writing in progress.

Real Involvement and Responsibility

When teachers work to involve students and promote their independence, they are really teaching students to be responsible for their own learning and giving them the tools to undertake it wisely and well. How else are they likely to develop the self-regulatory skills that are the hallmark of experts? It isn't likely, however, that students will become competent, realistic self-evaluators on their own. They need to be taught skills of self-assessment, have routine and challenging opportunities to practice, and develop internal feedback or self-monitoring mechanisms to validate and call into question their own judgments. For students to become independent learners, they need to develop a complicated combination of skills, attitudes, and dispositions. These don't emerge unaided; they are taught and developed over time, like any other complex set of skills. "The Case of Choices" that follows in this chapter is an excellent example of building independence, not only in specific tasks, but in life. Experts may have begun with some exceptional talents that gave them a head start, but they have had to learn the rest by setting goals, organizing their thinking and their lives, self-monitoring, and self-correcting. Each of these skills can be learned, not by posting them up as rules but from helping students engage in setting goals, organizing their world (in small pieces at first), monitoring their progress, and changing their plans based on what they learn, over and over again, during their years in school.

Recording and Reporting for Learning

Integrating new ideas in a discipline with what the students know, and using these new ideas to inform their learning, requires a different kind of recordkeeping and reporting. Instead of dedicating their recording and reporting time to a small number of "marking" and "report card" days, teachers will find that they need to make notes and keep records daily, sometimes on the fly, sometimes in a more orderly fashion. Recording becomes more descriptive, rather than judgmental. What did Jose do? What prompts did I use with Jesse? What artifacts show growth over time? Students become the prime clients for the data that are accumulating, not as statements of their value but as milestones in their learning.

Targeted Feedback

When feedback allows students to see the gap between their actual production and some reference point that makes sense to them, they are both motivated and able to work with their conceptions and make adjustments. The work of teachers is to provide current, accurate, and focused feedback, with examples and reasonable directions for the student to keep going. Informal feedback can refocus students' thinking and allow them to collect their thoughts and feelings so that they can carry on with less frustration and confusion. The examples that occur to me range from a teacher stopping to ask a formative question to class discussions where ideas are shared and challenged by the group.

More formal feedback for self-evaluation occurs when students meet with teachers to discuss where they are and where they are going, and to negotiate the procedures to get there. These less frequent and formal opportunities can provide chances to regroup, establish new or reaffirm existing skills if necessary, and come back to try again with renewed vigor and additional strategies.

Discussion, Challenge, and Reflection

Ideas are not transported ready-made into students' minds. As the Jojo story showed, new ideas emerge through careful consideration and reasoned analysis, and just as important, through interaction with text, pictures, and people. Learning is not private, and it isn't silent. It may happen in individual minds, but it is constantly connected to the world outside and the people in that world. Peers and parents can be strong advocates and contributors to this process, not as judges, meting out marks or favors, but as participants in this process of analysis, comparison, rethinking, and reinforcing that makes up learning. Consider activities like "fishbowls," where a few students discuss a problem and their analysis of it while the rest of the class sits in a circle around them, making notes of ideas, competing hypotheses, resources that might be useful, and suggestions for next steps. At the end of the discussion, the students from the circle write their ideas on sticky notes, and the fishbowl students take them and organize them as a starting point for their next discussion on the issue. Learning is a social activity. Peers and parents, when they understand their role and the situation is structured to support the process, can be key players as students grapple with what they believe to be true in relation to the views, perspectives, and challenges of others.

Practice, Practice, Practice

Like any other complex skill, self-evaluation is hard work that requires commitment and practice to become automatic. This usually necessitates trying something again and again, working at it, feeling uncomfortable for a while, and experiencing new responses.

"The Case of Choices"

In a secondary school in which I have worked, the staff decided that they would try to make the transition to secondary school more humane by keeping the ninth-grade students together as a group and working to bring some coherence to their program. The timetable was based on 70-minute periods, and the students traveled to each class as a group. The core program for the semester was mathematics, English, computer applications, and French. The students were being taught by four teachers who planned together and sometimes team-taught. Let me describe one day that I spent with them.

The day began like most secondary school days—the students were in their homeroom classrooms for attendance checks, announcements, and opening activities, all undercut by a din of whispers and sounds of people moving. I arrived with one of the teachers (Mr. Math) and sat at the back of his classroom. It struck me that this was no ordinary secondary school classroom. There were things on the walls: displays of students' work, a poster containing the expectations from the mathematics curriculum document. On a side table sat calculators (regular and graphing), manipulatives, resource books, and several computers. One corner of the room contained a round table surrounded by games, puzzles, and cards, some commercial, some homemade. As the announcements ended, the teacher began the class with a review of the "bellringer." He had gone into the class early and put open-ended mathematics questions on each of the tables (shared by four students) in the room. The whispering that I had heard was the students discussing the bellringer of the day. The question of the day was based on a current event in the community. There had been a hot-air balloon festival on the weekend, and several balloons were taking passengers up for rides. The question was, "How many people do you think went up in the hot air balloons over the weekend? Why?" The resource for the exercise was the morning newspaper, which had a story about the event that included an estimate of the number of people who attended and gave some details about size, capacity, and so on. The question did not have a "right" answer. The ensuing discussion included hypothesis generation, estimation, calculations, logic, debate, and attention to evidence. The amazing thing was that most of it happened before class started. The review was quick. Each table had a reporter who described the students' thinking and conclusions. The group voted on the best one, based on the quality of the arguments, and the winning table took a bow.

Later in the day, I went with these students to their computer applications class. Most of the students were sitting at the computers

> We have so much to gain by admitting students to the "secret garden" of assessment to empower them to direct and manage their own learning.
>
> —Broadfoot (2002)

working on spreadsheets, entering data, and calculating mortgage payments based on different interest rates and amortization periods. As I walked around, I realized that one group of five or six students was sitting in a corner working on something else. The students had their French text out and were clearly not doing spreadsheets. When I approached, I was surprised that the text was not whisked away. Instead, they continued, asking each other French vocabulary questions, seemingly oblivious to my presence. When I asked what they were doing, the answer was straightforward: "Studying for the French test next period."

"But what about the mortgage assignment?" I asked.

"Oh, we'll do that after school. We've chosen to spend this time on French," said a charming young woman, who then took me by the arm away from her hard-working peers and explained that their teachers believed in choices. At the beginning of the year, the teachers had told them that life was all about choices. "Outside of school, people don't tell you what to do every minute, and bells don't ring to tell you to do something else." So, the students were expected to make choices and then to live with the consequences. The teachers had talked about the curriculum in the four subjects for the semester and showed them how the assignments and classes would help them learn what they needed to know. The expectations were displayed on the classroom walls. Classes continued on the regular timetable. But students were responsible for their own choices about what they did and when. The teachers gave all of the students diaries so that they could organize their own time and helped them decide how to use the diaries to schedule and plan. Every day, a few students met with their homeroom teacher to review their plans and their progress and to make adjustments. When students didn't do their work, they weren't punished. They were reminded that they were responsible for their own decisions. But it was clear that they had made a choice to neglect their studies and that there would be consequences. Ultimately, of course, the consequence could be failing to achieve the requirements for completion of the course. Remember, this was school.

When I met with the teachers at the end of the day, I raised this issue of choices. For them, it was clear. "How else will they learn to make reasonable decisions if we don't teach them and then let them do it in an environment where there are limits and they are safe?" said one. "Sure," added another, "some students don't want to be more responsible for their learning. They are very happy to be receptacles for the 'stuff' of the course and discard it when the time is up and the test is done. That's not good enough for us. If someone is resistant, we need to find out what he's afraid of and find the right scaffolds to make it safe to take tiny risks."

Self-monitoring and self-adjustment protect students from the vagaries of the world around them. This group of teachers was determined to help the students develop and practice the habits of mind that would serve them in the future.

Ideas for Follow-Up

1.   Use a fishbowl technique in your study group. Each of you should come prepared to discuss the ways in which you use assessment to encourage students' self-reflection. The rest of the group listens intently and serves as a "critical friend," asking probing questions and offering constructive suggestions.

2.   Brainstorm as many ways as you can that teachers (and students) can record information about ongoing learning and use it to inform the next stage of learning.

CHAPTER 11

Using Assessment for Optimum Learning

Assessment is, and will continue to be, contentious in both public and political arenas. Moving toward assessment for and as learning will require educators to have courage and stamina, as well as motivation and capacity. This chapter is about how to get there. It has been written for teachers to stimulate thinking, challenge ideas, and inspire action.

In case anyone doubts it, considerable research evidence shows that teachers make a difference in students' learning (Wenglinsky, 2002). Although background characteristics do have an influence, they can be moderated and even overcome by high-quality, active teachers who press all of their students to grow, regardless of their backgrounds; adjust their classroom activities to accommodate the multiple levels of abstraction of the students; and engage students in their learning. Classroom assessment can be a powerful tool for teachers in their pursuit of high-quality learning for their students.

The good news is that teachers intuitively trust their own classroom assessments, prefer them to other assessment methods, and already use them for both instructional purposes and determination of students' grades (Rogers, 1991; Stiggins, 1994). Unless they are under close public scrutiny, schools and teachers pay little attention to externally imposed tests and go about their own business, using classroom assessment for their judgments. They believe that their own assessments and observations are direct, unmediated, and inherently valid, unlike external tests, which, they argue, are indirect, mediated, and inherently invalid (Broadfoot, 1994; Wilson, 1994).

The bad news is that teachers' trust in their assessment practices is not always justified, and the classroom assessments that teachers trust don't always promote learning. Assessment interacts with learning; the interaction can be a forward one to reflect and support learning goals or a backward one that diverts attention from learning or sets up barriers in the learning process. As Black (1998) says:

- Classroom evaluation practices generally encourage superficial and rote learning, concentrating on recall of isolated details, usually items of knowledge.

- Teachers do not generally review the assessment questions that they use and they don't discuss them critically with peers, so there is little reflection on what is being assessed.

- The grading function is over-emphasized and the learning function is under-emphasized.

- There is a tendency to use a normative rather than a criterion approach that emphasizes competition between pupils rather than personal improvement of each. (p. 111)

Changing assessment to reflect some of the principles included in this volume will be a challenge for teachers. They receive little information about assessment in teacher training, and when they do, the focus is often on Assessment *of* Learning for grading purposes. Their own histories and experiences have been the same. The process of assessment in most classrooms is a game (or battle), with teachers pitted against students. There are some explicit rules (e.g., no cheating, attendance at classes counts for 15%, etc.) and many implicit ones (e.g., teachers have the power to decide) in this game. Teachers create secret tests. Students try to imagine (guess) what the tests will include. Marking is a private affair, done late at night in rooms lit only by late-night television screens. Grade books are essential elements in the teacher's arsenal, giving the proof (or at least the illusion) of objectivity, precision, and accuracy. Even the idea of sharing the assessment process with students raises suspicion and challenges the teachers' position in the classroom.

> Assumption: Teachers' overriding moral purpose is to meet the needs of students, even when it conflicts with personal preferences.

Penetrating the myths and the realities about classroom assessment will be challenging. Assessment has never been straightforward or rational, or even very objective (no matter how neat and tidy the marking schemes and grade books look). It is a deeply personal and emotional experience for the students being assessed, the students' parents, and, often, the teacher (Earl & LeMahieu, 1997). It is spontaneous, idiosyncratic, unpredictable, context-dependent, time-bound, and group-influenced, and it leads to different responses depending on the student involved (Wilson, 1994). It is also constrained by the state, district, and school policies that require particular kinds of reporting or attach rewards or sanctions to student grades (Darling-Hammond, 1994). But these are not reasons to abandon classroom assessment and replace it with external assessment procedures. These are precisely the reasons why classroom assessment is so important and why changing it is worth doing—because it matters in students' lives.

Making radical changes to classroom assessment is risky business. Regardless of the dangers, this is not the time for timidity. Teachers have the chance to take charge of change and reformulate the nature of assessment and even of accountability in education. Once again, I have a preferred future. Assessment can become an instrument of learning. Accountability can be diverted from the accounting that emerges from large-scale assessment and external control to its rightful place in schools, as a conversation between educational professionals and those whom they serve—students and parents (Earl & LeMahieu, 1997). The evidence of success will be obvious and visible examples of learning, not through disembodied scores and league tables, but through the accomplishments of young people in their schooling and their lives.

In the rest of this chapter, I examine some of the things that educators can do to prepare for this future. None of them is prescriptive. Instead, they are designed to offer ways of thinking about the purpose of schools; the role that we, as educators, play in schools; and the challenges that we face if we hope to transform schools for students who will live the bulk of their lives in the 21st century.

Think About What You Believe to Be True

The changes in assessment that this volume advocates require some dramatic shifts in thinking. Don't forget—the belief systems and images of schooling that most of us hold come from our own history of learning and schooling. We are products of a factory model of schools and a culture dominated by Assessment *of* Learning. Changing attitudes and beliefs that have been with us for a lifetime is not easy. Watkins et al. (2001) suggest that everyone is in a constant state of consciousness and competence in relation to his or her learning in any area. The authors describe four possible states (see Table 11.1). It seems to me that it is important to revisit this matrix routinely

Table 11.1   Four Possible States of the Learner

	Unconscious of need to learn a specific skill or knowledge	*Conscious of need to learn a specific skill or knowledge*
Incompetent in relation to a specific skill or knowledge	I don't know that I don't know how to do it.	I know that I don't know how to do it.
Competent in relation to a specific skill or knowledge	I can do it but I'm not aware how.	I know how to do it and am aware of how I am doing it.

SOURCE: Watkins et al. (2001).

and decide which quadrant is the best representation, at present, of personal learning.

Beliefs About Learning and Teaching

As long as teachers assume that the "stuff of learning" is the content in texts and other resources, that teaching is transmitting that "stuff" to students, and that student learning either happens or it doesn't, it is unlikely that much will change in schools. Learning, as I describe it in Chapter 4, is an active and demanding process for students.

Beliefs About Assessment

Researchers who have been working with teachers committed to changing their assessment practices are finding that teachers have difficulty moving away from practices that are so ingrained that they have never even questioned them before. They believe that their testing has to be a formal, objective process that is uniformly administered and separate from teaching (Bliem & Davinroy, 1997, cited in Shepard, 2000; Torrance, 2001). Even when they engage in formative assessment, they often see it as extracting a product from students that they can then use for planning of teaching. This is a far cry from a process of consistently using assessment data to plan and respond on the fly to adapt teaching to the needs of their students and to promote student self-assessment. The first stage toward new practices (as is always the case in learning) is an awareness of personal enduring beliefs.

Learn About Learning

If schools are for learning, then knowing about learning for teachers is like knowing about anatomy for doctors. You have to know all there is to know. Unlike anatomy, there is a tremendous amount of new knowledge about learning, and more still to be discovered. We are still far from a complete understanding of how the mind works and how this complex human process of learning takes place. For teachers, this makes learning about learning an ongoing professional responsibility in order to do the job well. Focusing on the tools of teaching without an understanding of learning is short-sighted. Learning needs to come first.

Know Your Subject

Using assessment to guide students in their learning demands a great deal of expertise from teachers. Not only do they need to update their own organizational mental models with new knowledge in their subject discipline(s), some of which renders old knowledge obsolete, but they also have to have a deep and detailed understanding of the way that knowledge development typically happens in their discipline. Knowing what feedback to give assumes an understanding of what causes errors and a recognition of strategies to bring students face-to-face with their misconceptions in ways that make it difficult to continue to hold their existing views.

One of the most compelling and surprising findings in our evaluation of the National Literacy and Numeracy Strategies in England (Earl, Fullan, Leithwood, & Watson, 2000) has been the shallow subject knowledge on the part of the teachers. This is consistent with the findings of Cohen and Hill (2001) in their research on mathematics in California. Although teachers may have a command of the subject themselves, they often do not have the knowledge of the way that they learned it, and more important, how others have learned it or have stumbled along the way. Teachers need to be able to ask the right questions at the right time, anticipate conceptual pitfalls, and have at the ready a repertoire of tasks that will help students take the next steps. This requires a deep knowledge of subject matter. Imagine all that the teacher in "The Bog" example needed to know about early language development and the kinds of misconceptions and confusions she might anticipate in the children's work. In her analysis, she was not looking for right or wrong answers in the students' writing. She was looking for evidence (or the absence of evidence) about the kind of thinking in which Jonathon was engaged. She was trying to make his learning visible so that she could intervene and assist.

The same is true for "The Pool Table." It is only because the teacher has a deep and flexible understanding of the principles that underlie algebraic notation and logic that he was able to devise an open-ended task that engaged all of the students and gave him invaluable information about their thinking and preconceptions. From there, of course, he was able to move quickly to establish the next activities for individuals and groups that would challenge each one of them without leaving them floundering.

So, knowing your subject deeply and intimately is critical—not just the content but the conventions, structures, organizers, underlying concepts, standard and nonstandard procedures, typical misconceptions and misunderstandings, and whatever else makes the subject what it is.

Be an Expert Teacher

Pedagogical understanding is about putting the understanding of learning and content knowledge together with a repertoire of strategies and resources for effective teaching. Expert teachers know about learning and the subjects that they teach, and they have a deep knowledge of pedagogy. They are constantly applying what they know in these areas to the diversity in students' strengths, weaknesses, home background, cultural experiences, developmental stage, and learning styles that exists in their classroom context. Watching an expert teacher is like watching a master jazz musician. The core phrases remain constant, but the treatment, diversions, embellishments, and pacing are variable and flexible, dictated by the other musicians and the context. The product may be unpredictable; it is always complex; and it can touch the souls of very diverse listeners.

I had the fortune for several months to observe such a teacher regularly. In an interview, he described a unit of work that I was observing in his Grade 8 class this way:

> This class is really musical. So I chose *A Tale of Two Cities* to study in novel study. We went to see *Les Misérables* at the theatre and watched it on video, too. That brought us to social studies. We focused on the politics and social structures of the time. We had an in-depth talk about the justice systems in England and France and compared them and talked about why they were different from one another. Each group in the class is doing a project connected to one of the key themes in the novel. They are really great. One group is even writing an operetta.

As an observer in the class, I watched him work with individuals and groups during this unit. They were all approaching their agreed-upon tasks in different ways, using different resources. Some were writing critical reviews of *Les Misérables* for the school newspaper. Others were composing an epic poem about the plight of the poor. Of course, the operetta was in progress. One boy had decided that he wanted to work individually to compare the current Canadian justice system to the English and French ones that they had studied to see what had endured (given that Canada was originally settled by both cultures and remains an amalgam of the two) and speculate about why.

At the same time as these children were engaged in dramatically different activities, the learning expectations from the provincial curriculum were posted around the room. A poster board contained a web organizer centered on the expectations on which they were working in this unit. The whole class had participated in deciding which expectations they were going to address and what the prerequisite skills and knowledge would be to get there. Finally, each child or group had a small whiteboard on which the teacher had written the detailed expectations on which the particular individual or group was focusing during this part of the unit.

The students were busy and engaged in their work. The teacher (sometimes hard to spot as he moved around the active and jam-packed classroom) used his time giving on-the-spot directions, asking questions, providing support, identifying possible resources, challenging thinking, and supplying focused feedback. When the recess bell rang, most of the students continued with their work until they finished the immediate task. When they returned from their exercise break, they went back to it. The teacher was in the hallway, with me, considering the displays from the prior unit that adorned the walls.

Work Together

For some time, collaboration among teachers has been touted as a major contributor to effective schools and the improvement of schools (Fullan & Hargreaves, 1992). Assessment and learning are a natural focus for discussion among teachers. In fact, working together and reaching some shared decisions are essential if teachers are truly committed to using assessment for and as learning in schools and providing consistency and coherence for student learning over time and across grades. Talking with each other is the first stage of sharing interpretations of curriculum and expectations for students and giving teachers a chance to see the connections in and across the curriculum. They have to develop the big picture as a road map for the journeys that they will take with the students in the school, not just for the single semester or year that they have direct responsibility for a group, but for the duration of the students' time in school.

As teachers struggle with the challenge of providing descriptions of their students' learning, they find themselves doubting their judgment and suggestions. These doubts are no different from what teachers have experienced for years. They ask themselves questions such as, "How sure am I that I'm right?" and "How much confidence do I have that I'm giving a fair and accurate picture of this student?" One of the most powerful ways to gain confidence in assessment decisions is to share them. After working with a group of teachers that was engaged in the tough process of mapping expectations for students across several grades and subjects, I received a letter from one of them saying,

> Just wanted to let you know that we had our first parents' night this week and it was awesome. We showed them our charts (posted in the hall) and we talked about how the integrated units will work during the term. It felt really good to be able to show where the different skills were being addressed (including spelling) and to get them excited about the theme units as well. The best part was when I met with parents of my kids. I felt as if I could speak with some authority. It wasn't just me and the kids' work speaking. I could hear the group's voices in my head.

When teachers involve students in their own assessment, the need for whole-school approaches, as well as consistency and progression in targets, becomes even more obvious. As students move from one class to another across years or across subjects, it is essential that the opportunity for involvement be continued and that they see the way the learning intentions change, grow, and become more sophisticated. Otherwise, students are likely to be confused and suspicious of the system that changes the rules on such fundamental issues on a whim.

In a delightful book called *The Competent Classroom,* by Allison Zmuda and Mary Tomaino (2001), the authors describe their collaborative journey of aligning high school curriculum, standards, and assessment. They worked together to challenge each other and to hone and refine their skills as teachers. They found that a change in assessment strategies affected everything else, so they needed to make multiple adjustments. Their journey took them through discussing "essential questions" to guide the program, aligning curricular goals with their essential questions, developing and refining content standards and instructional objectives, bringing assessments into the mix, actually implementing a project, and using standards and assessments to calculate grades. Their vivid description of the process, with all its difficulties, is a wonderful example of planning at its best and collaboration that results in something bigger and better than either one could have created alone—collaboration that includes assessment of, for, and as learning.

Be Gentle With Yourself, But Don't Give Up

Even when teachers are willing to change and interested in changing their assessment practices, they find that it is not as easy as they thought it would be. Changing beliefs, practices, and habits is hard and frustrating. I liken it to using a seat belt in a car. When I learned to drive, seat belts were not mandatory. I learned to get in the car, start the engine, check where I was going, and drive away. When seatbelts became standard requirements, new drivers learned to get in the car, buckle up, and then start the engine. To this day, I follow my old habits, and I'm constantly scrambling to fasten the seat belt as I pull away. If my new car had a mechanism that meant the engine would not start until I buckled the belt, I would have the motivation to do it—I certainly know how to do it—and I would still spend the first few weeks (hopefully not months) cursing all and sundry when I got in and reverted to the old routine. If something this straightforward takes so much energy, thought, and practice, why would we ever assume that changing how we teach will be easy?

A good deal of research on the impact of professional development has demonstrated how difficult it is for teachers to actually implement new strategies (Joyce & Showers, 1982). Changing practices takes time and practice—time to construct an understanding of all of the ways that assessment can contribute to learning, and practice with new skills and approaches. It is likely that teachers will be faced with the prospect of adopting a whole new way of teaching and casting aside or unlearning much of what they have known and done confidently before. This requires a significant amount of practice and lots of scope for making mistakes. A classically trained violinist faced with a new piece composed for jazz fiddle is likely to have to practice harder to master the different rhythms and dynamics. An artist like Seurat would have developed his pointillist method through much trial and error and refinement of technique. Many of the artist's drawings and sketches hanging in exhibitions are practice attempts. Similarly, the play at the theatre has gone through a rehearsal period, and the rehearsal comes after the actors and actresses have already devoted significant time and a range of strategies to learning their lines (Stoll et al., 2002).

Self-Monitoring and Self-Development for You, Too

So, efficient and lifelong learning is about making connections, adding new ideas, organizing and reorganizing understanding, and, ultimately, self-monitoring and self-correction or adjustment. We've come full circle. As I said in Chapter 4,

> Learning is at the core of our being, as individuals and collectively. It is the key to equipping future generations to respond and survive in a frenetically and unpredictably changing world. We have not even approached the limits of what can be learned.

Using assessment for optimum learning for students is a process of growth, change, monitoring, and more change for teachers, along with their students. We are asking students to be brave, take risks, and learn more and better. We face the same challenge. Teachers need to understand their own learning and internalize learning habits of mind as well. This means showing students that you are a learner as well, and having a willingness to engage in in-depth explorations of your own learning—what motivates and influences it, what hinders it, and what it feels like to be on that learning curve.

> For teachers, going to school must be as much about learning as it is about teaching. They must have time each day to learn, plan lessons, critique student work, and support improvement as members of learning teams. . . . Staff development cannot be something educators do only on specified days in the school calendar. It must be part of every educator's daily work schedule.
>
> —Hirsch (2001)

Even those teachers who are well on the road to changing their practices will find that the process never ends. After the first blush of novelty and enthusiasm, how can you sustain the energy, the freshness, the ideas, and most of all, the engagement of your students in learning for the love of it? Changing education, as Michael Fullan (1991) told us many years ago, "is a process, not an event" (p. 19).

Get the Support You Need

New learning about assessment is not just a nice idea; it is an essential element in changing the role and power of assessment in schools. Assessment has been neglected in teacher training and avoided in policy debates. I think it is clear that there are many thorny issues and lots to learn. Competence and confidence using classroom assessment *for* and *as* learning are not skills or dispositions that teachers will acquire by osmosis. On the other hand, there is nothing in what I'm suggesting that teachers can't understand and internalize. Unfortunately, the learning curve is fairly steep and the time is short. In the best-case scenario, policymakers, universities, school districts, principals, and teachers themselves would all have a role to play in providing the support for teachers. The more likely scenario is one where teachers and administrators will have to take charge of their own learning and lobby for what they need.

Put It All Together

Making these changes to assessment and teaching is within the purview of teachers and schools. We have seen glimpses of it in many classrooms and schools in many countries. In a 5-year study of school improvement in Manitoba, Canada (Earl & Lee, 1998), we identified a pattern in schools that were successful in making significant, whole-school changes—a pattern of activity that we have characterized as a cycle of *urgency, energy, agency,* and *more energy.* Since that time, we have added *synergy* to the mix.

Something in a school prompted a group of teachers to feel a sense of *urgency* about changing the way it did business. This urgency was experienced as a surge of *energy* that could result in productive action or a tumble into despair. When the conditions were right, these bursts of energy led to an upward spiral with an increased sense of *agency* and productivity. The *synergy* of working together moved the teachers further. This, in time, released more energy, and the cycle went on.

Schools embarked on major change initiatives when they experienced a *call to action* or critical incident that resulted in a sense of *urgency.* Something happened in these schools that jarred them and forced them to believe that change must be made, and made quickly. The staff (and sometimes the students and the community) experienced something that compelled them to action. One school coordinator describes it this way: "We had an epiphany." For others, the realization was not so dramatic—just a gnawing feeling that something was amiss. Often, this experience resulted in a challenge to how teachers viewed the world or, perhaps more precisely, their school in relation to the world. The world was not as they had known it to be, and, therefore, the status quo was no longer acceptable or appropriate. When staff came to believe that their view of the world was at odds with what they wanted to achieve, they experienced a sense of dissonance and urgency. The urgency came in many ways, but whatever the source, the staff came to see their school, themselves, and their students through different lenses.

Once schools felt the urgency to change, staff members were energized. They experienced a surge of *energy* and creativity. The energy that comes from urgency can rouse anxiety and immobilize staff when a school is not able to respond, or it can be the impetus for action. Often, teachers had to go looking for ways to make the changes that they felt were necessary. When they found support or knew that they could get it, they reported having *agency* and expressed confidence about their ability to do what they had to do, or to get the training that they needed. Sometimes, the training preceded the confidence and contributed to it, and sometimes, it was the other way around. Building capacity both internally and through professional development was critical to continued movement. Either way, the teachers experienced growth in several different areas. They increased their knowledge and skills, changed their dispositions, and established positive views about themselves and their role in changing education. Working together created *synergy* as the teachers grew in confidence and continued to extend and enhance their professional capacities. The momentum that was generated created more *energy,* and the process continued.

For me, high-quality learning for more students, more of the time, is a compelling idea that has a real urgency attached to it. I believe that assessment can be the impetus to release the energy in schools that will stimulate action. Teachers and administrators can find the resources to build capacity and create agency by working together and utilizing the synergy that results from their mutual determination and shared knowledge. And these schools can travel the tiny steps that it takes to transform education from the inside out.

> We keep asking teachers to get on luxury liners and go to places they have never been and don't believe are any better than staying at home, and we wonder why they resist. In our experience, when teachers have an image of where they want to go, they will get there, any way they can, even if it means paddling a canoe.
>
> —Earl (1999)

References

Arter, J., & McTighe, J. (2001). *Scoring rubrics in the classroom: Using performance criteria for assessing and improving student performance.* Thousand Oaks, CA: Corwin.

Assessment Reform Group. (1999). *Assessment for learning: Beyond the black box.* Cambridge, UK: University of Cambridge School of Education.

Barton, P. (1999). *Too much testing of the wrong kind, too little of the right kind in K-12 education.* Princeton, NJ: Educational Testing Service.

Beare, H. (2001). *Creating the future school.* London: Routledge/Falmer.

Biggs, J. B., & Collis, K. F. (1982). *Evaluating the quality of learning: The SOLO taxonomy.* New York: Academic Press.

Biggs, J. B., & Moore, P. J. (1993). *The process of learning* (3rd ed.). Englewood Cliffs, NJ: Prentice Hall.

Black, P. (1998). *Testing: Friend or foe? Theory and practice of assessment and testing.* London: Falmer.

Black, P., & Wiliam, D. (1998). *Inside the black box: Raising standards through classroom assessment.* London: King's College School of Education.

Bloom, B., Hastings, J., & Madaus, G. (1971). *Formative and summative evaluation of student learning.* New York: McGraw-Hill.

Brandsford, J. D., Brown, A. L., & Cocking, R. R. (1999). *How people learn: Brain, mind, experience, and school.* Washington, DC: National Academy Press.

Broadfoot, P. (1994, October). *Assessment and evaluation: To measure or to learn?* Paper presented at the International Conference on Evaluation, Toronto.

Broadfoot, P. (1996). *Education, assessment and society.* Buckingham, UK: Open University Press.

Broadfoot, P. (2001). Editorial: New wine in old bottles? The challenge of change for educational assessment. *Assessment in Education: Principles, Policy & Practice, 8*(2), 109–112.

Broadfoot, P. (2002). Assessment for lifelong learning: Challenges and choices. *Assessment in Education: Principles, Policy & Practice, 9*(1), 5–7.

Brown, R. (1989). Testing and thoughtfulness. *Educational Leadership, 46*(7), 31–33.

Clarke, S. (2001). *Unlocking formative assessment.* London: Hodder and Stoughton.

Cohen, D. K., & Hill, H. C. (2001). *Learning policy: When state education reform works.* New Haven, CT: Yale University Press.

Costa, A. (1989). Reassessing assessment. *Educational leadership, 46*(7), 2.

Costa, A. (1996). Prologue. In D. Hyerle (Ed.), *Visual tools for constructing knowledge.* Alexandria, VA: Association for Supervision and Curriculum Development.

Costa, A., & Kallick, B. (2000). *Activating and engaging habits of mind.* Alexandria, VA: Association for Supervision and Curriculum Development.

Crooks, T. (1988). The impact of classroom evaluation practices on students. *Review of Educational Research, 58*(4), 438–481.

Csikszentmihalyi, M. (1990). *Flow: The psychology of optimal experience.* New York: Harper & Row.

Cuban, L. (1984). *How teachers taught: Constancy and change in American classrooms, 1890–1980* (1st ed.). Research on Teaching Monograph Series.

Cuban, L. (1988). A fundamental puzzle of school reform. *Phi Delta Kappan, 70*(5), 341–344.

Darling-Hammond, L. (1992, November). Reframing the school reform agenda. *The School Administrator,* pp. 22–27.

Darling-Hammond, L. (1994). Performance-based assessment and educational equity. *Harvard Educational Review, 64*(1), 5–30.

Dart, B. C., Burnett, P. C., & Boulton-Lewis, G. M. (1999). Classroom learning environments and students' approaches to learning. *Learning Environments Research, 2,* 137–156.

Earl, L. (1999). *The paradox of hope: Educating young adolescents* [Monograph]. Victoria, Australia: Incorporated Association of Registered Teachers of Victoria.

Earl, L., & Cousins, J. B. (1995). *Classroom assessment: Changing the face, facing the change.* Toronto: OPSTF.

Earl, L., Fullan, M., Leithwood, K., & Watson, N. (2000). *Watching and learning: Evaluation of the implementation of the national literacy and numeracy strategies first annual report.* London: Department for Education and Employment.

Earl, L., & Katz, S. (2002). Leading schools in a data rich world. In K. Leithwood, P. Hallinger, G. C. Furman, P. Gronn, J. MacBeath, B. Mulford, & K. Riley (Eds.), *The second international handbook of educational leadership and administration.* Dordrecht, The Netherlands: Kluwer.

Earl, L., & Lee, L. (1998). *Evaluation of the Manitoba School Improvement Program.* Toronto: Walter and Duncan Gordon Foundation.

Earl, L., & LeMahieu, P. (1997). Rethinking assessment and accountability. In A. Hargreaves (Ed.), *ASCD 1997 yearbook: Rethinking educational change with heart and mind.* Alexandria, VA: Association for Supervision and Curriculum Development.

Elmore, R. (1996). Getting to scale with educational practice. *Harvard Educational Review, 66*(1), 1–25.

Ertmer, P., & Newby, T. (1996). The expert learner: Strategic, self-regulated, and reflective. *Instructional Science, 24,* 1–24.

Firestone, W. A., Mayrowetz, D., & Fairman, J. (1998). Performance-based assessment and instructional change: The effects of testing in Maine and Maryland. *Educational Evaluation and Policy Analysis, 20*(2), 95–113.

Firestone, W. A., Winter, H., & Fitz, J. (2000). Different assessments, common practice? Mathematics testing and teaching in the USA and England and Wales. *Assessment in Education: Principles, Policy & Practice, 7*(1), 13–37.

Fullan, M. (1991). *The new meaning of educational change.* Toronto: OISE Press.

Fullan, M. (2000). The return of large-scale reform. *Journal of Educational Change, 1*(2), 5–28.

Fullan, M., & Hargreaves, A. (1992). *What's worth fighting for in your school?* New York: Teachers College Press.

Gardner, H. (1991). *The unschooled mind.* New York: Basic Books.

Gipps, C. (1994). *Beyond testing: Towards a theory of educational assessment.* London: Falmer.

Gipps, C., McCallum, B., & Hargreaves, E. (2000). *What makes a good primary school teacher? Expert classroom strategies.* London: Routledge/Falmer.

Goleman, D. (1995). *Emotional intelligence: Why it can matter more than IQ.* New York: Bantam.

Gronlund, N. (2000). *How to write and use instructional objectives* (6th ed.). Englewood Cliffs, NJ: Prentice Hall.

Haertel, E. (1999). Validity arguments for high-stakes testing: In search of the evidence. *Educational Measurement: Issues and Practice, 18*(4), 5–9.

Haney, W. (Ed.). (1991). *We must take care: Fitting assessments to function.* Alexandria, VA: Association for Supervision and Curriculum Development.

Haney, W., & Madaus, G. (1989). Searching for alternatives to standardized tests: Whys, whats and whithers. *Phi Delta Kappan, 70*(9), 683–687.

Haney, W., Madaus, G., & Lyons, R. (1993). *The fractured marketplace for standardized testing.* Boston: Kluwer.

Hargreaves, A. (1994). *Changing teachers, changing times: Teachers' work and culture in the postmodern age.* London: Cassell.

Hargreaves, A., Earl, L., Moore, S., & Manning, S. (2001). *Learning to change: Teaching beyond subjects and standards.* San Francisco: Jossey-Bass.

Hargreaves, A., Earl, L., & Ryan, J. (1996). *Schooling for change: Reinventing education for early adolescents.* London: Falmer.

Hirsch, S. (2001). We're growing and changing. *Journal of Staff Development, 22*(3), 10–17.

Hyerle, D. (1996). *Visual tools.* Alexandria, VA: Association for Supervision and Curriculum Development.

Hynes, W. (1991). *The changing face of testing and assessment* [Critical Issues Report]. Arlington, VA: American Association of School Administrators.

Jensen, E. (1998). *Teaching with the brain in mind.* Alexandria, VA: Association for Supervision and Curriculum Development.

Joyce, B., & Showers, B. (1982). The coaching of teaching. *Educational Leadership, 40*(1), 4–10.

Katz, S. (1999). Substituting the symbol for the experience: Exposing a fallacy in mathematics education. *Journal of Mathematical Behavior, 17*(4), 405–410.

Katz, S., Earl, L., & Olsen, D. (2001). The paradox of classroom assessment. *McGill Journal of Education, 36*(1), 13–24.

Katz, S., Sutherland, S., & Earl, L. (in press). Developing an evaluation habit of mind. *Canadian Journal for Program Evaluation.*

Lambert, N. M., & McCombs, B. L. (1998). *How students learn: Reforming schools through learner-centered education.* Washington, DC: American Psychological Association.

Leithwood, K., Jantzi, D., & Mascall, B. (1999). *Large-scale reform: What works?* Toronto: OISE/UT.

Lemann, N. (1999). *The big test: The secret history of the American meritocracy.* New York: Farrar, Straus and Giroux.

Linn, M., & Songer, N. (1991). Cognitive and conceptual change in adolescence. *American Journal of Education, 99*(4), 379–417.

Marzano, R. (2000). *Transforming classroom grading.* Alexandria, VA: Association for Supervision and Curriculum Development.

Marzano, R., Brandt, R., Hughes, C., Jones, B., Presseisan, B., Rankin, S., & Suhor, C. (1988). *Dimensions of thinking: A framework for curriculum and instruction.* Alexandria, VA: Association for Supervision and Curriculum Development.

Marzano, R., Pickering, D., & McTighe, J. (1993). *Assessing student outcomes: Performance assessment using the Dimensions of Learning Model.* Alexandria, VA: Association for Supervision and Curriculum Development.

McDonnell, L. (1994). *Policymakers' views of student assessment.* Santa Monica, CA: RAND.

National Council of Teachers of Mathematics. (2000). *Principles and standards for school mathematics.* Reston, VA: Author.

Newmann, F. (1996). Linking restructuring to authentic student assessment. *Phi Delta Kappan, 73*(6), 458–463.

Olsen, D. R., & Bruner, J. S. (1996). Folk psychology and folk pedagogy. In D. R. Olsen & N. Torrance (Eds.), *The handbook of education and human development.* Cambridge, MA: Basil Blackwell.

Perkins, D. (1992). *Smart schools: From training memories to educating minds.* New York: Free Press.

Perkins, D., & Unger, C. (Eds.). (2000). *Teaching and learning for understanding.* Mahwah, NJ: Lawrence Erlbaum.

Pollard, A., & Filer, A. (1999). *The social world of children's learning.* London: Cassell.

Popham, J. (1995). *Classroom assessment: What teachers need to know.* Boston: Allyn & Bacon.

Popham, J. (2002). Right task, wrong tool. *American School Board Journal, 189*(2), 18–22.

Rogers, T. (1991). Educational assessment in Canada. *Alberta Journal of Educational Research, 36*(2), 179–192.

Sadler, R. (1989). Formative assessment and the design of instructional systems. *Instructional Science, 18,* 119–144.

Sarason, S. (1996). *Revisiting "The culture of school and the problem of change."* New York: Teachers College Press.

Senge, P. (1990). *The fifth discipline: The art and practice of the learning organization.* New York: Doubleday.

Shepard, L. (1989). Why we need better assessments. *Educational Leadership, 46*(7), 4–9.

Shepard, L. (2000, April). *The role of assessment in a learning culture: Presidential address.* Paper presented at the annual meeting of the American Education Research Association, New Orleans.

Stevenson, H., & Stigler, J. (1992). *The learning gap: Why our schools are failing and what we can learn from Japanese and Chinese education.* New York: Summit.

Stiggins, R. (1990). Toward a relevant classroom assessment research agenda. *Alberta Journal of Educational Research, 36*(1), 92–97.

Stiggins, R. (1991). Assessment literacy. *Phi Delta Kappan, 72*(7), 534–539.

Stiggins, R. (1993, May). *Student-centered assessment.* Paper presented at the workshop sponsored by the Association of Educational Research Officers of Toronto.

Stiggins, R. (1994). *Student-centered classroom assessment.* New York: Merrill.

Stiggins, R. (1997). *Student-centered classroom assessment* (2nd ed.). Upper Saddle River, NJ: Prentice Hall.

Stiggins, R. (2001). *Student-involved classroom assessment* (3rd ed.). Upper Saddle River, NJ: Prentice Hall.

Stoll, L., Fink, D., & Earl, L. (2002). *It's about learning (and it's about time): What's in it for schools?* London: Routledge Falmer.

Sutton, R. (1995). *Assessment for learning.* Salford, UK: RS Publications.

Torrance, H. (2001). Assessment for learning: Developing formative assessment in the classroom. *Professional Journal for Primary Education, 29*(3), 26–32.

Torrance, H., & Pryor, J. (1998). *Investigating formative assessment.* Buckingham, UK: Open University Press.

Vygotsky, L. S. (1978). *Mind in society: The development of the higher psychological processes.* Cambridge, MA: Harvard University Press. (Originally published 1930)

Watkins, C., Carnell, E., Lodge, C., Wagner, P., & Whalley, C. (2001). *Learning about learning: Staff development resources from NAPCE.* Unpublished manuscript, London.

Weinstein, R. S. (1998). Promoting positive expectations in schooling. In N. M. Lambert & B. L. McCombs (Eds.), *How students learn: Reforming schools through learner-centered education.* Washington, DC: American Psychological Association.

Wenglinsky, J. (2002). How schools matter: The link between teacher and classroom practices and student academic performance. *Education Policy Analysis Archives, 10*(12), 1–28.

Whitty, G., Power, S., & Halpin, D. (1998). *Devolution and choice in education: The school, the state, the market.* Buckingham, UK: Open University Press.

Wiggins, G. (1989). Teaching to the (authentic) test. *Educational Leadership, 46*(7), 41–47.

Wiggins, G. (1993). *Assessing student performance.* San Francisco: Jossey-Bass.

Wiggins, G. (1998). *Educative assessment: Designing assessments to inform and improve performance.* San Francisco: Jossey-Bass.

Wiggins, G., & McTighe, J. (1999). *Understanding by design.* Alexandria, VA: Association for Supervision and Curriculum Development.

Wilson, R. (1994, May). *Back to basics: A revisionist model of classroom-based assessment.* Paper presented at the Canadian Educational Research Association, Calgary, AB.

Wilson, R. (1996). *Assessing students in classrooms and schools.* Scarborough, UK: Allyn & Bacon.

Wolf, D., Bixby, J., Glenn, J., & Gardner, H. (1991). To use their minds well: Investigating new forms of student assessment. *Review of Research in Education, 17,* 31–74.

Young, S., & Wilson, R. (2000). *Assessment and learning: The ICE approach.* Winnipeg, MB: Portage & Main Press.

Zmuda, A., & Tomaino, M. (2001). *The competent classroom: Aligning high school curriculum, standards, and assessment—A creative teaching guide.* Washington, DC: National Education Association.

Index

**CORWIN
PRESS**

The Corwin Press logo—a raven striding across an open book—represents the happy union of courage and learning. We are a professional-level publisher of books and journals for K-12 educators, and we are committed to creating and providing resources that embody these qualities. Corwin's motto is "Success for All Learners."